The American Weird

The American Weird

Concept and Medium

Edited by
Julius Greve and Florian Zappe

BLOOMSBURY ACADEMIC
LONDON • NEW YORK • OXFORD • NEW DELHI • SYDNEY

BLOOMSBURY ACADEMIC
Bloomsbury Publishing Plc
50 Bedford Square, London, WC1B 3DP, UK
1385 Broadway, New York, NY 10018, USA
29 Earlsfort Terrace, Dublin 2, Ireland

BLOOMSBURY, BLOOMSBURY ACADEMIC and the Diana logo are trademarks of
Bloomsbury Publishing Plc

First published in Great Britain 2021
This paperback edition published in 2022

Copyright © Julius Greve and Florian Zappe and Contributors, 2021

Julius Greve and Florian Zappe and Contributors have asserted their rights under the
Copyright, Designs and Patents Act, 1988, to be identified as Authors of this work.

For legal purposes the Acknowledgments on p. viii constitute an extension
of this copyright page.

Cover design: Eleanor Rose
Cover image © Keith Tilford

All rights reserved. No part of this publication may be reproduced or transmitted
in any form or by any means, electronic or mechanical, including photocopying,
recording, or any information storage or retrieval system, without prior
permission in writing from the publishers.

Bloomsbury Publishing Plc does not have any control over, or responsibility for, any
third-party websites referred to or in this book. All internet addresses given in this
book were correct at the time of going to press. The author and publisher regret any
inconvenience caused if addresses have changed or sites have ceased to exist,
but can accept no responsibility for any such changes.

A catalogue record for this book is available from the British Library.

A catalog record for this book is available from the Library of Congress.

ISBN: HB: 978-1-3501-4119-3
PB: 978-1-3501-8538-8
ePDF: 978-1-3501-4120-9
eBook: 978-1-3501-4121-6

Typeset by Deanta Global Publishing Services, Chennai, India

To find out more about our authors and books visit www.bloomsbury.com and
sign up for our newsletters.

Contents

List of Figures vii
Acknowledgments viii

1 Introduction: Conceptualizations, Mediations, and Remediations of the American Weird *Julius Greve and Florian Zappe* 1

Part One: Concept

2 A Doxa of the American Weird *Dan O'Hara* 15
3 The Oozy Set: Toward a Weird(ed) Taxonomy *Johnny Murray* 28
4 Validating Weird Fiction as an (Im)Possible Genre *Anne-Maree Wicks* 40
5 Woke Weird and the Cultural Politics of Camp Transformation *Stephen Shapiro* 55
6 The Weird in/of Crisis, 1930/2010 *Tim Lanzendörfer* 72
7 After Weird: Harman, Deleuze, and the American "Thing" *Daniel D. Fineman* 89
8 Concerning a Deleuzean Weird: A Response to Dan Fineman *Graham Harman* 105

Part Two: Medium

9 *Get Out*, Race, and Formal Destiny (On Common Weirdness) *Eugenie Brinkema* 121
10 From a Heap of Broken Images Toward a Postcolonial Weird: Ana Lily Amirpour's Western Landscapes *Maryam Aras* 139
11 "It Is in Our House Now": *Twin Peaks*, Nostalgia, and David Lynch's Weird Spaces *Oliver Moisich and Markus Wierschem* 154
12 Demolishing the Blues: Captain Beefheart as Modernist Outsider *Paul Sheehan* 173

13 Weird Visual Mythopoeia: On Matthew Barney's *Cremaster Cycle*
   Florian Zappe 187

14 Hidden Cultures and the Representation and Creation of Weird Reality in Alan Moore's *Providence* *Alexander Greiffenstern* 201

15 Alien Beauty: The Glamor of the Eerie *Fred Francis* 216

16 Conspiracy Hermeneutics: *The Secret World* as Weird Tale
   Tanya Krzywinska 230

17 Afterword: Weird in the Walls *Roger Luckhurst* 248

Contributors 259
Index 263

Figures

1	Based on the diagram of a double chiasmatic invagination of edges by Jacques Derrida © *Critical Inquiry* 1980	46
2	Skulltopus by China Miéville © *Collapse* 2009. Reproduced with the permission of China Miéville	48
3	Concave of the Old Weird	50
4	Locating the New Weird	51
5	The corrupted form of weird fiction	52

Acknowledgments

The editors would like to thank the following individuals without whom *The American Weird: Concept and Medium* would not have been possible: Lucy Brown, Graham Harman, Marleen Knipping, Susann Köhler, James Dowthwaite, Andrew S. Gross, Anca-Raluca Radu, Caro Franke, Hanna Riggert, and Jonah H. Greve—thank you for your input, inspiration, patience, and support! The text of Tanya Krzywinska's chapter, "Conspiracy Hermeneutics: *The Secret World* as Weird Tale," has previously been published in the 2014 issue of *Well Played: A Journal on Video Games, Value and Meaning*, 3 (2). Thanks go to Krzywinska for kindly granting permission to reprint these pages in the present book. Finally, the editors want to wholeheartedly express their gratitude to Keith Tilford for generously providing them with three phenomenal artworks for this volume—that is, for the front cover and for the two main sections of the book, *Part One: Concept* and *Part Two: Medium*.

1

Introduction

Conceptualizations, Mediations, and Remediations of the American Weird

Julius Greve and Florian Zappe

"The weird is the discovery of an unhuman limit to thought that is nevertheless foundational for thought. The life that is weird is the life according to the logic of an inaccessible real. . ."

—Eugene Thacker, *After Life*

"*KEEP Austin Weird,* it says on a popular bumper sticker for the city where I spend much of my time. That old Anglo-Saxon word for fate or destiny has taken on a lot of meanings. And, should you mention a coincidence to someone, they are likely to respond "Weird!" That kid next door who prefers to read rather than play is weird. How weird is that?"

—Michael Moorcock, "Foreweird"

How to conceptualize what is called "the weird" in American culture? What are its genre conventions in literary terms, and what are the dynamics that pertain to the contemporary mediations and remediations in the contexts of its nonliterary permutations: film, television, photography, video games, music, visual and performance art, and music, among others? In the spirit of Roger Luckhurst's invaluable essay "The Weird: A Dis/Orientation" (2017), we will start our reflections on what has been called "the American Weird" (see also Luckhurst 2015) with a digression: In her book *Our Aesthetic Categories: Zany, Cute, Interesting* (2012), Sianne Ngai thinks through the notions of "zaniness," "cuteness," and "the interesting" along the parameters of political economy and its aesthetic consequence. As Ngai contends, these notions, "for all their marginality to aesthetic theory and to genealogies of postmodernism, are the ones in our current repertoire best suited for grasping how aesthetic experience has been transformed by the hypercommodified, information-saturated, performance-driven conditions of late capitalism" (Ngai 2012: 1). For her, established concepts of aesthetic theory, such as "the beautiful" and "the sublime," are not sufficient to account for contemporary lived experience, caught as it is in the throes of affective labor, social networks, and the aesthetics and politics of media-technological modes of distribution. Different from traditional aesthetic theory in the wake of Kant, according to whose *Critique of Judgment* "[a]ffective states can either be judged beautiful or not beautiful, sublime (as in the case of 'enthusiasm') or nonsublime (as in the case of 'hatred')" (Ngai 2012: 57), Ngai's exposition places the supposedly "minor" or supposedly "less powerful evaluations" (53), such as *being cute*, and their pop culture and avant-garde manifestations center stage. Why is such an approach needed in the context of contemporary American literature and culture, including the experimental poetry of Gertrude Stein's *Tender Buttons*, the 1996 movie *The Cable Guy*, or the comedy show *I Love Lucy* (all of which are part of the "canon" that establishes Ngai's alternative or "minor" aesthetic categories)?

We agree that twentieth- and twenty-first-century American culture is, indeed, structured according to a distinct set of new aesthetic forms, functions, and categories that exceeds that of the Romanticist dichotomy of the beautiful and sublime, recapitulated via Nietzsche as Apollonian order versus Dionysian force and, and via French psychoanalytical criticism as *plaisir* versus *jouissance* (see Ngai 2012: 57). Contemporary American culture, to be sure, rests on a plethora of affective states that go beyond indifference versus difference. And Ngai's set of categories is idiosyncratic and extremely useful in the context of what she describes as late capitalism's commodity fetishism indexed by cuteness, the cultural investment in discursive production indexed by the interesting, and the "becoming-labor of performance" (233) that she reiterates via readings of the work of "performers like Lucille Ball in *I Love Lucy* and Richard Pryor in *The Toy*" (7). In the latter, for instance, zaniness "evokes the performance of affective labor—the production of affects and social relationships—as it comes to increasingly trouble the distinction between work and play . . . under what Luc Boltanski and Eve Chiapello call the new 'connexionist' spirit of capitalism" (7).

Thus, while Ngai's efforts in redefining today's aesthetico-political paradigm are on point in the contexts she discusses in her book, we would like to return to the initial set of questions voiced at the beginning of these remarks, namely by proposing the addition of "the weird" as yet another foundational aesthetic category of not merely, or predominantly, twentieth-century American culture, but in particular that of the new millennium. H. P. Lovecraft introduced the concept of the weird to describe a particular aesthetic quality of literature in his seminal essay *Supernatural Horror in Literature* (1927), based on what he termed humanity's "oldest and strongest kind of fear" or anxiety—that is to say, "fear of the unknown" (Lovecraft 1973: 12)—and "the creation of a given sensation" (16) related to such an aesthetics. To borrow Ngai's phrasing in our present context: "for all [its relative] marginality to aesthetic theory and to genealogies of postmodernism" (Ngai 2012: 1), the weird has been a haunting presence in American literature and culture. Originally referring to a particular form of genre fiction, the term by now refers to a broad spectrum of artistic practices and expressions. Hence, similar to Ngai's transmedial approach to the aesthetic proliferation of the cute, the zany, and the interesting, the weird, too, is a question of literary (and nonliterary) genre, of aesthetic categorization, as well as of a particular mode of experience. Like Ngai's categories, the weird—especially in the American context—provides a simultaneously colloquial and conceptual, a vulgar and philosophical dimension, as exemplified by the two epigraphs above and their respective definitions of the term, referring to the "unhuman limit" (Thacker 2010: 23) that is the basis of human thought and pointing to the merely strange instances that characterize human culture beyond the beautiful and the sublime: "How weird is that?" (Moorcock 2011: xi).

Given its central feature of "[a] certain atmosphere of breathless and unexplainable dread of outer, unknown forces" (Lovecraft 1973: 15), the weird is sometimes relegated as being merely one of many forms of genre fiction— in between horror and science fiction, as scholars most routinely characterize this form of literature. Yet with the multiple manifestations of weird American culture, many of which (and yet only a comparatively small number, compared to the rich diversity of cultures and subcultures) are examined in this book, it is key to realize the various extraliterary forms of cultural expression, those contemporary media ecologies that emerged in the wake of Lovecraft. Even S. T. Joshi, the eminent scholar of "the weird tale" (an expression taken from Lovecraft's *Supernatural Horror in Literature*, and used as the book title of Joshi's defining 1990 monograph on the topic), described this type of literature as not so much grounded in genre categorization, as in ontological claims: "the weird tale, in the period covered by this volume (1880–1940), did not (and perhaps does not now) exist as a genre but as *the consequence of a world view*" (Joshi 1990: 1, emphasis in the original)—a claim that he would repeat in the beginning of his sequel of sorts, *The Modern Weird Tale* (2001). This take on a type of narrative literature and medial expression that evades categorization and yet evokes an equally aesthetic and affective category in itself is also reflected in recent, albeit rather specialized, publications on the topic—Graham Harman's *Weird Realism: Lovecraft and Philosophy* (2012), Justin Everett and Jeffrey H. Shank's *The Unique Legacy of Weird Tales: The Evolution of Modern Fantasy and Horror* (2015), Carl H. Sederholm and Jeffrey Andrew Weinstock's *The Age of Lovecraft* (2016), and Mark Fisher's *The Weird and the Eerie* (2016). Nonetheless, the weird remains a comparatively understudied phenomenon. We want to single out Harman's and Fisher's books for a more careful analysis, because these are consistently argued monographs that develop highly useful and impactful theorizations of weird culture—Lovecraftian and otherwise—as can also be seen in the influence these studies have had on the contributions in the present volume, *The American Weird: Concept and Medium*.

Harman's *Weird Realism* (2012) galvanized the valorization of the weird as a philosophical category. His point of departure is, unsurprisingly, Lovecraft, in whom he sees not only a kindred spirit with regard to his own philosophical school (object-oriented ontology and speculative realism) but he even elevates him to the status of "a hero of object-oriented thought" (Harman 2012: 5). That praise is based on Harman's reading of Lovecraft as a "productionist author," as a "tacit philosopher" (one inevitably wonders if Lovecraft would have embraced such a label) who is "perplexed by the gap between objects and the power of language to describe them, or between objects and the qualities they possess" (3). In doing so, he renegotiates the relationship between epistemology and ontology in a way that corresponds with Harman's own philosophical viewpoint and thus offers a notion of realism that is indeed—for lack of a better word—*weird*.

Fisher's last book *The Weird and the Eerie* is a similarly important landmark in theorizing the weird (and its conceptual sibling, the eerie). Building on close readings of numerous manifestations of weird art—Lovecraft is, of course, on top of the list, David Lynch is also a key example but there are also artists and authors, such as Rainer Werner Fassbinder or Philip K. Dick—Fisher develops a theory of weirdness defined as the presence of the inappropriate, as "that *which does not belong*" (Fisher 2016: 10, emphasis in the original). To him, the weird is a multifaceted mode of artistic production and aesthetic experience that transcends the idea of genre. Put differently: in the conception of weirdness, the supernatural is wedded to the subcultural.

In spite of these monographs (and other studies on the topic), and in spite of the concept's undisputed significance and unbroken popularity, the weird has nonetheless remained surprisingly undertheorized so far. This volume therefore brings together perspectives from literary, cultural, media, and film studies, as well as from philosophy to provide an interdisciplinary framework to generate new approaches to answer our initial questions: How can the weird be conceptualized as a generic category, as an aesthetic mode, or as an epistemological and ontological position? What are the transformations it has undergone aesthetically and politically since its inception in the early twentieth century? Which strands of contemporary critical theory and philosophy have engaged in a dialogue with the discourses of and on the weird? And what is specifically "American" about this aesthetic mode? Luckhurst reminds us that

> [i]t is hard to define a national tradition (is there an "American weird" after all?), precisely because influences are often pulled together from multiple canons. The weird might just as well contain Théophile Gautier, Franz Kafka, Gustav Meyrink, or Bruno Schulz as Herman Melville and Edgar Allan Poe. At the same time, it seems entirely plausible to extend the American weird to run from Charles Brockden Brown to the sinister comics of Charles Burns, such as *X'ed Out* (2009), where weird affect crawls out of the gutters of his spookily disconnected panels, or the multimedia art of David Lynch, one of the best contemporary artists to grasp weird affect in cinema, TV, music, painting, and even his strip cartoon, "The Angriest Dog in the World." . . . As if reacting like a bewildered Lovecraft narrator, the weird seems to expand and contract strangely, leaving one unable to judge with any appropriate sense of scale. (Luckhurst 2015: 202)

Along these lines, *The American Weird* (re)frames the weird based on a broad spectrum of artistic manifestations and media practices, including the writings of Lovecraft, Caitlín Kiernan, and Jeff VanderMeer, the graphic novels of Alan Moore, the music of Captain Beefheart, the films of Lily Amirpour, Matthew Barney, Jordan Peele, and David Lynch, and the video game *The Secret World*. Our project is not so much invested in examining the concept of "weird media" Eugene Thacker describes as those devices facilitating the end point of communication—that is to say, "excommunication"—by pointing out the irredeemable gap between the two registers of the phenomenological "for us" and the ontological "in itself" (Thacker 2014: 132–3) in the weird literature of Frank Belknap Long or Clark Ashton Smith (even though authors like Smith are nonetheless important in the present context, as Johnny Murray's chapter will show). Rather, we are interested in the ways in which the philosophical and literary concept of the weird—*qua* medium—has been (and is) mediated and "remediated" by extratextual practices in US-American culture ("remediation" being understood in Jay Bolter and Richard Grusin's sense of "respond[ing] to, redeploy[ing], compet[ing] with, and reform[ing] other media" [Bolter and Grusin 2000: 55]).

The book is structured in two parts, *Part One: Concept* and *Part Two: Medium*. The chapters in Part One take up many of the already-existing threads of defining the weird as a mode and a genre, but they also attempt to fill in at least some of the gaps that remain open in the theoretical discourse. Part Two focuses on specific medial manifestations of the weird in word, image, and sound to illustrate the polymorphic instances of contemporary weird artistic production. Obviously, this does not mean that Part One ignores the question of the American Weird's media-specific forms of expression; nor is Part Two of the present book free of conceptual work, engaging with the philosophical, political, and ethical investment of the American Weird. The division of this book into concept- and media-focused parts, respectively, is meant to be helping the reader explore the volume, in terms of predominantly conceptual and mediological analyses, of the literary and extraliterary figurations of weirdness.

The opening chapter of the Part One takes up a historical perspective on the weird: Dan O'Hara's "A Doxa of the American Weird" retraces its development from the first English settlements in North America. O'Hara argues that a definition of the weird restricted to its nineteenth-century vernacular usage limits its scope and ignores the extent to which Puritan thinking in America from the time of the colonies onward already incorporated a conception of "weirding." The weird, whose etymology (*wyrd*) reveals one of its meanings in terms of a conception of fate (also noted by Moorcock in the second epigraph of this introduction), relates to the Puritan focus upon the invisible world, and to its US-American English association with witchcraft. It leads from early American millennialist doxa to the nineteenth-century concept of America's manifest destiny and, in its relentless orientation toward a utopian future, embeds ideas of technology as a means of transcendence into American culture throughout its history, from Cotton Mather and Jonathan Edwards in the seventeenth and eighteenth centuries to Chuck Palahniuk, Don DeLillo, and the Silicon Valley cults examined in their most recent novels. By presenting a brief history of Puritan influence upon American cultural thinking over the last 400 years, this chapter outlines a historical and uniquely American conception of the weird.

Johnny Murray's "The Oozy Set: Toward a Weird(ed) Taxonomy" claims that the weird's feasibility as a critical term in literary and cultural studies would benefit from a careful examination of its relationship with the related genre of the gothic, science fiction, fantasy, and horror. Such taxonomical analysis must confront the weird's disruptive tendency to breach boundaries, which it shares in various ways with the affiliated categories, each of which possesses its own transgressive propensities that together have contributed to a troublesome legacy of fierce debates concerning definition. Murray illustrates his argument with evidence from representative texts by Arthur Machen, William Hope Hodgson, Algernon Blackwood, H. P. Lovecraft, and Clark Ashton Smith, as well as by more recent practitioners of the weird such as Jeff VanderMeer.

Genre is also the central category in Chapter 4, Anne-Maree Wicks's "Validating Weird Fiction as an (Im)Possible Genre." Wicks aims to reveal how weird fiction is an exemplary genre with an authority that reaffirms and practices its understanding of genre by engaging with its own impossibility. Tracing the similarities and differences between genre discourse in the context of what has been called "the Old Weird" and "the New Weird," Wicks sides with contemporary feminist criticism, claiming that the law of genre cannot hold.

The following two chapters share a Marxist orientation. Stephen Shapiro's contribution "Woke Weird and the Cultural Politics of Camp Transformation" conceptualizes the weird based on a number of contemporary TV shows, for an investigation of what he calls "Woke Weird": a "decolonial" weird raising consciousness about the nexus of racial domination and capitalist exploitation. Drawing on Karl Marx's concept of *Zwittersubsumption*, he investigates the potentials of this wokeness with regard to a new set of cultural alliances and progressive social coalitions. Tim Lanzendörfer's "The Weird in/of Crisis, 1930/2010" tries to find an answer to the question of why the weird has (re)gained its popularity since the beginning of the current century and he takes an explicitly political position to answer that question. He takes two "temporal markers"—the years 1930 and 2010 as indicators for two periods in which weird fiction blossomed—as points of departure for his investigation of the weird as a literary mode indicative for severe socioeconomic crises in American culture (the "Great Depression" and the "Great Recession," as Lanzendörfer frames it), an understanding he tries to prove by interpreting Lovecraft's *At the Mountains of Madness* (written in 1931, published in 1936) (negotiating the crisis of "modernist liberal capitalism") and Jeff VanderMeer's Southern Reach Trilogy (2014) (negotiating the effects of neoliberal capitalism), all the while substantiating a conceptual difference between what he terms "the weird" and "Weird" (with a capital W), modeled after the Marxist capitalization of "History."

A philosophical conversation—in the form of Chapters 7 and 8—between Daniel D. Fineman and Graham Harman concludes Part One of the book. Fineman's "After Weird: Harman, Deleuze, and the American 'Thing'" brings two major philosophers of the continental school into a critical dialogue: namely, Harman and Gilles Deleuze—not, as Fineman insists, "to decide between the ontologies of Deleuze and Harman but to briefly reflect on what each can uncover in the unpacking of American literature" (Fineman, 90). His case studies in this context are Emily Dickinson (which he associates with Deleuze's weird) and H. P. Lovecraft (which he associates with Harman's weird). Fineman's siding with Deleuze provokes a response by Harman. His contribution, "Concerning a Deleuzean Weird: A Response to Dan Fineman," takes up the, as he calls it, "friendly dispute" (Harman, 105) and defends himself against the criticism brought forth in the preceding chapter.

The investigation into the multitude of media used by artists to engage with the weird—*Part Two: Medium*—is opened by Eugenie Brinkema's "*Get Out*, Race, and Formal Destiny (On Common Weirdness)," which provides an interpretation of Jordan Peele's 2017 film *Get Out* as an example for what she calls "*common weirdness . . . a weird that is not at all strange*" (Brinkema, 127) and that therefore allows Peele to engage with the everyday horrors of contemporary urban America: racism and the violence linked to it.

Maryam Aras's chapter also deals with the horrors of racialized othering. Her chapter, "From a Heap of Broken Images Toward a Postcolonial Weird: Ana Lily Amirpour's Western Landscapes," argues that in her two feature films *A Girl Walks Home Alone at Night* (2014) and *The Bad Batch* (2017), Iranian-American filmmaker Amirpour rearranges classic American genres such as the Western and the gothic movie in a weirded fashion. Both films make use of the weird as a basic principle of Amirpour's vision of America. The weird western landscapes of her work thus figure as spatial configurations that correspond and reframe the imaginary of Iranian-America.

In the next chapter, "'It Is in Our House Now:' *Twin Peaks*, Nostalgia, and David Lynch's Weird Spaces," Oliver Moisich and Markus Wierschem argue that David Lynch's and Frost's *Twin Peaks: The Return* may be read as a statement on popular contemporary revival TV shows. In reference to Lynch's earlier work, the weird spaces in the series parody the nostalgic aspect of other shows and propound storyworld logic. Moisich and Wierschem examine Lynch's use and creation of weird forms of spatiality in his work, via the Foucauldian concept of heterotopia and the Bakhtinian concept of the chronotope. Finally, this reading investigates *Twin Peaks: The Return* in the light of this conceptualization.

For the most part, the academic discourse on weirdness has largely overlooked music as a medial outlet for weird creativity. However, as Chapter 12 demonstrates, the music that Captain Beefheart and His Magic Band made between the late 1960s and the early 1980s is often seen as the epitome of the weird—deliberately misshapen tunes, disorienting rhythms, and strange vocal styles combined with lyrics that probe the hidden recesses of the American psyche. Paul Sheehan's "Demolishing the Blues: Captain Beefheart as Modernist

Outsider" examines the contradictory nature of Beefheart's status as a "modernist outsider," deeply committed to his own intuitive strangeness. The Beefheartian weird, Sheehan argues, provides nothing less than a radical relocation of the insurrectionist spirit of the continental avant-garde to the timeless imaginary of the American desert landscape.

Florian Zappe's chapter, "Weird Visual Mythopoeia: On Matthew Barney's *Cremaster Cycle*," approaches the weird yet from another perspective—that of avant-garde cinema. He argues that Matthew Barney's *Cremaster Cycle* offers a variation of the long tradition of weird mythopoeia. The complex and seemingly impenetrable Cremaster mythology evokes an experience that accords with Mark Fisher's definition of the weird that has its roots in the collapsing of established epistemological frameworks. The sensation of "weirdness" in view of the *Cremaster Cycle* is the product of the gap that opens between the mythological objects displayed on the screen and our habitual and prefabricated modes of reading them. In this, Zappe argues, Barney is a prototypical "productionist" artist (as defined by Harman) who uses a unique mythopoetic visual vocabulary to open up epistemological chasms.

In Chapter 14, Alexander Greiffenstern analyzes the different narrative strategies that Alan Moore employs in his Lovecraftian comic book series *Providence* (2015–17). Being more than an homage to the writer's work, *Providence* also ponders on ideas of writing and inspiration. According to Greiffenstern's "Hidden Cultures and the Representation and Creation of Weird Reality in Alan Moore's *Providence*," the power of texts for the creation of our reality plays an important role for Moore and issue of representation, the role of the media and political propaganda that are important in the setting of 1919, echo similar questions today. Moore's *Providence* negotiates the topics of racism and sexuality in terms of Lovecraft's work, which can also be read as commentary on the social fabric of contemporary America.

Fred Francis's chapter demonstrates that high fashion can also be a suitable medium for eccentric creativity. In "Alien Beauty: The Glamor of the Eerie," he focuses on a particular style of fashion called "alien beauty," represented by designers and design collectives such as Fecal Matter, Salvia, MLMA, and Aryuna and shows how their aesthetic has an astonishingly close kinship to central motifs of the canon of weird fiction and art. Arguing along the lines of Fisher's distinction between the weird and the eerie, Francis shows how these designers employ the disruptive qualities of these aesthetic modes to scrutinize the implicit normativity of the fashion industry regarding gender categories, beauty standards, and also the marketability of clothes.

The final analytical chapter of the volume—Tanya Krzywinska's "Conspiracy Hermeneutics: *The Secret World* as Weird Tale"—shows that the weird has also crept in the most recent of popular entertainment media. This chapter takes the multiplayer online game *The Secret World* (2012) as a starting point to delineate what she terms "weird games" by commending the aesthetic potential of the notion of weirdness for this medium. There is a complex form of adaptation going on, Krzywinska argues, whereby the weird mode crucially influences the today's grammar of the participatory and rule-based digital game form, in contradistinction to the established generic norms and conventions.

Finally in his "Afterword: Weird in the Walls," Roger Luckhurst reflects on the multiperspectival reading of the American Weird presented in this volume, eventually arguing for a decidedly political reading of weird media practices in the United States, in particular as they pertain to race relations in the Mexican-American borderlands. This is an argument that usefully and necessarily points in the direction of post-nationalist or even irreducibly localist forms of weird culture that equally problematize and confirm the centrality of weirdness in American culture. Thus, we do feel that this highly diverse set of perspectives on the American Weird makes a strong case for *weirdness* being a worthy candidate for joining the ranks of terms listed in *Our Aesthetic Categories*. That is to say, the *the weird* may adequately represent some of the fundamental issues of contemporary cultural and social life, including the anxieties caused by economic crises and ecological disasters. As if tacitly referring to the aesthetic-political thrust of Ngai's argument regarding the cute, the zany, and the interesting, yet coming from the present context of the American Weird, Luckhurst contends that the latter "has to be regarded as simultaneously high *and* low, a kind of war on the banality of middlebrow, mainstream literary culture. It is an acquired taste, messy, mean, and miscegenate, but for that very reason the weird continues to speak powerfully to our times" (Luckhurst 2015: 204)—which is, precisely, what the following chapters have set out to explore, demonstrate, and, eventually, prove.

References

Bolter, J. D., and R. Grusin (2000), *Remediation: Understanding New Media*, Cambridge, MA: The MIT Press.

Everett, J., and J. H. Shank (2015), *The Unique Legacy of Weird Tales: The Evolution of Modern Fantasy and Horror*, London: Rowman & Littlefield.

Fisher, M. (2016), *The Weird and the Eerie*, London: Repeater.
Harman, G. (2012), *Weird Realism: Lovecraft and Philosophy*, Winchester, UK: Zero Books.
Joshi, S. T. (1990), *The Weird Tale: Arthur Machen, Lord Dunsany, Algernon Blackwood, M.R. James, Ambrose Bierce, H.P. Lovecraft*, Austin, TX: University of Texas Press.
Joshi, S. T. (2001), *The Modern Weird Tale*, Jefferson, NC: McFarland & Company.
Lovecraft, H. P. (1973), *Supernatural Horror in Literature*, New York: Dover.
Luckhurst, R. (2015), "American Weird," in G. Canavan and E. C. Link (eds.), *The Cambridge Companion to American Science Fiction*, 194–205, Cambridge: Cambridge University Press.
Luckhurst, R. (2017), "The Weird: A Dis/Orientation," *Textual Practice*, 31 (6): 1041–61.
Moorcock, M. (2011), "Foreweird," in A. and J. VanderMeer (eds.), *The Weird: A Compendium of Strange and Dark Tales*, xi–xiv, New York: Tom Doherty Associates.
Ngai, S. (2012), *Our Aesthetic Categories: Zany, Cute, Interesting*, Cambridge, MA: Harvard University Press.
Sederholm, C. H., and J. A. Weinstock (2016), *The Age of Lovecraft*, Minneapolis, MN: University of Minnesota Press.
Thacker, E. (2010), *After Life*, Chicago and London: University of Chicago Press.
Thacker, E. (2014), "Dark Media," in A. R. Galloway, E. Thacker, and M. Wark, *Excommunication: Three Inquiries in Media and Mediation*, Chicago: University of Chicago Press.

Part One

Concept

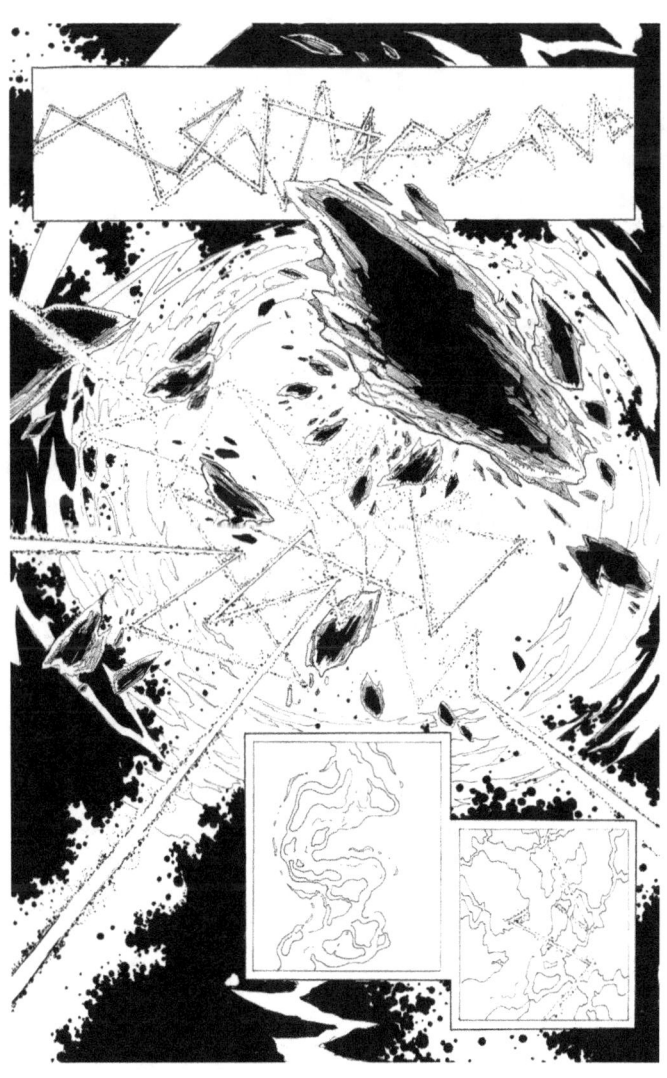

Untitled (acrylic on duralar 9" x 12") by Keith Tilford © 2010.

2

A Doxa of the American Weird

Dan O'Hara

The word "weird" had long fallen into disuse in England, barring in some of the northernmost dialects, when in the first decades of the seventeenth century Shakespeare reintroduced it from the Scots into the English language. It carried, at that time, a very definite sense of a destiny imminently manifest: it described both the foretelling and the *poeisis* of a future.

Probably first performed in 1606, and certainly first printed in 1623, *Macbeth* planted a word of power and movement into the vocabulary of the generation that boarded the *Mayflower*. Shakespeare had borrowed the word and its context from his habitual source, Holinshed's 1587 *Chronicles*:

> [C]ommon opinion was, that these women were either *the weird sisters*, that is (as ye would say) the goddesses of destinie, or else some nymphs or feiries, indued with knowledge of prophesie by their necromanticall science, bicause euerie thing came to passe as they had spoken. (Holinshed 1587: 171; emphasis added)

And in his turn, Holinshed had taken the idea of "the weird sisters" from the Scottish historian Boece's 1527 *Historia Gentis Scotorum*:

> [B]ecaus al thingis succeedit as thir wemen devinit, the pepill traistit and jugit thame to be weird sisteris. (Boece 1821: 259)

The Americans-yet-to-be of the seventeenth century therefore had a very different concept of "weirdness" from that which is taken for granted in the twenty-first century. The current vernacular use of "weird," associating the word with abnormality or strangeness, is a nineteenth-century British English misunderstanding: it is purely nominative, a noun or adjective describing a thing or a fixed state of affairs, and is often merely a synonym for a characteristically British ambiguity: the word "funny" (the British often have to ask each other "do you mean funny-haha or funny-peculiar?" and also often find a peculiar comedy in the weird collapse of one into the other). Fourteenth-century Scots, Jacobean English, and American English on the other hand all share a more dynamic, shifting, revelatory sense of the weird that has little to do with the strange or uncanny, and that is easily misunderstood if read through the superimposition of more recent reductive definitions.

The American concept of the weird bore an unhumorous earnestness with it ab initio: an apocalyptic sense of predestination and imminent revelation, and an apparently unrelated relation to wealth. Only in Scots English is there the concept of the "weirdless," meaning those who are idle and unprosperous.[1] In the reign of James I, the Scottish King of England and author of the treatise upon witchcraft *Daemonologie*, the "werd" or "weird"[2] was also, as in *Macbeth*, to do with the practice of witchcraft: the ordaining and prophesy of futures, and this witchcraft was no small part of the European godlessness that the Puritan colonists of America were keen to leave behind (see Stuart 1597).

Puritan Belief and Destiny

The first colonists in the seventeenth century were Puritans schooled in a tradition of millennial thinking that didn't initially have anything intrinsically to do with America. St. John of Patmos's Book of Revelation or St. Augustine's notion of the City of God were not the particular properties of these colonists; they were only an influence upon them because they were a major influence upon English religious thinking at the time the colonists left Europe. They were leaving a country which had recently undergone upheaval, in the shape of the Elizabethan reformation of the church, which founded a new, Protestant English church in the place of the Catholic church, which rejected Rome and the pope as corrupt, and which tried to create a Christian religion not dependent upon Rome and purified of some of its more corrupt practices. The most appalling excesses of Rome made it seem not ridiculous to believe that the papacy was in fact going through an apocalyptic phase itself. The protestants believed that the papacy might very well be the anti-Christ, so extreme were some of the corruptions, and much of the English literature of the time, such as John Foxe's *Actes and Monuments* specifically described Rome as the apocalyptic beast, to be destroyed by the English church. It was a time of holy war.

Puritans believed that the reformation hadn't gone far enough, that there were still corruptions in the English church, and that a new church was needed, in a new land. Their mission, therefore, was a religious one: they saw themselves leaving on an errand into the wilderness, going like Moses toward a promised land, and considering themselves God's chosen people. So is it that the small number of Puritans who left England and colonized "New England" took with them a vision of themselves as the people chosen to build a new Israel.

The idea of such a mission is a much older one than this. The Puritans were taking an ancient Judaeo-Christian mythology and applying it to themselves. But if we can understand that, first of all, they were escaping a situation in which they believed chaos and corruption had taken over Rome and then England, then perhaps we can understand why they might see themselves as having an important religious role. And if we consider that their explanation for the chaos and corruption of Rome would have to be a religious explanation itself, what would be more likely than the biblical narrative of apocalypse—that encoded in St. John's Book of Revelation—in which the anti-Christ had taken over the functions of the church and was leading people astray?

Almost by accident of the Puritans' beliefs, the land they colonized, America, became invested with the value of the new Jerusalem, the place where the true worshippers of the true Christ will prepare the ground for his return, when he will banish the false Christ who sits in Rome. The Puritans explicitly saw themselves in this light, giving themselves Old Testament names in an echo of Moses's people heading off into the wilderness: an identification reinforced by the simple fact that this New World was a long way away from Europe, and was in fact a wilderness, and furthermore was in the West, which traditionally had been held to be the location not of Eden (the place of beginnings, and therefore in the East, where the sun rises) but of destiny (paradise is usually sought, in literature, in the West; from the *Odyssey*, where heaven is reached via Hades, located in the West, to the *Lord of the Rings*, in which the Grey Havens are located over the western seas) (see Tolkien 1954/5). This new land, so separate, emphasized a sense of messianic destiny in its very geographical separateness. This separateness becomes most interesting in the nineteenth and twentieth centuries, when technologies such as the telegraph, the steam boat, the aeroplane, and the internet start to close distances. For, at the beginning, the belief that earthly paradise will be created in America through the millennium is a literal one founded on scripture, and much of the religious drive of the Puritans derives from this belief: that they should remain faithful so that millennium will come in America, because scripture prophesies the saints reigning with Christ on earth—therefore, they should try to be as holy as possible, so that they will become these saints. But later, in the eighteenth and nineteenth centuries, as America starts to obtain its modern shape, as Romanticism starts to encourage the notion of nature as a visionary heaven on earth, as Enlightenment ideas and modern science start to transform both society and the landscape, the American dream of the millennium starts to become less religiously literal, and more secular. It's from these roots that utopian thinking emerges: the idea that America can be a heaven on earth through prosperity, technology, and science, rather than through Puritan saintliness.

Millennialism and Technology

But there are also things lost, when America's idea of its own destiny as the promised land starts to become secularized. If you were a Puritan in the seventeenth century in America, you weren't just positively trying to be as saintly as possible in order to make sure that, when the millennium happened, you'd be sitting with Christ. You were also terrified that if you weren't holy enough, if you didn't obey God's commandments, the apocalypse would be your doom. Hence the great revivalist movements of the eighteenth century, with their frequent tone of hellfire and damnation preaching, which were intended to scare people into virtue because the stakes were so high, millennium being just around the corner. Ideas of a technological, secular utopia lack the element of fear that drives millennialism: utopian narratives are myths that dispense with the stick, leaving only the carrot. But these narratives are relatively recent, and as such they do not form the principal tradition of apocalyptic thought in America; they only emerge from and are influenced by it.

> 'Tis probable that the world shall be more like Heaven in the millennium in this respect: that contemplation and spiritual employments, and those things that more directly concern the mind and religion, will be more the saint's ordinary business than now. There will be so many contrivances and inventions to facilitate and expedite their necessary secular business that they shall have more time for more noble exercise, and that they will have better contrivances of assisting one another through the whole earth by more expedite, easy, and safe communication between distant regions than now. The invention of the mariner's compass is a thing discovered by God to the world to that end. And how exceedingly has that one thing enlarged and facilitated communication. And who can doubt but that yet God will make it more perfect, so that there need not be such a tedious voyage in order to hear from the other hemisphere? And so the country about the poles need no longer be hid to us, but the whole earth may be as one community, one body in Christ. (Edwards 1955: 207–8)

Jonathan Edwards is here in the early eighteenth century talking about America as the origin and missionary of the millennium. And Edwards is enthusiastic and positive about the millennium; his approach is not that of hellfire and damnation preaching, but more a kind of visionary ideal. Yet his vision is also starting to be tainted by a certain utopianism—for example, his enthusiasm for the mariner's compass, an article of technology, man-made, a product of scientific progress, a material thing which makes material life better. This is not a vision of a luminous and numinous heaven, but of a heaven on earth made by man for man with the help of science. And the "world" is to benefit from this new utopianism—how? It's telling again that he stresses communications technologies—already, it seems Edwards is beginning to see America's God-given role as an imperial power.

This kind of techno-millennialist vision emerges again during the time of the Civil War, which itself was seen as a kind of holy war: the North, the victorious Union armies, comprising in religious terms of the four main Protestant groups during the nineteenth century—the Baptists, Methodists, Presbyterians, and Congregationalists—really held the conviction that they were playing a part in bringing the millennium forward, fighting a part of the great war against Satan, creating a Redeemer Nation out of the divided North and South. It was at this time that the telegraph started to be used widely, and the way it is described by Joseph Brady in 1850 recalls Edwards directly:

> This noble invention is to be the means of extending civilization, republicanism, and Christianity over the earth. It must and will be extended to nations half-civilized, and thence to those now savage and barbarous. Our government will be the grand center of this mighty influence.... The beneficial and harmonious operation of our institutions will be seen, and similar ones adopted. Christianity must speedily follow them; and we shall behold the grand spectacle of a whole world, civilized, republican, and Christian. Then will wrong and injustice be forever banished. Every yoke shall be broken, and the oppressed go free. Wars will cease from the earth. Men "shall beat their swords into plough shares, and their spears into pruning-hooks. Nation shall not lift up sword against nation; neither shall they learn war any more"; for each man shall feel that every other man is his neighbor—his brother. Then shall come to pass the millennium, when "they shall teach no more every man his neighbor, and every man his brother, saying Know ye the Lord; for all shall know him, from the least of them unto the greatest." (Brady 1850: 61–2)

Edwards and by extension Brady, whose rhetoric is directly apocalyptic, both appear to see the millennium as actually happening in their own time. They regard America as already having started the process of millennium;

something is already under way. They see America as promising a different kind of millennium, one which is a process; not a realized utopia, or a sudden transformation of the earth into heaven, but a kind of slow political and social transformation. Their idea that millennium is a process suggests that America's development and the process of the millennium are one and the same thing; so, in America, material, political, social progress, and religious virtue are one and the same thing.

But how can Edwards or Brady regard the millennium as already having started if Christ hasn't shown up on earth yet? There are in fact two doctrines, called postmillennialism and premillennialism. Edwards and Brady are clearly postmillennialists: they believed that Jesus would return to earth after the millennium; hence, they can continue to believe in America's material progress as an instrument of God. Premillennialists insisted that Jesus had to return to earth before the millennium could begin, which latter belief somewhat reduces the incentives for trying to make material, scientific progress—why bother, if it's all going to be redundant when Christ arrives? The weakness of this position strengthened the postmillennialists, and, in doing so, strengthened the connection made widely in America between material value and Godly virtue.

This is only one of a number of paradoxes that inheres to millennialist thinking. For example, if you're hoping for the millennium to come, no matter which doctrine you follow, you still have to support the idea that before Christ's thousand-year reign on earth can happen, there will be a period when the anti-Christ rules the earth, the saints are persecuted, and there is a violent holy war preceding a day of judgment. In other words, there has to be darkness before there can be light, and in hoping for the light you must inevitably also hope for the darkness which precedes it. This paradoxical attitude toward the millennium grounds a contemporary strange attraction to apocalyptic narratives and films and images such as ruin-porn: we relish the apocalypse only with a little ambivalence of emotion, because we have the promise of a subsequent utopia.

A second paradox is that the millennium was conceived both as a promise, but also as a threat. America might have been seen as the promised land and the Puritans as God's chosen people, the elect; but they were also wary of failing to fulfill God's mission for them; and the hellfire vision of their punishment was derived from the Old Testament. However much, over the nineteenth and twentieth centuries, the stick was replaced by the carrot, this vision of hellfire persisted, and meant that millennium signified not just hope to America, but also a certain anxiety.

Most peculiar of all millennial paradoxes is the idea that the apocalyptic battle against Satan will not be one of the spirit, but a material, real battle. In America, God and guns go together. One of the battle-songs during the Civil War was a hymn written by George Duffield Jr. in 1858:

> Stand up, stand up for Jesus,
> The trumpet call obey;
> Forth to the mighty conflict
> In this His glorious day.
>
> Stand up, stand up for Jesus,
> The strife will not be long
> This day the noise of battle;
> The next the victor's song. (Christiansen 2007)

This sense of militancy persists in such movements as the Jesus Army, and infects mainstream American religious thinking. It's not only radical Islam that has a concept of Jihad, or holy war, but American Christianity too. In this, America's millennialists and Islam are almost long-lost twins; no other religion has this kind of militant self-image but these two. It's interesting to "read" apocalyptic Hollywood films in this light: How often do we have an avenging angel figure wielding a gun, fighting a righteous war, in films with no overt religious content? One can certainly read *Terminator 2* in this way, for example; but occasionally the eschatology of American culture manifests itself in less direct and more cryptic fashion.

Eschatology and Comic Apocalypse

In the film version of Thomas Harris's novel *Red Dragon*, the dragon of the title is the guiding obsession of a serial killer called the Tooth Fairy, whose real name is Francis Dolarhyde, who has the Blake painting *The Great Red Dragon and the Woman Clothed in Sun* tattooed on his back. The image of this tattoo is derived from William Blake's illustrations for his mythopoeic work of 1793 "America a Prophesy," which tells of seven warlike men who confront "Albions fiery prince" or "Albions angel," symbolized as the red dragon, "a dragon form clashing his scales" (Blake 2014: 199).

Blake is reworking mythic aspects of the Book of Revelations, the final book of the New Testament, a part of the New Testament added later, and written not by one of the four gospel writers but by another John, John of

Patmos. The place of this book in the Bible and indeed in Christian theology has always been dubious; but it has also been perhaps even more influential on ordinary people's religious thinking, especially in America, than even the Gospels. The red dragon appears in the Book of Revelations—or apocalypse—as a manifestation of Lucifer or Satan: it is the red dragon that St. Michael and the angels fight and cast out of heaven. On earth the great whore of Babylon arises, clothed in the red and gold of the sun, seated upon the red dragon. In John of Patmos' book, the red dragon is Satan, presiding over earth. He has to be cast out in an apocalypse before millennium is possible. But as D. H. Lawrence tells us, the symbol is much more ancient than the Bible, and stems from a different, probably Chaldean symbolism. Dragons appear in all old mythologies: in the Chinese certainly; and in the Norse, where it is a serpent eating its own tail, Ourobouros, curled around the roots of the tree of life, Yggdrasil, upon which lie the three realms of reality, Asgard, Midgard and Niflheim or Hel. Lawrence allies the fear of the red dragon in mythology with a fear of the unpredictable life spirit: "the dragon is the symbol of the fluid, rapid, startling movement of life within us. That startled life which runs through us like a serpent, or coils within us potent and waiting, like a serpent, this is the dragon" (Lawrence 1980: 123). And man has, as Lawrence says, always been aware of something potent within him but not entirely under his control, whether it be his sexual desires, his anger, his unconscious—all of the things which can appear to man to happen to him, as a part of the external world within him. It is libido or *élan vital*, the life spirit, though Lawrence prefers the more apocalyptic symbol.

Blake takes up the symbol of the red dragon of the Apocalypse, with its seven crowned heads. In the book of John of Patmos, these seven heads must be cut off by man before the dragon is cast out, and man can be free of Satan. But Blake unifies the dragons; he has a more nuanced concept of the natural power of the red dragon. In "America a Prophesy," Blake makes the red dragon symbolize Albion: that is, the ancient England, and the seven warlike men who must cast the red dragon down are all Americans including George Washington, Benjamin Franklin, Thomas Paine, and various historical defenders of American independence. Blake uses the symbolism found in the Book of Revelations to justify the American Revolution. England is the Satan, the red dragon which much be cast down. And once this has happened, then the millennium—the thousand-year reign of Christ on earth—can come to pass *in America*.

All of this literary history forms merely a tapestry in front of which Hannibal Lecter, the central character of *Red Dragon*, may play his part. Lecter is a

Lithuanian immigrant to the United States and a Europhile who loves the classical music and architecture of renaissance Europe, and who is very un-American in the sense of being in thrall to the old world. Set against him is the tooth fairy, Francis Dolarhyde—whose "hyde" or skin is not made of dollars, but a tattoo of the red dragon, and whose personality is itself split into two—the Dolarhyde who strives to love and the Dolarhyde who is convinced he is becoming the red dragon.

Such allusions explicitly invoke millennialist eschatology, speaking to an American filmgoing audience who won't know Blake but who certainly know the Book of Revelation. Blake was depicting the dragon as Albion against which America had to fight for its independence. Dolarhyde is allied with this evil, with the ancient Satan—or, in other words, the England which lost its colonies in the war of independence. What can it mean, then, that Dolarhyde is here allied with the symbol of Satanic English influence? The serpent symbolism isn't solely to do with Dolarhyde's distorted sexuality, nor to do with the red dragon within him, the split personality he cannot control.

There is a strange set of apocalyptic resonances being set up here, as in so much recent and more explicitly apocalyptic Hollywood film. America is figured as the city on a hill, the new Jerusalem, fighting the ancient dragon, or serpent, or Satan—which is sometimes England. America is an ex-colony, fighting not only for its independence but also for its holy or "manifest destiny" as the realm of the new thousand-year reign of Christ on earth.

In the nineteenth century, Herman Melville, James Fenimore Cooper, and Nathaniel Hawthorne all drew on the apocalyptic tradition to criticize the New England Puritan vision and its excessive idealism, and to satirize and undermine a corrosive overconfidence in America, her manifest destiny, and her material progress. In the twentieth century, a kind of comic apocalypse became the norm in American literature. Whereas apocalyptic films have been by and large realist in method, novels that are realist tended to be utopian or dystopian rather than apocalyptic: witness the delay in critical recognition for the richness of the tradition to which, for example, Octavia Butler's *Parable of the Sower* (1993) and Margaret Atwood's *The Handmaid's Tale* (1985) belong. Apocalypse, on the other hand, tends toward comedy, perhaps because the effect of the surreal in comedy lends an edge of doomy immediacy that utopian and dystopian novels often lack. Chuck Palahniuk presents us with comic apocalypses in most of his fiction: *Survivor* (1999) and *Fight Club* (1996) are two such novels. Nathanael West's *The Day of the Locust* (1939), or *Miss Lonelyhearts* (1933), like Herman Melville's *The Confidence-Man* (1857), presents a surrealistic comedy about the devil deceiving humanity in order to pervert it. The protagonist of Ralph Ellison's *Invisible Man* (1952) finds that America in the millennium is not actually a place of millennium for everyone—only for the whites—and so has to disguise himself, but in so doing keeps getting mistaken for a con man called Rinehart. Kurt Vonnegut's *Slaughterhouse-Five* (1969), part of the subtitle of which is as faux-antique as *The Confidence-Man: His Masquerade*—it reads *Slaughterhouse-Five, or the Children's Crusade*—is an apocalyptic comedy about the bombing of Dresden. Saul Bellow's *Mr. Sammler's Planet* (1970) is about the devil's cities being those of the northern United States. Joseph Heller's *Catch-22* (1961); Vladimir Nabokov's *Pale Fire* (1962); Thomas Pynchon's *Gravity's Rainbow* (1973); Tom Wolfe's *The Bonfire of the Vanities* (1987); Don DeLillo's *Underworld* (1997)—all of these novels are comic apocalypses; they all employ a kind of humor-in-horror as their principal tone and are all satirical in intent. They use the tropes of classical satiric comedies, which present situations in which everyone is fooled, or a fool: Ben Jonson's renaissance plays present situations in which the greed of devious swindlers (or "con-men") is matched only by the greed of their stupid victims.

These novels also all use one particular trope found in *The Confidence-Man*: metamorphosis. The mutation of one character into another, or the changing of form, is a common comic device: think, for example, of Bottom in *A Midsummer Night's Dream*, who is transformed into an ass. Only slightly different is the comic aspect of disguise (think of Viola in *Twelfth Night*, disguised as a boy), or the comic tale of mistaken identity (think of, perhaps, the 1979 movie *The Life of Brian*, where Brian is mistaken, much to his own distress and to our amusement, for the Son of God) (see Shakespeare 1632; Jones 1979). In such comedies we derive amusement from our knowledge of what the characters themselves do not realize. Clearly comedy, because it permits a distance from the real, also permits farcical, sometimes preposterous mutations, which mutations allow the author to present the characters' bemusement in the face of their own gullibility or naiveté. It permits a double level of humor in that we can laugh at the characters' ignorance of their own ignorance, and insofar as we may also laugh at a metalevel of humor, which they cannot appreciate (e.g., the visual and linguistic pun in Bottom being turned into an Ass).

The metamorphoses of the devil in *The Confidence-Man* therefore belong to a long tradition of low satirical comedy that hinges on reversals and questionings of identity. Apocalyptic comedies are full of doubles, masks, disguises, impostors, impersonations, deceit: where truth is manipulated for low ends, the characters' plausible simulation of the truth is enacted in their dissimulations.

The American Wyrd

This logic of humor-in-horror of the mutated, displaced, tainted, broken, deformed, or "different" body leads in two directions in American culture. One is toward the augmented future: the techno-millennialist future of Silicon Valley, of grinding and body hacking, of surgery and perfectability, but also of Arnold Schwarzenegger as Governor of California—or of the character Solomon in Harmony Korine's 1997 film *Gummo*, a white-trash hydrocephalic child working out with tied-together kitchen utensils. It is an excision of the taint the earliest Puritans feared they had brought with them to America from Europe—the deformity of the body, being via maternal impression the outward sign of spiritual corruption, the belief in which Anne Bradstreet documented in her poem "The Author To Her Book." The other is toward the totalizing linear millennialist vision of apocalypse, of a planet without humans—that is to say, without Americans. Only the first of these visions is currently being realized, which is why the American Weird is a millennial process—a verb or gerund—a weirding. It is a process of becoming. As a verb it cannot be; it can only do.

Whether such recent definitions of the weird as conform to its late-nineteenth-century British vernacular usage are adequate as general descriptive categories for British cultural expressions in the twentieth century remains a moot point. The notion of seeing the inside from the perspective of the outside was the explicit raison d'être of late-1970s literary Martianism, whose chief proponents were Craig Raine and Martin Amis: it rapidly became clichéd as a practice, as critics recognized that what presented itself as outside the British literary canon was very much a product of the inside.

But there is no question that the binary categories of inside/outside so essential to current formulations of the weird are both semantically inadequate and ahistorical for any concept of an American Weird, in ignoring the extent to which Puritan thinking in America from the time of the colonies onward already incorporated a conception of "weirding." The *wyrd*—OS *wurd*, OHG *wurt*, ON *urðr* (Timmer 1941: 24), all of which are roots of the modern German *werden*—as a concept of fate in Anglo-Saxon poetry and onward relates to the Puritan focus upon the invisible world, and to its US English association with witchcraft. It leads from early American millennialist doxa to the nineteenth-century concept of America's manifest destiny and, in its relentless orientation toward a utopian future, embeds ideas of American technology as a means of transcendence into American culture throughout its history. It cannot work if it is a stable concept: if it signals that previous concepts and frameworks are obsolete, and we recognize that signal, then it has already rendered itself obsolete. The American Weird must change to be: it has to be dynamic, nonessential, a nonconcept, a moving shadow.

Notes

1 "WEIRD I. *n.* 5. (2) (iii) *weirdless, wa(i)rd-, weard-*, unfortunate, unprosperous, esp. as implying one's own incompetence, hence inept, incapable, shiftless, improvident, managing one's affairs badly, thriftless, gen. of persons" (SND 1931–75).
2 "We(i)rd, *n.* 1. c. A person or entity viewed as the instrument of destiny; one of the Fates. d. *pl.*= We(i)rd sisteris *n. pl.*" (DOST 1937--2002).

References

A Dictionary of the Older Scottish Tongue (1937–2002), London: Oxford University Press. Abbr. as DOST.
Atwood, M. (1985), *The Handmaid's Tale*, Toronto: McLelland and Stewart.
Bellow, S. (1970), *Mr. Sammler's Planet*, New York: Viking.
Blake, W. (2014), *The Complete Poems*, ed. W. H. Stevenson, London: Routledge.
Boece, H. (1821), *The History and Chronicles of Scotland*, vol. 2, trans. John Bellenden, Edinburgh: W. and C. Tait.
Bradstreet, A. (1678), "The Author to Her Book," in *Several Poems*, 2nd edn, Boston: John Foster.
Brady, J. (1850), "The Magnetic Telegraph," *Ladies Repository*, 10.
Butler, O. E. (1993), *Parable of the Sower*, New York: Four Walls Eight Windows.
Christiansen, R. (2007), "The story behind the hymn," *Telegraph*, 25 September.
DeLillo, D. (1997), *Underworld*, New York: Scribner.
Edwards, J. (1955), *The Philosophy of Jonathan Edwards: From His Private Notebooks*, ed. Harvey G. Townsend, Eugene: University of Oregon Press.
Ellison, R. (1952), *Invisible Man*, New York: Random House.
Foxe, J. (1563), *Actes and Monuments of these Latter and Perillous Days, Touching Matters of the Church*, London: John Day.
Gummo (1997), [Film], Dir. Harmony Korine, USA: Fine Line Features.
Harris, T. (1981), *Red Dragon*, New York: G. P. Putnam's Sons.
Heller, J. (1961), *Catch-22*, New York: Simon & Schuster.
Holinshed, R. (1587), *Chronicles of England, Scotland and Ireland*, vol. 5. http://www.cems.ox.ac.uk/holinshed/.
Lawrence, D. H. (1980), *Apocalypse and the Writings on Revelation*, ed. Mara Kalnins, Cambridge: Cambridge University Press.

Melville, H. (1857), *The Confidence-Man: His Masquerade*, New York: Dix, Edwards & Co.
Monty Python's Life of Brian (1979), [Film], Dir. Terry Jones, UK: Handmade Films.
Nabokov, V. (1962), *Pale Fire*, New York: G. P. Putnam's Sons.
Palahniuk, C. (1996), *Fight Club*, New York: Norton.
Palahniuk, C. (1999), *Survivor: A Novel*, London: Jonathan Cape.
Pynchon, T. (1973), *Gravity's Rainbow*, New York: Viking.
Red Dragon (2002), [Film], Dir. Brett Ratner, USA: Universal Pictures.
Scottish National Dictionary (1931–75), Edinburgh: Scottish National Dictionary Association. Abbr. as SND.
Shakespeare, W. (1623), *Mr. William Shakespeares Comedies, Histories, & Tragedies*, London: William Jaggard and Edward Blount.
Stuart, J. C. (1597), *Daemonologie, In Forme of a Dialogue, Divided into three Books*, Edinburgh: Robert Walde-graue.
Terminator 2: Judgement Day (1991), [Film], Dir. James Cameron, USA: Carolco Pictures.
Timmer, B. J. (1941), "Wyrd in Anglo-Saxon Prose and Poetry," *Neophilologus*, 26 (1): 24–33.
Tolkien, J. R. R. (1954/5), *The Lord of the Rings*, London: Allen & Unwin.
Vonnegut, K. (1969), *Slaughterhouse-Five; or, The Children's Crusade, a Duty-Dance with Death*, New York: Delacorte.
West, N. (1933), *Miss Lonelyhearts*, New York: Avon.
West, N. (1939), *Day of the Locust*, New York: Random House.
Wolfe, T. (1987), *Bonfire of the Vanities*, New York: Farrar, Strauss, Giroux.

3

The Oozy Set

Toward a Weird(ed) Taxonomy

Johnny Murray

Despite its increasing prominence, "the weird" remains a somewhat nebulous term, a "nascent critical classification" (Simmons 2013: 3) that is yet to be firmly established in the cultural lexicon. China Miéville asserts that the weird "has had a colossal impact across work in all media, with under-investigated generically problematizing implications" (Miéville 2009: 510). Such problematizing implications would seem to arise at least in part from the weird's evident hybridity, which exacerbates contentious questions of taxonomy within the fields of "genre" fiction, theory, and studies. The present chapter argues that the weird's viability as a critical term with shared meaning and utility would benefit from a careful examination of its relationship with those genres which contribute to its hybrid makeup and with which it frequently is conflated in much cultural discourse to date—namely, the gothic, science fiction, fantasy, and horror. Such taxonomical analysis must confront the weird's disruptive tendency to rupture limits, a tendency shared in varying ways and degrees by the affiliated genres as well, each of which possesses transgressive propensities that together have contributed to a complex legacy of "boundary disputes and definition wars" (Attebery 1992: 11).

What *is* the weird? Ann VanderMeer and Jeff VanderMeer suggest that it involves "the pursuit of some indefinable and perhaps maddeningly unreachable understanding of the world beyond the mundane" (A. and J. VanderMeer 2011: xv). Miéville describes it as "an off-handedly predatory unknowable, a bad numinous, manifesting often at a much closer scale, right up tentacular in your face" (Miéville 2012: 381). Weird stories deal with outlandish things hopelessly beyond human comprehension, bringing us into contact with the radically alien, the utterly inconceivable, or as Arthur Machen puts it in his seminal weird novella *The Great God Pan*, "that for which we have no name" (Machen 2018: 53). Such a stress upon ineffable, incomprehensible phenomena presents certain challenges for critical analysis. Roger Luckhurst remarks that the weird "is hard to define because it focuses on the Horrors of the hard to define" (Luckhurst 2013: xvi). But if the weird is to flourish as a critical concept, it behooves us to search for some degree of shared understanding of what it is and how it works, lest it lose its distinctive semantic flavor and dissipate into a critically impoverished vagueness.

What happens if we attempt to explicate certain features that appear to be essential to the weird at its most prototypical? I contend that a thorough analysis of characteristic weird texts by prominent weird authors such as Machen, Algernon Blackwood, William Hope Hodgson, H. P. Lovecraft, and Clark Ashton Smith reveals recognizable elements of the gothic, science fiction, fantasy, and horror coalescing to produce a hybrid form that partakes of, but cannot be reduced to, each of the others. Of course, this begs the question of what is meant by the terms *gothic*, *science fiction*, *fantasy*, and *horror*, a question complicated by the lack of critical consensus surrounding each term. "The notion of what constitutes Gothic writing," observes David Punter, "is a contested site" (Punter 2000: vii). In the field of science fiction studies, according to Carl Freedman, "no definitional consensus exists" (Freedman 2000: 13). Brian Attebery contends that fantasy "always seems larger than any theory that tries to encompass it" (Attebery 1992: 5). Matt Hills notes the "monstrous outpouring of academic thought" devoted to horror, a "range of academic 'answers' [that] have raised further problems" (Hills 2005: 1). To further vex matters, each of the genres under discussion possesses a tendency to breach boundaries of various sorts in various ways. Victoria Nelson describes the gothic as "a consummate violator of boundaries" (Nelson 2012: 5). David Seed proclaims that science fiction has a "tendency to question limits and boundaries" (Seed 2011: 123). Fantasy, argues Rosemary Jackson, "is preoccupied by limits, with limiting categories, and with their projected dissolution" (Jackson 1981: 48). Roger Salomon maintains that "violation of various kinds is the principal action of horror narrative" (Salomon 2002: 130). This shared propensity to transgress poses difficulties for any rigorous effort to differentiate these genres. Given this situation, an approach that avoids rigid categories seems to be called for.

My strategy, therefore, will be to treat these genres as *fuzzy sets*—that is, classes defined not by partitions but by central prototypes (see Rosch 1978: 35–7). Thus, I will focus upon cores rather than borders, essences rather than edges. Deborah Kapchan and Pauline Turner Strong observe that the "study of genre brings us face to face with boundaries" (Kapchan and Strong 1999: 243), but the use of fuzzy sets enables us to subvert the strict dichotomies of traditional categorization. As Mark Currie points out, "the fuzzy set is one which approximates much more closely than the categories of classical logic could to the actual activities of categorization and recognition taking place in the human mind and in language" (Currie 2004: 120–1). Approaching the gothic, science fiction, fantasy, and horror as fuzzy sets, I will identify specific features widely considered to be principal characteristics of each genre and will demonstrate how those features merge into something irreducibly and unmistakably weird. In this way, I hope to suggest a flexible yet workable method of distinguishing the weird from its affiliated genres (as well as the latter from one another) while at the same time respecting the transgressive qualities of each and eschewing the pointless and counterproductive policing of borders.

I will begin with the gothic. Alan Lloyd-Smith declares that "one of the great strengths of the Gothic is its ability to articulate the voice of the 'other'" (Lloyd-Smith 2004: 8). "Gothic writing," affirms Sue Chaplin (2011: 260), "has been concerned often, one might say invariably, with representations of 'otherness.'" The encounter with the other is the prototypical element that I will focus upon here. Such encounters in gothic narratives typically evoke a sense of the uncanny in the characters as well as (ideally) in the reader. As Glennis Byron and David Punter state, "Phenomena of the uncanny form the background and indeed the *modus operandi* of much Gothic fiction" (Byron and Punter 2004: 286). The uncanny provides us with a clue regarding the nature of the other as it is portrayed in gothic texts. In his groundbreaking essay on the topic, Sigmund Freud proposes that "the uncanny is that species of the frightening that goes back to what was once well known and had long been familiar" (Freud 2003: 124). While Freud's psychoanalytical interpretation of the phenomenon is certainly debatable, it foregrounds what seems to be a key aspect of the experience: the disturbing sense of a *return* of some sort. The uncanny "would appear to be indissociably bound up with a sense of repetition or 'coming back,'" writes Nicholas Royle (2003: 2), "the return of the repressed, the constant or eternal recurrence of the same thing, a compulsion to repeat." In other words, the uncanny involves a feeling of *hauntedness*. Thus, we might describe the other that is encountered in gothic texts as a haunting other, and the encounter itself might more accurately be termed a reencounter.

The weird shares the gothic's concern with alterity. Weird fiction is, after all, notoriously typified by the presence of entities so radically different from normality that they are, to borrow a characteristic phrase from H. P. Lovecraft, "impossible to describe" (Lovecraft 2014: 404). But unlike the haunting other of the gothic, which in some sense has been known or encountered previously, the weird other at its most paradigmatic is completely unprecedented. "The whole experience whose verge we touched was unknown to humanity at all," proclaims the narrator of Algernon Blackwood's "The Willows" (Blackwood 2002: 50). "It was a new order of experience, and in the true sense of the word *unearthly*." The protagonist of H. P. Lovecraft's "The Whisperer in Darkness" expresses a similar sentiment: "Never before had I seen anything so strangely and unmistakably alien to this world" (Lovecraft 2014: 404). "The hauntological," contends Miéville, "is the recurrence of that which we know and wish we did not," whereas "the Weird is the assertion of that we did not know, never knew, could not know, that has always been and will always be unknowable" (Miéville 2012: 380). Miéville emphasizes that "Lovecraft's pantheon and bestiary are absolutely *sui generis*" (Miéville 2005: xiv). Weird entities, in their utter novelty, differ from such gothic figures as the titular antagonist of Bram Stoker's *Dracula*, the reanimated creature in Mary Shelley's *Frankenstein*, or the specter of Peter Quint (whether or not a projection of the governess) in Henry James's *Turn of the Screw*. Vampires, zombies, and ghosts are long-established folkloric figures that return again and again in gothic texts. They are cultural as well as literal revenants. The weird, conversely, introduces a radically *new* other, an other that is unprecedented rather than haunting. This leads us to the weird's kinship with science fiction.

In his study of science fiction, Adam Roberts asserts that "the particularities of the 'novum' distinguish SF from other forms of imaginative literature" (Roberts 2000: 7). *Novum* is a term coined by Darko Suvin to designate the essential conceptual content within any given science fiction text which differentiates it from the world of the reader. As Suvin puts it, "SF is distinguished by the narrative dominance or hegemony of a fictional 'novum' (novelty, innovation) validated by cognitive logic" (Survin 1979: 63). A novum could take the form of a technological innovation such as teleportation, for example, or highly advanced artificial intelligence. It could involve a divergence from the historical past, or a speculation into the near or distant future. It could consist in a sociopolitical structure distinct from those currently known in the world, as in any number of utopian or dystopian texts. An SF novum could be anything, really, so long as it remains within the realm of the conceivably possible—otherwise it would arguably lose its very science fiction-ness. For, in the words of Roberts, "nova are grounded in a discourse of possibility" (Roberts 2000: 7).

Such a "discourse of possibility" is where science fiction and the weird diverge. Istvan Csicsery-Ronay Jr. tells us that "the sf novum is the material condensation of a conceptual breakthrough" (Csicsery-Ronay Jr. 2008: 59). Damien Broderick affirms the centrality of "cognitive breakthrough" in science fiction (Broderick 1995: 33). The weird shares science fiction's focus on cognitive breakthrough, but in the weird the breakthrough becomes one which paradoxically short-circuits cognition, as it involves something that should be impossible according to prevailing conceptions of reality. If the SF novum is grounded in possibility, the weird shatters that grounding. "More and more, I felt that I was being alienated from the realms of all rational experience or conjecture," remarks the protagonist of Clark Ashton Smith's "The Uncharted Isle" (Smith 2014: 40). "I searched everywhere for a proof of reality," the narrator of "The Willows" tells us, "while all the while I understood that the standard of reality had changed" (Blackwood 2002: 29). The unprecedented other encountered in a weird story—its version of the novum—contravenes the accepted "standard of reality." As Lovecraft declares of the monstrous entity in "The Dunwich Horror," the weird novum is "an impossibility in a normal world" (Lovecraft 2014: 386). Thus, the weird reveals its affinity with fantasy, which also traffics in the impossible.

According to Kathryn Hume, "fantasy is any departure from consensus reality" (Hume 1985: 21). W. R. Irwin maintains that "fantasy is based on and controlled by an overt violation of what is generally accepted as possibility" (Irwin 1976: x). Contrary to science fiction, fantasy seems to operate in a discourse of *impossibility*. Such a notion raises questions, of course, about what is or is not deemed possible, and by whom. Irwin defers to the "evidence of senses and reliance on authority, individual or collective, so generally trusted as to produce consensus" (Irwin 1976: 62). The notion of "consensus reality" is helpful, but what of those aspects of reality regarding which there is a significant lack of consensus? For instance, if a given text includes accounts of angels and demons, does its status as fantasy or not change with each reader, depending upon the reader's particular religious convictions?

A solution proposed by Carl Freedman is to consider the viewpoint not of the reader but of the text, so to speak. "The crucial issue for generic discrimination," Freedman argues, "is not any epistemological judgment external to the text itself on the rationality or irrationality of the latter's imaginings, but rather . . . the attitude of the text itself to the kind of estrangements being performed" (Freedman 2000: 28). Traveling faster than the speed of light, for example, is generally considered to be impossible according to the laws of physics as currently understood in the scientific community, but it is a common trope found in numerous texts that are widely accepted as science fiction. Such travel is treated in the texts as scientifically plausible, which is perhaps the crucial matter insofar as the reading experience is concerned. Were a faster-than-light journey to be represented in a text not as a function of technology but rather of supernatural agency or magic, on the other hand, then it would likely be a marker of fantasy instead.

Fantasy texts tend to treat their novel imaginings with an attitude characterized not by scientific plausibility but by *wonder*. Gary Wolfe notes "the strong affective element that accompanies and sometimes overpowers the cognitive in fantasy" (Wolfe 2004: 225). A similarly "strong affective element" exists in the weird as well. The weird, as we have seen, explicitly represents its unprecedented other as an impossibility, and the presence of such impossibility induces a powerful sense of astonished awe in those who encounter it. In a characteristic response, the protagonist of Smith's "The City of the Singing Flame" laments the inadequacy of language in the face of such an encounter: "There are no words to convey the incomprehensible wonder of it all" (Smith 2014: 63). In *The Great God Pan*, a doctor performs ethically dubious experimental surgery on the brain of a young woman named Mary in an effort to enable her to perceive things beyond the world of matter, which results in an experience that initially appears congruent with the kind typically represented in and engendered by fantasy: "[Her eyes] shone with an awful light, looking far away, and a great wonder fell upon her face, and her hands stretched out as if to touch what was invisible" (Machen 2018: 15). What happens next in Machen's narrative, though, illustrates a key difference between fantasy and the weird: "But in an instant the wonder faded, and gave place to the most awful terror" (Machen 2018: 15). If fantasy is "a fiction evoking wonder" (Manlove 1975: 1), the weird is its disturbing cousin, a fiction in which the impossible arouses not just wonder but intense dismay as well.

"Fantasy," observes S.T. Joshi, "never truly inspires the sentiment of ontological horror" (Joshi 1990: 9). Talking animals, for instance, are often depicted as charming peculiarities in certain types of fantasy tales—think of the White Rabbit, the Cheshire Cat, and so forth in Lewis Carroll's *Alice's Adventures in Wonderland*—but that does not tend to be the case in weird fiction, or at least not entirely. "What would your feelings be, seriously," asks a character in Machen's "The White People," "if your cat or your dog began to talk to you, and to dispute with you in human aspects? You would be overwhelmed with horror. I am sure of it. And if the roses in your garden sang a weird song, you would go mad" (Machen 2018: 263). The impossible unprecedented other in weird fiction evokes a potent, ambivalent affect, a heady blend of awe and distress. "It was extraordinary," proclaims the protagonist of William Hope Hodgson's "The Hog," "and at the same time, exquisitely horrible and vile" (Hodgson 2019: 187).

In addition to elements of the gothic, science fiction, and fantasy, then, the weird employs features of horror as well.

"Horror," suggests Xavier Aldana Reyes, "is largely defined by its affective pretences. Horror takes its name, in other words, from the effects that it seeks to elicit in its readers" (Reyes 2016: 7). The very word derives from the Latin verb *horrēre*, meaning *to bristle* or *to shudder*. Affective response is fundamental to horror: what it *is* is inextricable from what it *does* to its audience. As Noel Carroll stresses, "works of horror are designed to elicit a certain kind of affect" (Carroll 1990: 15). This affect involves something more complex than just fear. Matt Hills describes it as an "ambiguous intermingling of anxiety/pleasure" (Hills 2005: 66). Terror and aversion mix with the compelling interest generated by the anomalous, the monstrous, the transgressive. Subtending this mixture is the primal appeal of the corporeal, for horror is intransigently physical. As Jack Morgan phrases it, "the horror imagination is somatic" (Morgan 2002: 7). Horror addresses our bodies as well as our minds, and in doing so provokes a holistic response with emotional, intellectual and physiological aspects. "We watch horror," writes Douglas Cowan, "and we are fascinated by it for the *frisson*, the physical and psychological shiver it generates in us" (Cowan 2008: 17). Engrossment, fear, empathy, disgust, curiosity, abhorrence, goosebumps, muscular tension, raised heart rate, altered breathing—all of these elements and more combine in an amalgamated affect which might be termed the *horror frisson*.

The weird traffics extensively in a similar sort of frisson. Like horror, the weird is designed to induce a powerful, complex reaction in its characters and its audience. Weird texts are overloaded with affective descriptors detailing the effects of confronting things "beyond all human ken" (Smith 2014: 6). The phenomena encountered in "The City of the Singing Flame," for instance, arouse a "vertiginous, overpowering bewilderment" in the protagonist, "an awe with which something of actual terror was mingled; and, at the same time, . . . an obscure but profound allurement" (Smith 2014: 55–6). Faced with the weird, characters react in vehement yet equivocal ways marked by extreme disturbance and fascination. "I was torn betwixt a longing to flee and a feverish mixture of burning curiosity and driving fatality," avows the narrator of Lovecraft's "The Shadow Out of Time" (Lovecraft 2014: 762). If the text is effective, a corresponding response is experienced by the reader as well.

Where the weird might be considered to distinguish itself from horror is in the evocation of a specifically *numinous* frisson. The numinous, in the pioneering formulation of Rudolf Otto (1958: 29), is "the 'wholly other,' something which has no place in our scheme of reality but belongs to an absolutely different one, and which at the same time arouses an irrepressible interest in the mind." As a *mysterium tremendum et fascinans*, a fascinating, awesome, overpowering mystery, the numinous lurks in the very essence of weirdness. Indeed, according to Otto, awareness of the numinous "first begins to stir in the feeling of something 'uncanny', 'eerie', or 'weird'" (Otto 1958: 14). The numinous inspires petrified awe at the presence of something that is totally beyond ordinary reality. As Rainer Maria Rilke famously states in the *Duino Elegies*, "Every angel is terrifying" (Rilke 1989: 151). The terror and astonishment induced by the numinous is commensurate with its preternatural power and indicative of the dire peril it poses for those who encounter it. "There are in the world things not of reason, but both below and above it," declares Gilbert Murray (1897: 272). "These things are Gods or forms of God: not fabulous immortal men, but 'Things which Are', things utterly non-human and non-moral, which bring man bliss or tear his life to shreds without a break in their own serenity." The enormous danger posed by contact with numinous forces, the likelihood of having one's life capriciously "torn to shreds" as Murray puts it, is a conception with cultural roots extending deep into antiquity. The weird taps into this venerable root system with a vengeance.

In weird stories, characters and readers are confronted with numinous phenomena manifesting as awesome, horrific, impossible, unprecedented others. "It was as if the veil of another universe than ours had been drawn back," asserts Smith (2014: 67) in "The City of the Singing Flame." The metaphor of an ontological "veil" is one that recurs frequently in weird fiction. In *The Great God Pan*, Machen (2018: 10) writes of "lifting the veil" between the mundane world and the numinous realm beyond: "The ancients knew what lifting the veil meant. They called it seeing the god Pan." Encountering the numinous, as weird stories such as this remind us, is not without its hazards. "No human eyes could look upon such a vision with impunity," Machen pronounces (2018: 53). "When the house of life is thus thrown open, there may enter in that for which we have no name." The experimental brain surgery mentioned earlier has disastrous consequences in Machen's novella. The symbolically named Mary is not only rendered hopelessly insane by her apparent encounter with the beyond but impregnated with what the story represents as a living embodiment of the numinous who will grow up to wreak havoc in fin de siècle London. As Guillermo del Toro remarks in his forward to a collection of Machen's fiction, "The price of lifting the veil and glimpsing the face of Pan is high and real" (del Toro 2011: viii).

Blackwood utilizes a similar veil metaphor in "The Willows": "The frontiers of some unknown world lay close about us. It was a spot held by the dwellers in some outer space, . . . a point where the veil between had worn a little thin" (Blackwood 2002: 49). In the weird, the borders of the ordinary world are breached by something "wholly different in kind" (Blackwood 2002: 52), something ineffable, inconceivable, and absolutely overwhelming. "Such forces cannot be named, cannot be spoken, cannot be imagined except under a veil and a symbol," proclaims Machen (2018: 47) in *The Great God Pan*. In "The Call of Cthulhu," Lovecraft insists that "the Thing cannot be described—there is no language for such abysms of shrieking and immemorial lunacy, such eldritch contradictions of all matter, force, and cosmic order" (Lovecraft 2014: 155).

In Blackwood's "Sand," the protagonist feels a petrifying "veneration touched with awe" upon witnessing an "army of dark Splendours" materializing from the sands of the Saharan desert: "He was conscious of a wild desire to run away, to hide, to efface himself utterly, his terror, his curiosity, his little wonder, and not be seen of anything. But it was all vain and foolish. The Desert saw him. The Gigantic knew that he was there" (Blackwood 2002: 337, 346, 335). Blackwood's capitalization of key words such as "Splendours," "Desert," and "Gigantic" highlights the prodigious significance of the weird, attesting to its numinosity. Hodgson employs the stylistic technique of selective capitalization to similar effect throughout "The Hog," in which the titular phenomenon is variously referred to as "some dreadful unknown Horror . . . some tremendous invisible Power . . . some monstrous Presence" (Hodgson 2019: 178–9). The weird involves no ordinary horror but rather Horror-with-a-capital-H, and as such it provokes a commensurate response. As the narrator of "The Willows" recounts, "what I felt of dread was no ordinary fear. It was infinitely greater, . . . more profoundly disturbing than anything I had known or dreamed of" (Blackwood 2002: 49). The awesome, horrific, impossible, unprecedented other that is revealed by the weird—that *is* the weird—induces an "ecstatic horror," as Smith phrases it, an "abominable rapture" (Smith 2014: 29).

Like the gothic, the weird is concerned with otherness—but an otherness that is unprecedented rather than haunting. Like science fiction, the weird introduces conceptual novelty—but a novelty that is impossible rather than possible. Like fantasy, the weird represents the impossible—but an impossible that evokes horror as much as wonder. Like horror, the weird elicits a powerful, ambivalent frisson—but a frisson with a pronouncedly numinous character. The weird thus takes certain estranging elements essential to its constituent genres and gives them each a further twist, so to speak, estranging the very estrangements in such a way that their generic associations are thoroughly contaminated with one another and subsumed into something new—something *weird*.

Viscous things, according to Michel Chaouli, possess a "structure imperiling structurality" (Chaouli 2003: 58). The weird performs such imperilment in myriad ways and on multiple levels, as I have endeavored to illustrate. In its unremitting estrangement and inextricable hybridity, the weird perhaps could be characterized as an *oozy set*: an amorphous, amoebic class that relentlessly infects and incorporates everything it comes into contact with (including the reader). Slime, as Jean-Paul Sartre memorably writes, "leaves its traces upon me. The slime is like a liquid seen in a nightmare, where all its properties are animated by a sort of life and turn back against me" (Sartre 1992: 777). The weird epitomizes this sort of contagious, disturbing dynamism. The weird consists in, exists by, weirding, and can therefore be understood as a verb as much as a noun or an adjective. Thus, the "weird" unsettles even its own grammatical status as a word.

If the "only good classification is a living classification" (Bowker and Star 1999: 326), then a good, useful taxonomy of the weird must be a weird—indeed, a weirded—taxonomy. In explicating the weird's taxonomical ooziness, my aim is to contribute toward a deeper shared understanding of what it might mean for a text to be weird(ed), without resorting to the kinds of fixed definitions that are antithetical to the weird's very nature. In such a way I hope to augment the viability of the weird as a critical concept.

References

Aldana Reyes, X. (2016), "Introduction: What, Why and When Is Horror Fiction?," in X. Aldana Reyes (ed.), *Horror: A Literary History*, 7–17, London: British Library.
Attebery, B. (1992), *Strategies of Fantasy*, Bloomington: Indiana University Press.
Blackwood, A. (2002), *Ancient Sorceries and Other Weird Stories*, ed. S. T. Joshi, London: Penguin.
Bowker, G., and S. L. Star (1999), *Sorting Things Out: Classification and Its Consequences*, Cambridge: MIT Press.
Broderick, D. (1995), *Reading by Starlight: Postmodern Science Fiction*, London: Routledge.
Byron, G., and D. Punter (2004), *The Gothic*, Oxford: Blackwell.
Carroll, N. (1990), *The Philosophy of Horror: Or Paradoxes of the Heart*, New York: Routledge.

Chaouli, M. (2003), "Van Gogh's Ear: Toward a Theory of Disgust," in F. S. Connelly (ed.), *Modern Art and the Grotesque*, 47–62, Cambridge: Cambridge University Press.

Chaplin, S. (2011), *Gothic Literature*, London: York Press.

Cowan, D. E. (2008), *Sacred Terror: Religion and Horror on the Silver Screen*, Waco: Baylor University Press.

Csicsery-Ronay Jr., I. (2008), *The Seven Beauties of Science Fiction*, Middletown: Wesleyan University Press.

Currie, M. (2004), *Difference*, London: Routledge.

del Toro, G. (2011), "Foreword," in *The White People and Other Weird Stories*, by A. Machen, ed. S. T. Joshi, vii–ix, London: Penguin.

Freedman, C. (2000), *Critical Theory and Science Fiction*, Hanover: Wesleyan University Press.

Freud, S. (2003), *The Uncanny*, trans. D. McLintock, New York: Penguin.

Hills, M. (2005), *The Pleasures of Horror*, London: Continuum.

Hodgson, W. H. (2019), *The Weird Tales of William Hope Hodgson*, ed. X. Aldana Reyes, London: British Library.

Hume, K. (1985), *Fantasy and Mimesis: Responses to Reality in Western Literature*, London: Routledge.

Irwin, W. R. (1976), *The Game of the Impossible: A Rhetoric of Fantasy*, Urbana: University of Illinois.

Jackson, R. (1981), *Fantasy: The Literature of Subversion*, London: Routledge.

Joshi, S. T. (1990), *The Weird Tale*, Holicong: Wildside Press.

Kapchan, D. and P. T. Strong (1999), "Theorizing the Hybrid," *The Journal of American Folklore*, 112 (445): 239–53.

Lloyd-Smith, A. (2004), *American Gothic Fiction*, London: Continuum.

Lovecraft, H. P. (2014), *The New Annotated H.P. Lovecraft*, ed. L. S. Klinger, New York: Liveright Publishing.

Luckhurst, R. (2013), Introduction to *The Classic Horror Stories*, by H. P. Lovecraft, vii–xxviii, Oxford: Oxford University Press.

Machen, A. (2018), *The Great God Pan and Other Horror Stories*, ed. A. Worth, Oxford: Oxford University Press.

Manlove, C. N. (1975), *Modern Fantasy: Five Studies*, Cambridge: Cambridge University Press.

Miéville, C. (2005), Introduction to *At the Mountains of Madness*, by H. P. Lovecraft, xi–xxv, New York: Modern Library.

Miéville, C. (2009), "Weird Fiction," in M. Bould, A. M. Butler, A. Roberts, and S. Vint (eds.), *The Routledge Companion to Science Fiction*, 510–15, London: Routledge.

Miéville, C. (2012), "On Monsters: Or, Nine or More (Monstrous) Not Cannies," *Journal of the Fantastic in the Arts*, 23 (3): 377–92.

Morgan, J. (2002), *The Biology of Horror: Gothic Literature and Film*, Carbondale: Southern Illinois University Press.

Murray, G. (1897), *A History of Ancient Greek Literature*, New York: D. Appleton and Co.

Nelson, V. (2012), *Gothicka: Vampire Heroes, Human Gods, and the New Supernatural*, Cambridge: Harvard University Press.

Otto, R. (1958), *The Idea of the Holy*, trans. J. W. Harvey, Oxford: Oxford University Press.

Punter, D. (2000), "Introduction: The Ghost of a History," in D. Punter (ed.), *A Companion to the Gothic*, vii–xiv, Oxford: Blackwell.

Rilke, R. M. (1989), *The Selected Poetry of Rainer Maria Rilke*, trans. S. Mitchell, New York: Vintage.

Roberts, A. (2000), *Science Fiction*, London: Routledge.

Rosch, E. (1978), "Principles of Categorization," in E. Rosch and B. B. Lloyd (eds.), *Cognition and Categorization*, 27–48, Hillsdale: Lawrence Erlbaum Associates.

Royle, N. (2003), *The Uncanny*, Manchester: Manchester University Press.

Salomon, R. B. (2002), *Mazes of the Serpent: An Anatomy of Horror Narrative*, Ithaca: Cornell University Press.

Sartre, J.-P. (1992), *Being and Nothingness*, trans. H. E. Barnes, New York: Washington Square Press.

Seed, D. (2011), *Science Fiction: A Very Short Introduction*, Oxford: Oxford University Press.

Simmons, D. (2013), "H.P. Lovecraft: The Outsider No More?," in D. Simmons (ed.), *New Critical Essays on H.P. Lovecraft*, 1–10, New York: Palgrave Macmillan.

Smith, C. A. (2014), *The Dark Eidolon and Other Fantasies*, ed. S. T. Joshi, London: Penguin.

Suvin, D. (1979), *Metamorphoses of Science Fiction: On the Poetics and History of a Literary Genre*, New Haven: Yale University Press.

VanderMeer, A., and J. VanderMeer (2011), Introduction to *The Weird: A Compendium of Strange and Dark Stories*, eds. A. VanderMeer and J. VanderMeer, xv–xx, London: Corvus.

Wolfe, G. K. (2004), "The Encounter with Fantasy," in D. Sandner (ed.), *Fantastic Literature: A Critical Reader*, 222–35, Westport: Praeger.

4

Validating Weird Fiction as an (Im)Possible Genre

Anne-Maree Wicks

Critical scholarship argues that the mixing of genres like horror, gothic, and science fiction validates weird fiction as a mode. In "The Law of Genre," however, Jacques Derrida declares that genres are not to be mixed. For Derrida, "it is a law of the law of genre" that allows a participant to be "faithful" because, "by its very nature, the law invites and commits" the mixing of genres (Derrida 1980: 57). In other words, what Derrida is implying is that for a genre to be considered whole and pure its announced boundaries must remain unpenetrated. This authority that the law of genre commands creates the desire to transgress its boundaries while paradoxically reaffirming faithfulness. The law thus positions itself as "the invisible center" of genre, and genre, then, invites and transgresses the law (74).

This chapter aims to reveal that when specific types of literary criticism speak of weird fiction, or of weird fictions that belong to a specific set of rules and standards, they speak with an authority that eliminates any proposition of a possible corruption. The cause of corruption, although confirming a genre's "essential purity," is driven "by accident or through transgression, by mistake or through a lapse" (57). Derrida describes this mistake as a participation without belonging, caused by a confusion produced from a rereading of history and genre-theory. This mistake of participating without belonging is not questioned but rather accepted within critical scholarship. Within this investigation Derrida speaks of Gérard Genette, who "demonstrates the stringent necessity of this distinction" in terms of "the confusion of modes and genres" (62). A mode is conceptualized in this context as a text that has been deemed impossible and threatens to deform the law of genre. More specifically, Derrida agrees with Genette that a mode is a theme of a genre. Derrida's and Genette's division between mode and genre is justified by the law of genre. Both accounts are "faithful" to the law in order to eliminate confusion and prevent corruption of the law and its boundaries. While a mode may not belong to a specific genre, it nonetheless relies on the law for the justification of its existence, thereby participating without belonging. Literary criticism of genre-theory refuses to address the impossibility, the corruption, when genres *do* mix—an occurrence that simultaneously does not "fit in" to the law of genre and rejects the categorization of a literary mode.

This "fitting in" can be read as a sex act in the law of genre, which helps us to consider a crucial problem in Derrida's theory. It is important to note that in progressing with this discussion, my argument aligns with feminist critics like Gayatri Chakravorty Spivak who take issue with Derrida's emphasis of genre as *moi*, as masculine (Spivak 1997: 64). Coupling *moi* with the feminine *la loi* (the law), Derrida explains how genre controls and gives "birth to the law," insinuating that the law of genre partakes in a sex act in order to produce something new (1980: 76). Although Derrida is quick to defend that "female personhood must be reduced out" and that the gendered language used is only "figural," Spivak points out that "the strength of his own methodology will not allow such a totalizing exclusion and binary opposition to stand" (1997: 65). And yet Derrida claims that, when coupled with the feminine, he, that is, Derrida's masculine use of "I," is capable of controlling and therefore giving birth to the law and all of its authoritative representatives (1980: 76).

The masculine genre that Derrida speaks of excludes female personhood, but it is precisely Spivak's point that he nonetheless uses feminine characteristics. The feminine represents the law because it is the only identifiable and fetishized corruption in masculine sexuality. It is necessary to establish this feminist tension in approaching Derrida's analysis of the law of genre because, accordingly, the critical scholarship of weird fiction occupies the masculine role in its attempt to define it. This risks instantiating the law of the phallus to expel and validate the Old Weird and the New Weird to create something that indeed "fits in" to the law of genre.

Derrida's analysis asserts that modulation is trans-jurisdictional. Critical scholarship fetishizes the corruption of weird fiction by penetrating an impossible boundary. Although the possibility of corruption is not universal and causes the law of genre to fail, it is precisely the failure that becomes successful in the scholarship's fetishization of corruption. It is the feminine that exposes and represents this failure, thus positioned as instrumental to the law of genre. Significantly, it is the fetishization of corruption that legitimizes weird fiction to exist as a genre proper because it speaks with an authority that reaffirms and practices its understanding of genre by engaging with its own impossibility. This chapter reveals how weird fiction is a genre that belongs to itself with participation in other genres and/or the law, a taking part in all limitations, having a membership in all sets, a genre of its own.

Corruption

To treat the Old Weird as an indicator of an event for weird fiction causes an aporia in the law of genre. This becomes particularly true when we regard the critical scholarship's alignment with the masculine in order to generate the New Weird as a mode of the Old Weird. As discussed, for Derrida and Genette a mode cannot be created from within a genre that has been deemed impossible and corrupt. Moreover, to claim the Old as a genre of its own contradicts New Weird scholarship's intent on remaining faithful to the law of genre. Weird fiction altogether is considered a mode of other genres such as horror, gothic, and/or science fiction. Benjamin Noys discusses this predicament as a problem with high modernism set on a "direct confrontation and replication of the racist and anti-Semitic strategies of the Old" (Noys 2016: 231). The New aims to mix "high modernism and the weird" in order to produce "a new form of collage 'text' that destabilizes both, probing the toxic core of anti-Semitism and racism that links them together," while simultaneously "remain[ing] active" (233). Noys makes an interesting point that Derrida's "law is constitutively impossible" and that weird fiction's ability to "'cross a line of demarcation,' to threaten the genres they inhabit through its own resources and so to threaten the concept of genre itself," is therefore possible (250). However, despite the New Weird's attempt to destabilize the limitations of the Old, the critical scholarship continues to repeat its mistake of corruption in the reification of the Old. It is for this reason that, in much the same way that the law of genre treats a mode, the New participates in the Old's conventions without belonging to it.

What is at stake in the critical scholarship's treatment of weird fiction is its separating of the Old and the New. It is with this separation, however, that the mistake of corruption is repeated: the New is categorized by the Old. Categories help recognize a mode of a specific genre, or, more to the point, a mode requires a "trait common to these classes of classes" in order to be "precisely the identifiable recurrence of a common trait by which one recognizes, or should recognize, a membership in a class" (Derrida 1980: 63). When critical scholarship speaks of the New, it speaks directly to the traits commonly found and recognized in the Old. For example, S. T. Joshi emphasizes:

> It seems as if the whole approach to weird fiction today is flawed in its very conception. The purpose of most modern weird writing seems to be merely to frighten. . . . If weird fiction is to be a legitimate literary mode, it must touch depths of human significance in a way that other literary modes do not; and its

principal means of doing so is the utilization of the supernatural as a metaphor for various conceptions regarding the universe and human life. (2001: 2)

Joshi's nostalgic notions of the Old coordinate his treatment of the New, positioning it as an impossible occurrence that threatens to deform the law of genre. Joshi's fidelity to the Old suggests that the New is troubling and perhaps altogether impossible. The corruption that presents itself in Joshi's argument is thus quickly repaired by a separation, by the New's "conception" that displaces its belonging and thereby eliminates its impossibility; there is no threat to the Old's limitations. However, because the law of genre commands faithful participation, the New is limited to the conventions presented by the identifiable traits of the Old. Although critical scholarship refuses to acknowledge the New's efforts to belong to itself without participation in the Old, to reject the "self-conscious 're-marking' of its own genre status" (Luckhurst 2015: 200), the scholarship maintains that it is "flawed in its very conception," or, more to the point, there is a corruption *within* weird fiction itself. For if, as the critical scholarship claims, weird fiction "is not just a term to describe the mode of Horror, but to describe where Horror is going" (Strantzas 2016: xiii), the conflict and questioning of impossibility should not appear here if weird fiction itself is to be regarded as a mode. There should be no questioning of weird fiction's existence when the scholarship has already delimited it as a mode.

Some scholars (see, for example, Jeff VanderMeer's "Moving Past Lovecraft") aim to rescue weird fiction from what it perceives to be the corruption of the Old and New. To be a category defined in relation to the Old does not imply that the New is not its own content. Rather, this discussion reveals how critical scholarship displaces the New to participate in the Old's limitations to justify their mistaken corruption of weird fiction. The most prominent example of mending this mistaken corruption that stands out to me among modern scholarship is that of Ann and Jeff VanderMeer's 2011 anthology *The Weird: A Compendium of Strange and Dark Stories*. Indeed, the VanderMeers' definition, notably relying on Lovecraft's, insists that weird fiction "represents the pursuit of some indefinable and perhaps maddeningly unreachable understanding of the world beyond the mundane" (2011: xv). The VanderMeers' view, in suggesting that the Old and New are inconsequential, is that weird fiction is a movement that rejects and dominates the Old and New, and abolishes any limitation that the law of genre announces. They position the weird as separate from the Old and New, thereby troubling the all-too-easy demarcations within the critical scholarship: "The Weird has again fragmented, perhaps in preparation for a future coalescing of a Next Weird or perhaps not . . . the Weird will endure" (xx).

Noys and Murphy offer a different perspective than the VanderMeers' attempt to rescue weird fiction. Where the VanderMeers attempt to impose a chaotic dynamism of the weird genre, Noys and Murphy prefer a path of skeptical postmodernism, asserting that the critical scholarship is "still too freighted with cultural value to assess the weird, which retains its 'pulpy' origin in eroding or even corrupting the 'literary' in 'literary fiction'" (2016: 128–9). Although Noys and Murphy are clear that it is New Weird scholarship that causes the impossibility of corruption, and indeed the corruption as shown by the VanderMeers, they overlook the fact that when weird fiction is in discussion of the law of genre it falls into the Old's limitations, which are being announced *as* the corruption, due to its very "retaining" of an "origin." Whether the critical scholarship's obedience to the law favors the Old or the New, it nonetheless signifies that the fault or corruption lies in the origin of weird fiction.

To investigate the law of genre through the cultural value that rejects weird fiction's pulp origins would risk corruption of the gothic, horror, or science fiction genres, because "these forms have been treated as natural" (Derrida 1980: 60). It is tempting to agree with the scholarship that weird fiction is a mode, rather than to compel the law to permit corruption. This is why the scholarship appears fixated and almost stuck on the "undefinable" weird, such as the volumes of Michael Kelly's *Year's Best Weird Fiction*. In each volume of *Year's Best*, we receive a "Foreword" from Kelly himself, in which he actively reinstates that weird fiction cannot be defined because it "is a diverse mode of literature" (2015 vii), but nonetheless recognizable "as an unceasing distortion and buckling of ambient space and time . . . A feeling" (2017: viii). Kelly's hesitant definition of weird fiction is followed with an "Introduction" by the volume's guest editor. The third volume, with Simon Strantzas as the guest editor, articulates a clear rejection of weird fiction that speaks to the previous volumes that do not "address *my* weird fiction" (2015: xi). Strantzas's use of "my" validates his faithful participation in the law of genre, in which he refuses the corruption of Horror: "weird fiction may be Horror-without-malignancy" (xi). Both Kelly and Strantzas, and the writers of *Year's Best* for that matter, all participate in a standard of weird fiction that rejects all previous notions of it. Within this movement of modern weird fiction, the separation between the Old and New appears once again. However, in Kelly's movement there is a direct severance of weird fiction itself: its modern writers are consciously writing *a* weird fiction that rejects its origin. But for a "mode of literature" to claim to be weird fiction is the crucial problem for the law of genre: How can weird fiction be a genre of its own when its announced (Old) limitations and practiced (New) categories are rejected?

If weird fiction's existence cannot be confirmed, it is because no limitation has been drawn to separate it from the genres within which it is claiming participation. Derrida speaks of this limitation as the "enigma" that is drawn "as soon as the word 'genre' is sounded" (1980: 56). Derrida goes on to explain that once a genre is announced, the limitation must not be disrespected. This is why we see scholarship like Wasson's and Adler's treating weird fiction, specifically the New Weird, as a validation of "relaxed genre strictures" because it "give[s] evidence of a rapid hybridization between horror, gothic, science fiction and . . . 'dark fantasy'" (2011: 22). The attempt, within the scholarship, to respect the limitations of horror, gothic, and science fiction, confuses weird fiction's limitations (the law) as a corruption of limitations. This permission of corruption, this taking part in all limitations as a limitation, is unique to weird fiction precisely because it participates without belonging.

It is through this participation without belonging that the scholarship risks and, in fact, altogether disrespects the limitations of weird fiction—limitations that are announced by the authority of the Old, as presented in the New. When confronted with their mistake of corruption, the scholarship attempts to rescue weird fiction; that is, corruption is fetishized. But this fetishization rejects weird fiction as a movement that is separate from the Old and New. Derrida speaks to this impossibility, referring to tracing a simple path of corruption as limitless: the temptation and "fetishizing" of corruption is key in understanding the course of the critical scholarship's concern with defining weird fiction, to separate the New from the Old, and to create an absolute meaning of weird fiction. It is my aim to reveal that, as shown by Derrida's diagram below, weird fiction cannot exist without the Old and New.

Old and/or New

Derrida denotes a set definition or decision of an account (in this case corruption) as impossible. Derrida's diagram of "a double chiasmatic invagination of edges" reveals how a weird fiction movement is impossible within "simple borderlines of this corpus, of this ellipse unremittingly repealing itself within its own expansion" (1980: 71). In explaining Derrida's diagram, I examine it as he depicts it: as a whole form that implies modulation, which will later become useful in dissecting weird fiction's limitless form.

Derrida's diagram depicts two overlapping waves in demonstration of the impossibility of following a set definition or decision of corruption. In this context, the key to Derrida's argument is that there is no definite definition of the law of genre. It is therefore impossible to normalize corruption in this account; that is, in order to trace corruption it is required to include "a modal structure within a vaster, more general corpus . . . concerning edge, borderline, boundary, and abounding which do not arise without a fold" (69). If we were to trace a weird fiction movement, from a point that the critical scholarship argued as the beginning, it would reveal the impossibility when rejecting the limitations of the Old and the New. Derrida structures this impossibility as the result of corruption:

For example, if we follow the strand of A, it is likely to become B. However, what Derrida does in complicating this decision from A to B is incorporating multiple folds that rupture a simple path: for example, C and D are A if A is a *and* b, and/or vice versa. The products of impossibility that Derrida depicts (what is validated and rejected by the law of genre) is marked by C and D. C and D represent corruption, produced by the repetition of a movement that, "in this permanent revolution of order, it follows, doubles, or reiterates it in advance" (71). C is the result of when two or more drawn limitations come together, functioning as the center or a sort of womb that conceives and also delimits corruption. C validates corruption by producing D, which is an external possibility within corruption. D is hypothetical, functioning as the Other that is formed outside of C. D is the subject of C, a corrupted space that validates Derrida's point of impossibility; that is, otherness can only exist outside of corruption when corruption itself becomes delimited.

What Derrida's diagram gives is a vector of the law of genre that not only expels corruption but also validates it from within. This paradox, and what Derrida himself suggests, lies in the exclusion of "linking all these complications to pure form or one suggesting that they could be formalized outside the content" (74).

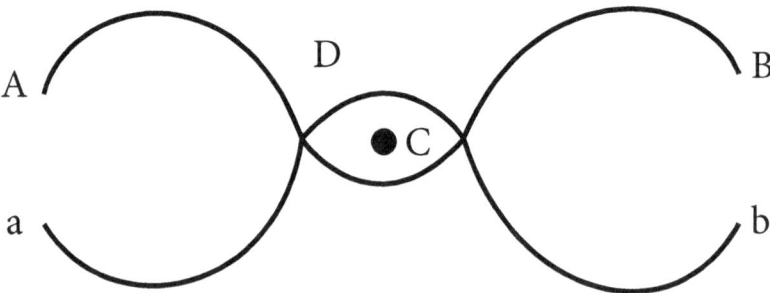

Figure 1 Based on the diagram of a double chiasmatic invagination of edges by Jacques Derrida © *Critical Inquiry* 1980.

Derrida, in faithful participation of the law of genre, invites and commits the existence of corruption (C and D)—taking particular attention with Derrida's use of genre as masculine (overlooking, indeed, the center "womb" and its feminine connection). However, it is important to investigate—at this Derridean symbolic level—the paradox that expels and validates the Old and New. Weird fiction cannot exist as the result of C; the paradox rejects weird fiction as a pure form outside the Old and New. Because the critical scholarship is obedient to the law of genre, it cannot link the Old and the New (from A to B) to create a pure form of weird fiction. However, due to the scholarship's desire to transgress the law of genre, the corruption of the Old and New cannot be ignored.

Critical scholarship like that of Joshi, Strantzas, the VanderMeers, and Kelly trouble the law of genre by ignoring the paradox. From what has been discussed, it is clear why weird fiction is mistaken as a mode: it is the reification of the Old through modern scholarship's concerns of the New (a new, separate weird fiction movement) that is viewed as the corruption. In so doing, the critical scholarship overlooks its mistake of rejecting and separating the Old and the New. The weird fiction movement that the critical scholarship aims to give birth to is based precisely on the corruption it aims to fix. A question worth asking, then, is not "*what* is weird fiction, but *why*?" (Strantzas 2016: xii). In other words, why are the Old and New necessary to weird fiction? An answer to this question in the context of Derrida's diagram becomes possible through a connection made by China Miéville, of "the contradiction between Weird and hauntological" (2009: 124).

In "M. R. James and the Quantum Vampire: Weird; Hauntological: Versus and/or and and/or or?," Miéville argues that there can be no Old and/or New. Miéville allows us here to build on Derrida's argument that corruption is limitless by questioning the very possibility of a delimited corruption. The separate stimuli that cause corruption—the linking complications that create the "multiple folds" and "center" (C) of Derrida's diagram—affect the entire form. The whole form of weird fiction is therefore complicated by the corruption of the Old and/or the New. In other words, is weird fiction Old Weird and New Weird *and* Old Weird or New Weird? Or is it Old Weird and New Weird *or* Old Weird or New Weird? But how is the critical scholarship to read this complication? The answer is found in the paradox that expels and validates corruption from within itself. In other words, to evoke the and/or complication which grants "teratological specificity," Miéville offers the figure of a skulltopus.

Much like Derrida's diagram of two overlapping waves that reveal the impossibility of tracing one specific strand of an account, Miéville reveals how the skulltopus is on the verge of something new. It is liminal but it is not the new thing, because the skull and the octopus are viewed as separate. The skulltopus is formed of two separate but identifiable stimuli, the skull and the octopus, which are combined into a single figure, a weird whole. However, instead of rejecting the paradox, Miéville questions both stimuli in their attempt to form something new.

Our understanding enables the skulltopus to exist purely on the basis that the two stimuli exist separately. However, because the merged object is created by the separate stimuli, it cannot exist completely and independently without the association. For Miéville, this "'separateness' has become dominant, not because there is a 'drive to separate,' but as a corollary of the oscillating efficacy of as-simon-pure-as-possible Weird and/or hauntology, for thinking our fraught and oppositional history" (2009: 128). Even when one stimulus dominates the other, there is no corruption of one or the other. It is Miéville's conclusion that, while "opposed but not separable, the traces of the Weird are inevitably sensible in a hauntological work, and vice versa" (128). However, what Miéville seems to

Figure 2 Skulltopus by China Miéville © *Collapse* 2009. Reproduced with the permission of China Miéville.

overlook is that while the form of a skulltopus may be the result of an attempted understanding of corruption, in the Derridean sense, what it achieves in spite of the two stimuli that respect one another's limitations, is a (im)possible existence. It creates ambiguity, otherness. Weird fiction lingers in this ambiguity; and indeed, Miéville's point is that weird fiction troubles genre-theory by forming itself outside but within the law of genre. We can now understand Derrida's concern with the impossibility as the result of corruption. Corruption is permitted by the law of genre if the corruption itself is impossible. Weird fiction is the Other, permitted by the law of genre precisely because it is formed by corruption. Weird fiction is limitless in its ability to belong to itself as a genre with participation in all limitations without belonging.

Fetishizing Corruption

Weird fiction appears, then, as a genre that engages with its own impossibility. Derrida's and Miéville's examples give answer to the impossibility of understanding corruption. The ambiguity of weird fiction as a genre is misleading for critical scholarship that transgresses the law of genre by seeking a definition and understanding of its corruption. When faced with corruption, however, scholars such as the VanderMeers question the creation of C, that is, in creating something new they reject the separate stimuli that create the new thing. In other words, the critical scholarship becomes excessive in permitting the corruption of the Old and New in assuming a firmer sense of understanding.

Significantly, the critical scholarship has concerned itself exclusively with definition and ownership of that definition. For example, the VanderMeers' earlier anthology, *The New Weird*, claims that the New has "unintentionally created a movement" and "is still mutating *forward* through the work of a new generation of writers" (2008: xviii). The issue with claiming a New movement contradicts the corruption of the Old from which weird fiction relies upon for understanding. Mark Fisher agrees with this assertion in his book *The Weird and the Eerie*, in which he insists that "any discussion of weird fiction must begin with Lovecraft" (2016: 16). In desiring a definition and understanding of weird fiction, the critical scholarship is in competition—reinforcing Derrida's point of impossibility of tracing a set definition. There can be no set definition because it is impossible to normalize the corruption of the account that, in itself, creates the movement that the critical scholarship are claiming. The point overlooked is that weird fiction cannot exist without association with the Old and/or the New.

Both the Old's and New's drawn limitations cannot be corrupted, otherwise the new movement cannot be identified as a whole, pure form by the law of genre.

Fetishizing weird fiction into existence by attempting to define its history and limitations, as well as its potentialities, risks Old phallogocentric progressions that, indeed, retain its pulp origin in the sense of a particularism. As I have articulated, the course of weird fiction becomes complicated and corrupted in three successive forms; in explaining it I will not limit it to the whole form as was shown with Derrida. The separate forms of the Old and New cannot be corrupted in forming something new, as was shown by Miéville. At its most elementary level, at its origin, weird fiction begins with the Old. It is worth mentioning, however, that in tracing weird fiction's corruption the Old does not function as the beginning but rather as the course critical scholarship begins with in understanding weird fiction as a form of literary expression.

The Old presents a separate "mode" of writing that first appeared in the pulp fiction era between the years of 1880 and 1940. With a slow rise in popularity, its linear progression upward in the graph, the Old saw publications in pulp magazines such as *Weird Tales*. From this, of course, came the Lovecraftian homage, which affected its popularity and writing standards after Lovecraft's death in 1937. In reaching a concave, the Old struggled to recover its momentum and identity as a mode, contributing to its death in 1940. The Old is placed on the upward slope of the graph to attest its identification as a mode that is separate from genres such as gothic, horror, or science fiction. On this level, where the Old has been separated from any connection to other genre's limitations, it is not corrupted or corruptible and therefore justified by the critical scholarship as a

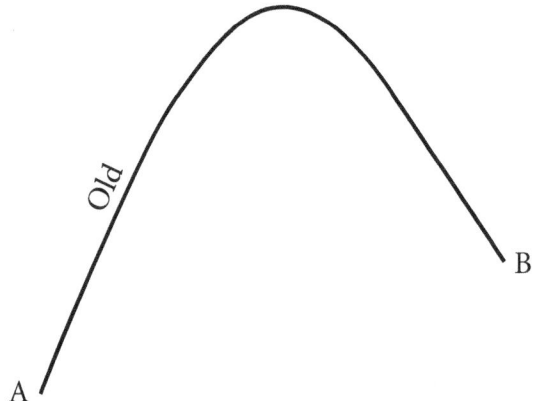

Figure 3 Concave of the Old Weird.

mode because it does not belong to a specific genre but does rely on participation for the justification of its brief existence.

The paradox lies, then, in the question of the Old's belonging. At this most basic level of tracing weird fiction, the Old's belonging is successful only to itself. However, the Old by itself cannot be claimed as a genre without a drawn limitation. Weird fiction's existence cannot be confirmed by the Old, moreover, because there has been no limitation drawn. This therefore leads us to consider the *birth* of the New, the second stage in the critical scholarship's understanding:

After a forty-year gap after the Old Weird's death, weird fiction is revived by the New Weird's emergence. The New recovers from the Old's downward concave by separating itself, and identifying itself in mainstream publishing of novels instead of pulp magazines. In so doing, the New attracted attention in critical reorientation in terms of both scholarship and writing. Significantly, the New saw works by women writers, which is a point often sidelined by scholarship like Joshi who are set on a fidelity to the Old. It is for this reason that, although both the Old and New are parallel to each other, they do not act in symmetry.

This therefore complicates the simple path of a mode that "wears itself out around genreless modalisations" (Derrida 1980: 63). This apparent complication, as shown in the separation between the Old and New (creating a and b), occupies the critical scholarship's desire to transgress the law of genre. Due to the Old's failure, the scholarship reanimates its limitations through the New, fetishizing it as corruption. This corruption has drawn itself as a limitation of the Old, or, as Derrida puts it, "with the inevitable dividing of the trait that marks membership, the boundary of the set comes to form, by invagination, and internal pocket larger than the whole; and the outcome . . . remains as singular as it is limitless" (59). The question that arises from the singular and limitless form is: Where do the Old and New come together to create the "invagination" and "womb," the

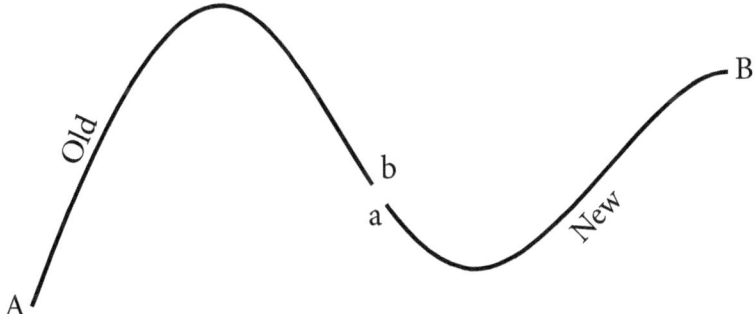

Figure 4 Locating the New Weird.

invisible center? To understand this ambiguity the critical scholarship attempts to locate the precise moment of corruption.

It perceives the separation between the Old and New as the disruption in their understanding, viewing it as the break in a "trend" that "is dead, or moved on to new realms" (Jones 2010). This break in the trend, as was Miéville's point of separateness, is the critical scholarship's tracing weird fiction's "fraught and oppositional history" through the Old into the New. The same cannot be said of the New, however, because it is not capable of corrupting the Old. The Old is positioned as the authority that the New reanimates in its movement to create something new. Zombie-like in its reanimation of the Old, the New treats corruption as discourse. It is an interesting connection, in fact, between the New's zombification of the Old and the Haitian and South African notions of zombies. For example, the Old can be read as "a corpse in tattered rags, trailing remnants of necrotic flesh as it rises from the cemetery in a state of trance-like animation, entirely subservient and beholden to the authority of some unknown master" (Niehaus 2005: 192). Isak Niehaus notes that this "mass-mediated popular culture[d]" figure signifies the "fear of becoming a zombie, the loss of individual freedom implied by enslavement, and 'expedition of the dead'" (192). The fear of domination in the discourse about zombies constitutes a collective, whole figure. Justin D. Edwards agrees with Niehaus in identifying this collective figure as a "zombie terrorist" that appears "within an era of globalization that . . . death is failure" (2015: 4).

To be dominated constitutes failure or, more specifically, domination equates to death. If death is viewed as failure, then the same can be said about the critical scholarship's view of the Old. The Old's death in 1940 is viewed by the critical scholarship as failure, and the New's domination over the Old signifies its fear of failure. But if the scholarship cannot separate the Old and New, thereby

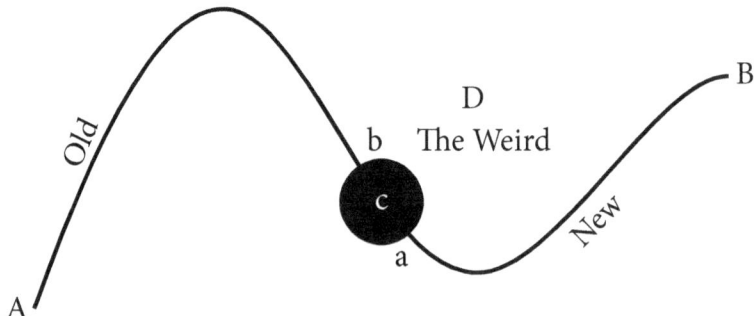

Figure 5 The corrupted form of weird fiction.

demonstrating that each maintains its limitations, the two become entangled producing a collective figure, the new movement. An (im)possible existence is thus the result of their impossible yet zombie-like corruption:

The Old and New are like the human skull and the octopus, brought together in an attempt to form something new. While deformed and unsettling, the new form that the Old and New create engages with corruption to express impossibility and attempts to delimit it. It is impossible to determine where the Old and New connect, except through their relation to the Weird. While it is impossible to determine their direct connection and/or separation, it is the Weird that validates both. The Weird, as the result of respecting limitless limitations, stands allusively but nonetheless attached to this "new" merged form: the Weird account. It stands to reason that the Weird emerges from the ambiguity, the "or-ness," between the Old and New. The Weird does not allow the Old and New to merge and instead acts as the "betwixt and between," the shadow that is cast between the two stimuli, connecting but separating them, controlling but not dominating.

In this way, in which corruption reconstructs genre-theory, it becomes clear how weird fiction operates as a genre proper. The law recognizes itself in the corrupted product of weird fiction's (im)possible existence, in its otherness. But this logic is complex and perhaps contradictory to Derrida's point that tracing a simple path of corruption is impossible. However, it is important to recognize and understand the complexities of corruption, which validates weird fiction as a genre. For example, an important feature of the corruption in this final stage of understanding is its position on the downward concave from the Old to the New. The problem with this positioning is what happens to the creation of C and D—what is the product of the Old's and New's corruption. As a result of corruption, C is positioned where the Old and New were once separated, forming the invisible center of the law that regulates weird fiction as a genre.

The relationship between the Old and New is not a relationship between a genre and a mode. It is a relationship that reveals a corruption that undoes the Old phallogocentric limitations while creating a space for something new, which speaks to the feminist tensions that arise from Derrida's genre-theory. It is this new space, this new movement that the critical scholarship insists upon, that occupies both sides of the Old-New spectrum. Instead of forming the overlapping waves like Derrida's diagram, weird fiction is thus revealed as deformed like Miéville's skulltopus. Weird fiction is an (im)possible genre that is capable of corruption while incapable of being a pure form outside the law of genre.

References

Derrida, J. (1980), "The Law of Genre," *Critical Inquiry*, 7 (1): 55–81.
Edwards, J. D. (2015), "Zombie Terrorism in an Age of Global Gothic," *Gothic Studies*, 17 (2): 1–14.
Fisher, M. (2016), *The Weird and the Eerie*, London: Repeater Books.
Jones, T. O. (2010), "Dig the New Weird," *New York Public Library*, 4 June. Available online: https://www.nypl.org/blog/2010/06/04/dig-new-weird (accessed April 4, 2017).
Joshi, S. T. (2001), *The Modern Weird Tale*, Jefferson: McFarland & Company.
Kelly, M. (2015), "Foreword," in K. Koja and M. Kelly (eds.), *Year's Best Weird Fiction*, 2nd vol., vii–ix, Pickering: Undertow Publications.
Kelly, M. (2017), "Foreword," in H. Marshall and M. Kelly (eds.), *Year's Best Weird Fiction*, 4th vol., vii–viii, Pickering: Undertow Publications.
Luckhurst, R. (2015), "American Weird," *The Cambridge Companion to American Science Fiction*, 3 (14): 195–205.
Miéville, C. (2009), "M.R. James and the Quantum Vampire: Weird; Hauntological: Versus and/or and and/or or?," in R. Mackay (ed.), *Collapse IV*, 105–27, Falmouth: Atheanæum.
Niehaus, I. (2005), "Witches and Zombies of the South African Lowveld: Discourse, Accusations and Subjective Reality," *Journal of the Royal Anthropological Institute*, 11 (2): 191–210.
Noys, B. (2016), "Full Spectrum Offense: Saboy's Reverbstorm and the Weirding of Modernity," *Genre: Forms of Discourse and Culture*, 49 (2): 231–53.
Noys, B., and T. S. Murphy (2016), "Introduction: Old and New Weird," *Genre*, 49 (2): 117–34.
Spivak, G. C. (1997), "Displacement and the Discourse of Woman," in N. Holland (ed.), *Feminist Interpretations of Jacques Derrida*, 43–72, Pennsylvania: The Pennsylvania State University Press.
Strantzas, S. (2016), "Introduction," in S. Strantzas and M. Kelly (eds.), *Year's Best Weird Fiction*, 3rd vol., xi–xiv, Pickering: Undertow Publications.
VanderMeer, J. (2008), "The New Weird: 'It's Alive?,'" in A. VanderMeer and J. VanderMeer (eds.), *The New Weird*, ix–xviii, San Francisco: Tachyon Publications.
VanderMeer, J. (2012), "Moving Past Lovecraft," *Weird Fiction Review*, 1 September. Available online: http://weirdfictionreview.com/2012/09/moving-past-lovecraft/ (accessed March 27, 2017).
VanderMeer, A., and J. VanderMeer (2011), "Introduction," in A. VanderMeer and J. VanderMeer (eds.), *The Weird; A Compendium of Strange and Dark Stories*, xv–xx, New York: Tor.
Wasson, S., and E. Alder, eds. (2011), *Gothic Science Fiction 1980–2010*, Liverpool: Liverpool University Press.

5

Woke Weird and the Cultural Politics of Camp Transformation

Stephen Shapiro

During the January 2017 Women's March in Charlotte, North Carolina, a few days after Donald Trump's inauguration, Jenny Sowry's twenty-two-month-old daughter lifted a small brown cardboard poster with nothing but multicolored crayon scrawls on its surface (Wanshel 2017). The image circulated on social networks, and Twitter user @mumbles_j (2017) commented: "I feel like #WokeBaby just gave us something powerful here but our third eye ain't ready for the truth." Can we consider these inscrutable runes as part of our moment's emergent weird canon? After all, we live in weird times, which seem to be getting weirder with every turn of the screw.

The category of the weird has been reactivated in cultural studies, not least through the advocacy of China Miéville, Ann and Jeff VanderMeer (2008), and Mark Fisher's *The Weird and the Eerie* (2016). H. P. Lovecraft's rapid move from the paraliterary margins to cultural touchstone has been accelerated by his influence on a strand of American philosophy, known as "object-oriented ontology" (Harman 2012) and mainstream filmic work, like Guillermo del Toro's Oscar-winning *The Shape of Water* (2017). In this resurgence, the image of Cthulhu rising from the oceanic depths now seems as iconic as Moby Dick's looming.

It is not simply that the weird has come into prominence again, but also that its authors and audiences have undergone a radical transubstantiation. For work that was previously to be overwhelmingly created for and consumed by "white," heteronormative men, the weird today has become one of a cluster of genres (e.g., science fiction) that have their most vibrant practitioners and readers within the overlapping categories of nonwhite, women's, and less heteronormative subjects. We need to take this metamorphosis seriously for what it may illuminate about the ways in which cultural products simultaneously register and help constitute new sociopolitical alignments and coalitions. In short, the weird today shows how the rattling of old bones can rustle up a new progressive counter-hegemony.

Here I want to explore this transformation by initially noting the presence of a cluster of prestige television series that exemplify what I call "Woke Weird," in that they use the weird as a means of coming to consciousness about the intersection of racial domination and capitalist exploitation. These televisual narratives are decolonial in spirit as they deploy weird devices as a means of recalling a long history of capitalist primitive accumulation and corporate imperialism in order to frame the entanglement between racialized bodies (and the territories they inhabit) and capitalism's grasping power, the concatenation of the bonds of chains and the bonds of profiteering exchange, in order to spark the viewer's left political sensorium.

These televisual narratives incongruously combine different temporalities to restage the past in order to register the onset of contemporaneous social instabilities and rearrangements. They become weird precisely as a means of critiquing "business as usual," with the hierarchies of everyday class and social subordination otherwise meant to be taken as commonsensical and unremarkable. To understand this culture of political transformation, we need a new definition of the weird, its procedures and moments of historical appearance. Here I suggest that this definition can be extrapolated from Marx's lesser-known comments on subjection (subsumption) within *Capital* and its preparatory notebooks. By reconsidering these lesser-known comments by Marx, we may see how the weird might confront the new far right's revanchism, as it enables a wokeness that could lead toward a new set of cultural alliances and progressive social coalitions.

Examples of this weird, decolonial television include *The Red Road* (2014–15, Sundance TV); *Frontier* (2016–present, Netflix); *Taboo* (2017–present, BBC), and, to a lesser degree, *Siren* (2018–present, Freeform), *Cleverman* (2016–17, Sundance TV), and *The Terror* (2018–present, AMC). Each shares the formal element of a barely articulate, overly musculated mixed-race male leading figure (such as Jason Momoa in *Frontier* and Tom Hardy in *Taboo*) experiencing aspects of mental fugue. This collision of muscular fitness and psychic imbalance is used as the narrative instrument to excavate the effects of frontier and colonial seizure capitalism committed by consumer goods corporations, such as the early nineteenth-century tea trade of the East India Company (*Taboo*), the eighteenth-century fur trade of the Hudson's Bay Company (*Frontier*), and the more recent events such as the Ford Motor Company's 1980s dumping of toxic car paint on the reservation of the multiracial Ramapough Lenape Nation in Upstate New York. Without seeking to present a focused reading of each series, I cluster them in order to ask a world-systems perspective question: Why there has been this nearly simultaneous spate of prestige television that foregrounds heterogeneous figures that bear the combined and uneven development of cartel-like imperialist capital? What are the contemporary social pressures that screen capital's past crimes through weird pulses that collapse normative psychology?

This question requires an understanding of the contrast between periodization and periodicity. As a result of the dominant forms of historiography from the Enlightenment-era onward, much work has gone into determining how we can periodize history, to see it as a sequence of uniquely differentiated units of social time. Periodicity, on the other hand, searches for the presence of capitalism's recurring features that reappear over multiple cycles of social reproduction. Even while capitalism's dynamism means that it adapts and changes shape over time, in order to overcome the barriers to profit that it sets for itself, capital also has familiar and repeating aspects that can be charted as similar or analogous moments across individual long spirals of time (Deckard and Shapiro 2019). Thus, each historical moment has both particular (and periodizable) features and more general (and periodic) ones. These two aspects coexist, but a concern for periodicity allows for a different kind of comparative cultural studies, one that slices through wrinkled strata of time, a wormholing of history that does not depend on contiguous temporality. Such a gesture differs from the recent turn to "deep time" studies, which may greatly expand their brackets of temporality, but usually still depend on the search for periodization, even if one highly difficult to discern within the scope of human observation.

While Marx did not fully flesh out a theory of periodicity, perhaps because he imagined that he would do so in his planned-for, but never delivered, analysis of the world market, he did leave enough commentary that telegraphs his understanding of periodicity in ways that will also help our own on the weird. On the one hand, Marx believes that periodicity only really emerges as a feature after the agents of capital can ensure recurring phases of expanded reproduction as a result of having fully cemented their social dominance, roughly from the last third of the eighteenth century. On the other, if periodicity only becomes normative when capitalism has become fully established, Marx recalls Sismondi's "deeper insight" that is precisely within the most highly developed forms of capital that antediluvian forms of coerced labor, such as feudal-like *corvée* and chattel slavery, become recalled and resituated (Marx 1990a: 345). For instance, Black American slavery in the nineteenth-century cotton plantations became "a factor in [the] calculated and calculating system" of British textile factories (Marx 1990a: 345).

These two seemingly contradictory features of periodicity—its appearance only in modern times, alongside its resurrection of prior ones—exemplifies what Marx in *Capital (Vol. I)* calls the *Zwitterformen* of subjection (subsumption), as that which links otherwise different social modes and temporalities (Marx 1990a: 645; Marx 1983: 415).

Zwitter Subjection (Subsumption)

"Subsumption" (*Subsumtion*) is a liminal term for Marx's *Capital*; he uses it only about a half-dozen times in the first German edition (1867). With each succeeding edition and translation, Marx either progressively reduced its use or replaced it for other terms, like "subordination" (Marx 1987; Marx 1989a; Marx 1991). By the last edition personally overseen by him (the French edition of 1872–5), the term has been entirely removed, as well as several passages that had contained it (Marx 1989b).[1] Only after Marx's death did Engels restore "subsumption" to the third and fourth German editions, whence it has entered all the English translations. Yet following the trajectory of Marx's revisions, we can read the term's erasure as a result of his increasing realization that two distinctive yet intertwined meanings were caught within his use of the term, a bivalence that he may have felt was clouding his desired clarity of exposition for the first volume. On one hand, Marx uses "subsumption" in a temporal sense to characterize phases in the historical expansion of *capital* as an economic practice. On the other, he uses it to characterize changing relations of subjectivity within *capitalism*, as a mode of hierarchical socialization. It may be for the more sociological purpose that all the English translations, with the exception of Ben Fowkes's most recent one, translate the term as "subjection," rather than "subsumption," a practice I will henceforth follow.[2] Marx himself seems to authorize this understanding of subjectivities within changing "governmentality" (to use Foucault's term) as he revised the first edition's phrase "*Die Subsumtion der Arbeit unter das Kapital* [the subjection of the work under Capital]" to read in the second, and ensuing editions, as "*Die Unterordnung* [subordination] *der Arbeit unter das Kapital* [the subordination of the work under Capital]" (Marx 1983: 592; Marx 1989a: 644).

In a basic sense, subjection (*Subsumtion*/subsumption) can be contrasted to sublation (*Aufhebung*). Whereas the latter is used by Marx to indicate a dialectical transformation that leads inexorably to a historical exit from capital, a move toward an *outside*, the former involves a nondialectical transformation usually within capital, or, in any case, a bringing of relations *inside* capital. While the movement from one mode of subjection to another involves a transformation, this metamorphosis involves a cementing of capitalism's hold on subjects, not its dissolution. Hence, "subjection" (subsumption) as a term captures Marx's interest in the process of human subordination within capital, an inclusion that involves different forms of subjectivity than those found in the precapitalist societies. Thus, Marx primarily uses "subjection" (subsumption) as his term to consider forms of compulsion as they historically differ in the movement from feudal or seigniorial power to capitalism. Precapitalist hierarchy depends on master/slave (serf, etc.) relations of personal "domination and dependency [*Herrschafts- und Abhängigkeitsverhältnissen/Herrschafts- und Knechtschaftsverhältnissen*]" in contrast to capitalism's impersonal "supremacy and subordination [*Über- und Unterordnung*]" of the worker by the capitalist boss through the exchange of wages for labor power (Marx 1990a: 1021, 1026; Marx 1987: 109–10; Marx 1988: 93, 97).[3]

The primary source for contemporary discussions of subjection (subsumption) is the so-called missing chapter of *Capital*, a manuscript first published in 1933 in Russian and German, and in English in 1976, translated by Rodney Livingstone, under the title, "Results of the Immediate Process of Production" (Marx 1990a: 941). This chapter was initially intended by Marx as a transitional one leading from the first volume of *Capital* toward volumes 2 and 3. Here, Marx tightly aligns the distinction between *formal subsumption* and *real subsumption* to his already-introduced categories of absolute surplus value and relative surplus value. Formal subjection is linked to the lengthening of the working day, which creates absolute surplus value. Real subjection is tied to the transformation of work processes that creates relative surplus value. The creation of an otherwise seemingly redundant term, "formal subjection," for what had otherwise been covered by "absolute surplus value" seems to have been used by Marx as his way to differentiate a more sociological aspect of disempowerment from a more technical practice of labor exploitation.

Furthermore, as the chapter's title, the "*the immediate process of production*," makes it clear, Marx insists that real and formal subjection solely exist in the figure of productive capital, and not in either of the figures of money or commodity capital, which are seen as the spheres of circulation, rather than of production (Marx 1990a: 1007). Thus, "formal subjection" and "real subjection" were terms only meant for discussions of the single figure of productive capital, not for capital as a whole formed by the interconnection of commodity, money, and productive capital. As such, the distinctions between formal and real subjection not only cannot be extrapolated to convey changes elsewhere in the expanded circuit of capital, but they also poorly handle capitalism's wider scope.

Patrick Murray argues that Marx elsewhere indicates the presence of eight different forms of subjection, which cover aspects of capital outside the sphere of production (Murray 2016: 337). Some of these other forms of subjection are the *Zwitterformen*, mentioned in a passage that exists in all the German editions of *Capital*. As Marx discusses the replacement of formal subjection by real subjection, he briefly mentions the existence of

> certain hybrid forms [*Zwitterformen*], in which although surplus labor is not extorted by direct compulsion from the producer, the producer has not yet become formally subordinate to capital. In these forms, capital has not yet acquired a direct control over the labor process.... The predominance of this form of exploitation in a society excludes the capitalist mode of production, although it may form the transition to capitalism, as in the later Middle Ages. Finally, as in the case of modern "domestic industry," certain hybrid forms are reproduced here and there against the background of large-scale industry, though their physiognomy is totally changed. (Marx 1990: 645; Marx 1987: 480)

This form of subjection does not belong to the direct compulsion (*direkten Zwang*) seen in "slavery, serfdom, vassalage and other forms of subjection," as the "relation between buyer and seller (or borrower or lender) is not bound by relations of servitude and domination [*Knechtschafts- und Herrschaftsverhältnisse*]" (Marx 1990: 1027–8; Marx 2010: 118; Marx 1982: 2152). Instead, it involves more independent activity, such as seen with "self-sustaining peasants, farmer who only have to pay a rent on what they produce, either the state or landlord; rural or domestic industry or *independent handicraft*" (Marx 1990: 1028–9). On the other hand, neither is it an aspect of fully fledged capitalism, since there it does not allow for the freedom to commodify labor through waged labor power, so there is no formal subjection within capitalist supremacy and subordination. Consequently, this form of subjection is both *outside* and *within* capital; "in social formations which precede the bourgeois mode of production; and on the other hand, they reproduce themselves within the latter and are in part reproduced by the latter itself" (Marx 2010: 117). These forms of subjection are *within* capital, but not within the figure of production, as they exist in the spheres of circulation. They are also not wholly *outside* capital, as they are found within the border conditions of primitive accumulation, where "previous forms of production [become] the sole and the original [primitive] forms of capital [*in frühren Productionsformen als die einzigen and ursprünglichen Formen des*

Capitals]" (Marx 2010: 118; Marx 1982: 2152). These are forms that indicate work processes altered by their proximity to capital's magnetic force and by the intervening forces of precapitalist forms of money and commodity capital such as usurers and merchant's trade.

One of Marx's examples here is the Indian *ryot* (peasant or tenant farmer), who mortgages his crop to a usurer "*before it is grown.*" The *ryot* is not a wage laborer, nor is the usurer "an industrial capitalist." The *ryot* "is his own employer" [written in English in the original] and "thus is not subsumed as a wage labourer to the owner of the conditions of production." Yet the force of capital is present as "the usurer appropriates . . . the whole of the surplus value created by the *ryot*" while also stunting any further independence or development: "This form heightens the exploitation of the producer . . . without in any way, with the introduction of capitalist production. . . . It is a form which makes labor sterile, places it under the most unfavorable economic conditions, and *combines together capitalist exploitation without a mode of capitalist production* . . . the means of production have ceased to belong to the producer . . . but they are nominally subsumed to him, and the mode of production remains in the same relations of small independent enterprise, only the relations are *in ruins*" (Marx 2010: 118–19, emphasis added). It is "*debt slavery* in distinction to *wage slavery*" (118–119). In short, this form is work that seems to be formally outside of capitalism's protocols but is nonetheless driven by its force. Importantly, this bivalent condition does not necessarily have a clear developmental trajectory, and these forms *are not necessarily transitional*. Marx believes that while they "may form the transition to capitalism [*den Uebergang bilden kann*]," they also may be caught in nondialectical stasis.

Yet, Marx also says that not only may these forms persist within advanced capitalism, as a residual feature of the past, but that they may also continue to recur and be sporadically reproduced. The example of the forms now given by Marx does not involve an earlier mode of textile production in South Asia, but a more contemporaneous European example: workers who have been made redundant from the introduction of new machinery. The reserve army of labor, made unemployed by technologically advanced capitalism, survives outside of waged labor in "dreadful forms of production" in which becoming a waged worker, even if over-worked, "appears as a redemption," a freedom from precarity (Marx 2010: 220). An illustration of this kind of work done by those ejected from waged labor is "jobbing work," where "middlemen and sweaters" make "colossal fortunes" by subcontracting, much as happens today in the so-called gig economy.

Murray separates these two kinds of subjection by distinguishing "one [that Marx] calls the transitional [*Uebergangsform*], [and] the other accompanying [*Nebensform*]," and he explains that the first involves "a bridge to modern capitalist relations," while the other "refers to forms that keep appearing alongside established capitalist firms" (Murray 2016: 316). But Marx does not suggest that he considers these forms as sequential and periodized. Instead, he suggests a form of subjection that is not merely inaugural or persistent, but also *reproduced by and recurrent within* capitalism, especially with the rise of fictitious capital (money-dealing capital) and the investment in new technologies, machinery, or scientific processes that create unemployment. Marx does not imply a temporal distinction of periodized sequence between the transitional and accompanying forms, but a periodicized entanglement and simultaneity, where the conditions of primitive accumulation, the extensification of capitalist relations, is interlinked with the production of surplus labor through the intensification of capitalist relations by new machinery.

The twisting together of the conditions of seizure capitalism on capital's frontiers and unemployment at home exists in ways that *Capital*'s English translations have obscured. What Marx writes as *Zwitterformen* has been variously translated as *hybrid* or *intermediate* (Marx 1990a: 645; Marx 1990b: 455; Marx 1909: 455; Marx 1930: 553). Yet neither is correct, especially as Marx elsewhere uses *Mittelding* for "intermediate" (Marx 1987: 308). The *Zwitterform* is more accurately translated as the hermophoditic or intersex form. Marx's referent here might be Tiresias, whose gender change made for the ability to see forward and backward in time so as to gain a greater perspective on historicity. With the *Zwitterform*, Marx indicates a form of subjection that neither is merely mixed (hybrid) nor is an evolutionary midpoint (intermediate), but co-functioning, operating equally, within two different formations, one that is outside capital and another that is within it, so as to connect two otherwise incommensurate social formations.

Following on this, we can see that the most full initial elaboration of the *Zwitterform* is Leon Trotsky's description of combined and uneven development (Trotsky 1971).[4] In surveying Russia's conditions at the turn of the twentieth century, Trotsky described a social ecology marked by the sudden introjection of fixed-capital investments, including transport and communication, by West European cartels into a Russia without either a dominant middle class or a large urban industrial proletariat, a country still largely operating as if serfdom had not been abolished. He observes the collision of the very advanced with the very underdeveloped: "[T]he appearance in Russia of modern capitalist industry in a completely primitive economic environment . . . a huge Belgian or American industrial plant surrounded by dirt roads and villages built of straw and wood which burn down every year." This created a temporality that simultaneously staged "the most primitive beginnings and the most modern European endings" (Trotsky 1971: 33). In this sense, *Zwitterform* subjection might be easily read as "combined and uneven subjection," the mode in which the historical fragments of past forms exist *alongside* modern implementations of new industry. The combined and uneven subjection creates its own figurations of the clash between advanced capital and hinterland regions, some of which are gothic, while others are weird.

The Weird's *Zwitterform*

The *zwittering* of capital's transformations helps explain the recent prevalence of the Woke Weird in new televisual forms, not least as it helps us toward a new definition of the weird, one that marks its difference from gothic and foregrounds its cultural alteration of the patterns of subjection. As I have elaborated elsewhere:

> Weird tales tend to cluster, or achieve a density of appearance at moments of the first instantiation of an incipient downward phase of economic (and social) contraction. The weird registers initial perceptions of what ought not to be present—i.e. capitalism in crisis—in times otherwise dominated by wealth creation and continuing expansion, those moments when rising inequality begins to be sensed even though these social divisions have been dogmatically claimed to have been overcome. Narratives that foreground the seepage of other, seemingly inexplicable lifeworlds and temporalities into the everyday are tremblors before the onset of larger transformations within the capitalist world-system. In their precognition and premediation of this economic transformation, they also reveal a greater fundamental truth about capitalism's production of surplus value, which is that it always works through conditions that mix proletarian and semi- or non-proletarian labor in ways that combine waged work with forms of coerced or unpaid labor, as well as labor in pre- or weakly-capitalist forms, like the Zwitterforms. The Weird is the narrative form that tends to become more prevalent at the first pulses of change, the inflection from boom to bust times, the switchover between capitalism's systole and diastole that creates a time-space for capitalism's mixed nature of labor relations to become acknowledged, even if through strained narratives. These tales often deploy bizarre sensorium juxtapositions because no commonsensical (or dominant-rational) language is readily available or allowed to express such inconvenient truths about the oncoming decline or overall heterogeneous composition of capital. (Shapiro 2016: 241–2)

This claim is linked to, but differs from, one that contends that gothic's cultural predicates appear in clusters at times when the world-system is forcibly incorporating new regions into its dynamic (Shapiro 2008). The collision of folk religion and customs with capitalist modes of production, especially in extractive and monoculture agricultural capital or new transportation and communication industries, results in the creation of invented traditions, where the monsters are described in what seem to be folk traditions, but are actually new constructions that register globalizing conditions in local-seeming idioms. While gothic may present the haunting of the present by past crimes of appropriation and destruction, the weird explores why the present does not see these crimes in the first place. It highlights how contemporary formations of knowledge production are themselves barriers to comprehending the past. Unlike gothic, the weird has a greater self-awareness about the creation of dominant epistemology and the ideological barriers to the structuration of knowledge that created an initial sense of frightful bewilderment in the first place. The weird's double consciousness about the combined and uneven subjections of two different social systems means that weird tales often void their own potential scariness, especially as they invite their reader, very early on, to be in on the project of resisting or overcoming gothic blockages of knowledge. The weird's boundary collapse belongs as much to critical epistemology as it does to any critical ontology.

Any discussion that considers the weird as a matter mainly of understanding the ontology or being-ness of the nonhuman simply misplaces the center of the weird's gravity. Despite what they often *say* about the difficulty of cognizing otherness, weird tales rarely find it difficult to then do so to the reader. Weird tales instead highlight the difficulty that official institutions, and their curation over what are admissible truth statements, have in acknowledging the presence of incongruity within their normative speech. This tension arises since these institutions seek to avoid not only a discussion of exploitation and domination but also their own complicity in helping to erase the traces of past and ongoing violence. Due to this pressure against honest speech, weird tales often register the force of the normative on their sentence line as much as any depiction of nonhuman subjectivity. Critical ontology may offer useful insights into the weird, but these are often preliminary propositions, rather than fundamental or radical ones.

A similar incompleteness appears in Mark Fisher's recent discussion of the weird in relation to the eerie. Unexpectedly, Fisher's discussion of the weird lacks the cultural materialist insight that otherwise characterizes his writing. By falling back to transhistorical, quasi-psychoanalytic categories, and not asking why the weird (and the eerie) have become unexpectedly popular now, Fisher's definitions fall short of being immediately usable for contemporary cultural politics, or, at least, remain unusable until they are modified and revised.

Fisher considers both the weird and the eerie as boundary forms, which "allow us to see the inside from the perspective of the outside" (Fisher 2016: 10). The weird is neither horrific nor suspenseful but inchoately understood due to an extreme juxtaposition or jarring catachresis. The weird is that *"which does not belong"* (13). It creates a "sensation of *wrongness*: a weird entity is so strange that it makes us feel that it should not exist, or at least it should not exist here" (15). To create the mood of fascination, "albeit a fascination usually mixed with a certain trepidation," Fisher argues that the "form that is perhaps appropriate to the weird is montage—the conjoining of *two or more things which do not belong together*" (11).

Unlike the weird's introjection of the foreign outside into the familiarly domestic (*heimlich*), the eerie for Fisher is the expulsion from an enclosed space to a vanishing point perspective: "A sense of the eerie seldom clings to enclosed and domestic spaces; we find the eerie more readily in landscape partially emptied of the human. What happened to produce these ruins, this disappearance? What kind of entity was involved?" (11). For Fisher, "the eerie is fundamentally tied up with questions of agency. What kind of agent is acting here? Is there an agent at all?" (11). An initial response might question the similarity of Fisher's depiction of the weird as a problem of composition, the disordering of the domestic, mundane, and quotidian, and of the eerie as a problem of the unseen or vanished agent, to older forms of criticism that invoked a cis-gendered division between the so-called female gothic of entrapment, told in hysteric tones, and the male gothic, told in paranoid ones, about anonymous pursuit through empty spaces (Moers 1977). By echoing these older claims, Fisher encodes the weird as feminized, since it seeks to prevent border collapse caused by unwelcome penetration, while he has the eerie as similarly evoking the explorer fantasy of an unpeopled land that will offer no resistance to settler colonization.

Against such a binary oppositional definition that contemporary criticism would be loath to reinscribe, a more materialist version may help. In what Fisher categorizes as eerie, these are better seen as the experience of the detritus of fixed capital's catastrophic crisis of (total) devalorization. This recalls Marx's definition of fixed capital as that which is used up, bit by bit, over multiple cycles of capital's realization (Marx 1992: 238). In this way, items like the built environment or monumental machinery ought, within capital's expectations, to depreciate through a knowable schedule of amortization, a linear and foreseeable consumption, leading to the item's scheduled replacement. When we see these objects abandoned before their value can be fully consumed, we experience the eerie as a form of capitalist apocalypse, an affect resulting from the radical devaluation of fixed capital by its drastic abandonment before it could be incrementally devalorized over time. In this sense, the eerie is produced by an amnesia of the weird, a forgetting of historical *zwittering*, where questions about agency replace ones of epistemic awareness. Instead of wondering about the weird's putative ontology, we might instead prefer to ask about its counter-hegemony, its constitutive action of new arrangements of progressive collectivity. By this, I mean namely the weird's Camp utopia.

Weird Is Camp for Heterosexual (Men)

If the material we call weird is often neither horrific nor scary, and frequently predictable in its plot revelations, then it functions less as gothic and more in the way of Camp. Susan Sontag's "Notes on 'Camp,'" as an early attempt to define Camp, still has a trick to teach us about how we can read contemporary consumers of the weird. Sontag likens Camp to the historical emergence, in the eighteenth century of a taste for "gothic novels, Chinoiserie, caricature, artificial ruins, and so forth" (Sontag 2009: 280). The "essence of Camp is its love of the unnatural . . . of the exaggerated, the 'off' of things-being-what-they-are-not" (Sontag 2009: 275, 279). Camp "sees everything in quotation marks. It is not a lamp, but a 'lamp': not a woman, but a 'woman.' To perceive Camp in objects and persons is to understand Being-as-Playing-a-Role" (Sontag 2009: 280). As the "sensibility of failed seriousness, of the theatricalization of experience," Camp stands for the dogged celebration of "character . . . as a state of continual incandescence . . . a person being one, very intense thing" in opposition to abstract, moral seriousness on ethics—the Hebraic Prophet cannot be the Wildean dandy (286–7). For Sontag, Camp is ultimately "a mode of enjoyment, of appreciation-not judgment. Camp is generous. It wants to enjoy. It only seems like malice, cynicism . . . [but] Camp taste is a kind of love, love for human nature" (291).

Sontag's notes do not explicitly draw link how this sensibility's esoteric bonds mainly exist as a "private code, a badge of identity even, among small urban cliques" (275). Eve K. Sedgwick later made Sontag's claims more specific to queerness, as she argues that Camp's performance enacts more than simply an awareness of identity for internal aesthetic gratification; it functions as a medium that enables a longing for and recognition of possible community, or what

Jose Muñoz would later call cruising for utopia (Sedgwick 1990; Muñoz 2009). Thus, Sedgwick makes a distinction between kitsch and Camp, similar to the one Sontag made between what she called naïve and deliberate Camp. Kitsch, for Sedgwick, is the notion that the viewer looks at an object, say pink flamingos or garden gnomes, and critically imagines that there are debased consumers who actually think that these objects have positive aesthetic value. Hence, to label an object as kitschy is to denounce its (usually working-class) owners as naïve, unsophisticated, and certainly without (bourgeois) taste.

Citing Robert Dawidoff, Sedgwick contends that Camp has the viewer of an object not only gain pleasure from viewing but also imagining that there might be others who do so as well. Unlike kitsch-attribution, Camp-attribution asks, "*What if*: What if the right audience for this were exactly *me*? . . . And what if, furthermore, others whom I don't know or recognize can see it from the same 'perverse' angle" (Sedgwick 1990: 156). The Camp viewer may think, "What if whoever made this was gay too?" For Sedgwick then, Camp is the flare signal that doesn't merely support *individual character*, but also provides a marker for the existence of a potential collective, even, or especially, in its absence. Unlike Sontag, who sees Camp as a production of urban ghettoes of spatial proximity, Sedgwick sees it as a phenomenon that overcomes distance and personal isolation. Or, to mix Fisher's and Sedgwick's arguments, Camp helps brings those outside (of the closet) into incongruous contact with those viewers perhaps still *inside*, due to heteronormative constraints, acting as a kind of social *zwitterlng*.

While Sontag admits that Camp has been "peculiarly suited" to the situation of the nonheterosexuals, and has historically been enacted by its members, there is nothing in its logic that limits it to these groups. Indeed, the weird today may function as an ersatz Camp for heterosexual, cis-men, who might not otherwise feel entirely comfortable with considering themselves as having a queer preference or taste. For example, Lovecraft and his work have become campy through websites like @cthulhu4america, children's coloring books, and other fan merchandise. This transvaluation exists alongside the transformation of Lovecraft's materials for the purposes of woke Black-oriented narratives, such as Victor LaValle's *The Ballad of Black Tom* (2016) or Matt Ruff's telling the tale of Jim Crow America through a landscape fashioned as *Lovecraft Country* (2016). Though Lovecraft himself would likely have been appalled at being turned into a dandy Warhol, the collective-building nature of his work was always present, for Lovecraft's writing was openly communal, as seen with his willing sharing of a so-called Cthulhu mythos among other writers, his collaborations, often discounted as ghost-writing, and his vast body of personal letters that he wrote to other writers across America to link otherwise isolated and underrecognized figures into a self-making community.

The historical conditions that interweave acts of violence on peripheralized peoples and precarious employment on the formerly enfranchised has created the terms and conditions for a new wave of the weird. If the weird appears more often at moments of transformation, factions begin to realize the structural conditions that have led to their disempowerment and, consequently, begin to scramble patterns of cultural taste. This incipient consciousness has had limited prior awareness leads to considering what lies beyond the previously considered norms. Or, to use a Lovecraftian phrase, a look at the mountains of madness. In these times of combined and uneven subjection, such as is our own, the social *zwittering* has led to renewed figurations of "changed physiognomy," as seen with the recent Woke Weird television series. As such, today's Woke Weird television has produced tales of mixed-race, muscular men lacking mental equipoise as a way of cognizing the shared periodicity of historical and contemporary, neoliberal capitalism. These cultural productions not only register the moment's ongoing catastrophes as similar to ones in the past, but may also look toward the future, by laying the grounds for incongruous coalitions and counter-hegemonies. Here the Woke Weird often deploys Camp as an attitude that seeks to bring together groups that might otherwise be thought as existing in opposition to one another: white, heterosexual men, disenfranchised nonwhites, and sexual and gender minorities.

A Cultural Front Politics

What catachrestic political possibilities may be possible as a result of the crosshatching of Woke Weird and Camp Weird? Dale Beran, writing on the role of the internet communications of 4chan, argues that this lifeworld emerges from a particular substrate or demographic of younger, largely white, male posters who have created a particular style of internet memes, like Pepe the Frog (Beran 2017). This group blends and blurs with the Alt-right and other extreme right-wing, post-truth formations, but Beran believes that the 4chan world is best compared to that of the Japanese *hikikomori*—"meaning 'pulling inward, or being confined'—teens and adults who withdraw from society into fantasy worlds constructed by anime, video games, and now the internet" (Beran 2017). The 4chan group's extreme insensitivity and tactless confrontationalism masks, for Beran, their own sensitivity as "particularly lonely, sex starved man-boys, who according to their own frequent jokes, lived in their parents' basements."

Recognizing themselves as failures—"men without jobs, without prospects, and by extension (so they declaimed) without girlfriends"—these men feel humiliated and rejected, and project their expression of powerlessness through resentment against groups who they see as having privileged status, even in the absence of economic wealth, for example women or those interested in social (or environmental) justice, and so on. The basement dwellers are weird in that they are not simply *losers*, but, according to Beran, *they know themselves* as losers. They belong, particularly, to the millennial generation that was raised on neoliberal predicates of aspirational entrepreneurship and competitive rewards, but now sense that this vision has also placed them structurally within a social fragility that ought not to have occurred. This is the generation to whom the promise of postwar, Fordist upward mobility is now little more than a bitter joke.

Their ire is thus directed against the "seriousness" of groups, like women or liberals, who, in spite of everything, still hold onto utopian claims for social betterment, or those who have "learned different ways to cope with the same problem," such as the hipsters, whose "sexual adventures, both gay and straight, were totally disconnected from their earning potential and all social expectations." Beran argues that while a critique of sex binary differences by feminism and queer theory *ought* to be enabling for the basement dwellers, they see it as disrespectful and furthering their abjection. Beran, however, believes that the basement dwellers can be "un-nazified." The question is how?

Could the Woke Weird, with its combination of muscle men and decolonial and anti-capitalist critique, be the kind of *Zwitterform* that might bring the basement dwellers into a new cultural front? The weird uses materials with which they are already familiar, but does so in Camp-like ways that may allow for the establishment of a new, albeit incongruous, coalition of cultural and social interests. In a later piece, Beren claims such a movement has indeed begun (Beran 2019). For with all its contradictions, the weird may turn out to be one of today's most politically progressive forms. Maybe #wokebaby's runes might open our third eyes, after all, as a weird way out of this moment's ruins.

Notes

1 The passages which appear in Marx 1990a, 645–6, would have been inserted into *Le Capital* (Marx 1989b: 441–2).
2 The prior complete translations of *Capital* Volume I are Marx 1990b, Marx 1909, and Marx 1930. Although Fowkes prefers to translate *subsumtion* as subsumption,

he is not wholly consistent and sometimes uses "subjection" as do the prior English translators. Compare Marx 1990: 616 and Marx 1883: 469.
3   Aveling and Moore use "dominion and servitude" (Marx 1990b 127). Fowkes is inconsistent and sometimes translates the phrase as "domination and servitude" (Marx 1990a 247).
4   For discussions of combined and uneven development for literary studies, see Shapiro and Barnard 2018 and WReC 2017.

References

@mumbles_j (2017), 22 January. Available online: https://twitter.com/mumbles_j/status/823199061381672962 (accessed March 11, 2019).

Beran, D. (2017), "4chan: The Skeleton Key to the Rise of Trump," 14 February. Available online: https://medium.com/@DaleBeran/4chan-the-skeleton-key-to-the-rise-of-trump-624e7cb798cb (accessed March 17, 2019).

Beran, D. (2019), "Why Does 8chan Exist at All?," 4 August. Available online: https://medium.com/@DaleBeran/why-does-8chan-exist-at-all-33a8942dbeb2 (accessed August 28, 2019).

Deckard, S., and S. Shapiro (2019), "World-Culture and the Neoliberal World-System: An Introduction," in S. Deckard and S. Shapiro (eds.), *World Literature, Neoliberalism, and the Culture of Discontent*, 1–48, London: Palgrave.

Elyse Wanshel, E. (2017), "This #WokeBaby Made Her Own Adorable Sign for the Women's March," *The Huffington Post*, 23 January. Available online: https://www.huffpost.com/entry/toddler-protest-sign-womens-march-washington-charlotte_n_58861fcce4b096b4a2330682 (accessed March 11, 2019).

Fisher, F. (2016), *The Weird and the Eerie*, London: Repeater Books.

Harman, G. (2012), *Weird Realism: Lovecraft and Philosophy*, Alresford, UK: Zero Books.

LaValle, V. (2016), *The Ballad of Black Tom*, New York: Tor.com.

Marx, K. (1909), *Capital: A Critique of Political Economy*, trans. E. Untermann, Chicago: Charles H. Kerr and Company.

Marx, K. (1930), *Capital: Volume I*, trans. E. and C. [Gertrude Mary Davenport] Cole, London: J. M. Dent and Sons.

Marx, K. (1982), *Zur Kritik der Politischen Ökonomie. Manuskript 1861–1863*, Berlin: Dietz Verlag.

Marx, K. (1983), *Das Kapital: Kritik der Politischen Ökonomie. Erster Band. Hamburg 1867*, Berlin: Dietz Verlag.

Marx, K. (1987), *Das Kapital: Kritik der Politischen Ökonomie. Erster Band. Hamburg 1872*, Berlin: Dietz Verlag.

Marx, K. (1988), "Sechstes Kapitel. Resultate des unmittelbaren· Produktionsprozesses," in *Ökonomische Manuscripte. 1863–1867*, 24–130, Berlin: Dietz Verlag.

Marx, K. (1989a), *Das Kapital: Kritik der Politischen Ökonomie. Erster Band. Hamburg 1883*, Berlin: Dietz Verlag.
Marx, K. (1989b), *Le Capital: Paris 1872–75*, trans. J. Roy, Berlin: Dietz Verlag.
Marx, K. (1990a), *Capital: A Critique of Political Economy*, vol. I, trans. B. Fowkes, London: Penguin.
Marx, K. (1990b), *Capital: A Critical Analysis of Capitalist Production. London 1887*, trans. S. Moore and E. Aveling, Berlin: Dietz Verlag.
Marx, K. (1991), *Das Kapital: Kritik der Politischen Ökonomie. Erster Band. Hamburg 1890*, Berlin: Dietz Verlag.
Marx, K. (1992), *Capital: Volume II*, trans. David Fernbach, London: Penguin.
Marx, K. (2010), *Marx & Engels Collected Works: Volume 34, Marx 1861–64*, London: Lawrence & Wishart.
Moers, E. (1977), *Literary Women*, New York: Anchor Press.
Muñoz, J. E. (2009), *Cruising Utopia: The Then and There of Queer Futurity*, New York: NYU Press.
Murray, P. (2016), *The Mismeasure of Wealth: Essays on Marx and Social Form*, Leiden: Brill.
Ruff, M. (2016), *Lovecraft Country*, New York: Harper Perennial.
Sedgwick, E. K. (1990), *Epistemology of the Closet*, Berkeley: University of California Press.
Shapiro, S. (2008), "Transvaal, Transylvania: *Dracula*'s World-system and Gothic Periodicity," *Gothic Studies*, 10 (1): 24–47.
Shapiro, S. (2016), "The Weird's World-system: The Long Spiral and Literary-Cultural Studies," *Paradoxa*, 28: 240–61.
Shapiro, S., and Barnard, P. (2018), *Pentecostal Modernism: Lovecraft, Los Angeles, and World-Systems Culture*, London: Bloomsbury.
Sontag, S. (2009), "Notes on 'Camp'," in *Against Interpretation and Other Essays*, 275–92, London: Penguin.
Trotsky, L. (1971), *1905*, trans. A. Bostock, London: Penguin.
Vandermeer, A., and J. VanderMeer, eds.. (2008), *The New Weird*, San Francisco: Tachyon Publications.
Warwick Research Collective [WReC] (2015), *Combined and Uneven Development: Towards a New Theory of World-Literature*, Liverpool: Liverpool University Press.

6

The Weird in/of Crisis, 1930/2010

Tim Lanzendörfer

By the time the reader turns to this chapter in the collection, it is undoubtedly commonplace to say that the weird is back; and to name the names involved in this return philosophically (Eugene Thacker, Graham Harman, or Mark Fisher) or literarily (Jeff VanderMeer, China Miéville, Thomas Ligotti, or Victor Lavalle, say—but the number is great) is a fairly repetitious endeavor. What is maybe left to do is give an answer to the question of "why?" that differs from the major accounts. What is it that drives the specifically contemporary fascination with the weird, and how are we to understand its relation to a wider history of weird fiction that goes back a century or so: chiefly to a fraying patch of literary production centered around the 1920s, but going back to the pre–First World War writings of such authors as Algernon Blackwood, and extending into the late 1930s and early 1940s in work by August Derleth and others (see Miéville 2009 for a brief but forceful summary of this history)?[1]

In what follows, I will propose a by no means radical though avowedly Marxist framing of this return, which will, I hope, nonetheless helpfully advance the discourse around the weird and the Weird alike. The convention of distinguishing between the "weird" and the "Weird"—namely, the merely weird and what I call the specifically Weird that reflects concrete socioeconomic crisis moments—has not yet been proposed (so quotations will usually be lowercase no matter which weird is meant!), and, indeed, seems to run counter to some of the arguments raised in this book. My argument, essentially, is twofold: first, I argue that we must understand the contemporary return of the Weird in both philosophy and literature as registrations of an impossibility of speaking about an unintelligible—and, importantly, socioeconomically volatile—reality's possible others, in historically specific constellations that do not always exist (although interest in the weird may do so, in either its Old or New forms). In simple terms, the Weird is a form that appears at moments of crisis because of its capacity to think nonsupernatural apparent outsides to socioeconomic systems that appear to be failing. It is this that ties together the philosophical turn to object-oriented ontology and the return of, concretely, capital "W" Weird fiction in the contemporary moment. Second, however, I contend that such a reading of the Weird requires us to understand this Weird as distinct from the merely weird, whether Old or New: the claim here is that while lots of things may be weird, to speak meaningfully of the specific work that the Weird does (as opposed to the more general work all things weird do) requires us to locate it temporally and historically, that is to say both in time and in those times' socioeconomic contexts, or their shared History.[2] Or, more pithily, not all things that are weird are Weird. This view makes the capital-W Weird, as it were automatically, Marxist: to understand the distinction between the weird and the Weird, we require the Marxist theoretical lens.

Drawing on and expanding China Miéville's understanding of weird fiction as the "literature of crisis" (2009: 514), I want to understand the Weird as a specific literary moment, rather than a "mere" genre or form, one which is "an expression of upheaval and crisis" (513) and thus located at a specific sociohistorical, and indeed socioeconomic, moment. In so doing I offer a more concrete idea of what we are to make of the return of the Weird in the contemporary moment, which is best appreciated through but in fact goes beyond the H. P. Lovecraft renaissance that has often been remarked upon.

In order to do so, I want to link two moments in Weird fiction: "1930," a temporal marker that is supposed to indicate the latest reach of the "Lovecraft event," "the singularity of Lovecraft's fiction in its knotting together of art, science, and politics" (Noys 2007: 1), and our own moment, here indicated by the temporal marker "2010." Both of these dates should be understood, as I have indicated earlier, as centers around which the production of Weird fiction flourishes, rather than as naming singular moments in time, but also as making explicit reference to an "after" of the inflection points of a general crisis, in these cases the Great Depression and the Great Recession, respectively. These crisis moments are, of course, more expansive than the singular dates by which we usually enter them into a historical chronology (October 24, 1929, "Black Friday," and September 16, 2008). In the first case, we need to understand the larger crisis—the modernist crisis itself, if we care to echo Alan Wilde (1979)—as well underway before the First World War demonstrated how easily civilization can shatter, growing in strength well before the Great Depression signaled (again) the limits of capitalism's promise of improvement, and still ongoing before the Second World War ended with the certain possibility of humanity's self-immolation. And in the second case, we could name at least the period between the oft-cited end of the long-1990s, September 11, 2001 (see Wegner 2009), and the onset of the concrete moment of economic crisis as the larger duration in which the contemporary Weird's crisis began to manifest. We should also understand that it is still ongoing and perhaps now, with a right-wing populist advance guard in charge of the biggest countries in the western hemisphere, the United States and Brazil, more noticeable than at any time since the ostensible end of the Great Recession.

My argument, then, will read the Weird's contemporary resurgence explicitly against the socioeconomic and sociopolitical backdrop of our times: a broad perspective, as befits a broad field of writing, but one which I will signpost here by recourse to only two writers (and nods to others). I am going to start with a short discussion of the weird as it is currently theorized by a number of writers: Miéville, Mark Fisher, and Graham Harman, especially, in order to lay the theoretical groundwork for what I do in the following. Then, I will seek to situate the specific moments of the capital-W Weird that I have identified above: "1930" and "2010." In the first of these, I will read Lovecraft's novella *At the Mountains of Madness*, written in 1931 and first published in 1936, as a late but eloquent and thorough response to the larger modernist crisis, but also as specifically readable against the economic upheaval of its immediate past and present. *At the Mountains of Madness* seeks to correlate technological developments, foundational racial conflict, idealism about progress, and the realization of immutable outside forces, in a registration of the global anxieties of its time. From there, I want to turn in the section on "2010" to Jeff VanderMeer's Southern Reach trilogy of novels, *Annihilation, Authority*, and *Acceptance* (2014). While superficially—that is to say, obviously, rather than depthlessly—concerned with the relationship between man and nature, with the Anthropocene threat of climate change, the series may be more appropriately read more broadly, I think, and be understood as very much akin of Lovecraft's *At the Mountains of Madness* in its all-encompassing registration of the crisis of the contemporary. Read against one another, the two texts will, I hope, elucidate my claim that the Weird is historically specific, but will, at the same time, illustrate the meaningful differences between the moments which are registered in each text.

The Weird: Theories

The contemporary resurgence of interest in the weird, and in theorizing the weird, is tied to the resurgence of interest in Lovecraft's writing that I will also address later, and probably bespeaks not just the dearth of previous theorizations that is largely the consequence of a fairly belated acceptance of popular fiction as objects of literary study but also the recognition that it is surprisingly fundamental to our sense of the contemporary. I will engage three major theorizations of the weird in what follows, and then offer my own rereading of them to arrive at a more particular sense of the Weird. Specifically, I want to engage Fisher, Miéville, and Harman, who approach weird fiction from signally different angles as regards both their objects—cultural, literary, philosophical—and their political agenda—leftist, Marxist, and (at best) liberal, respectively. What emerges from these theorizations is what I would understand as an aesthetically similar reading of the weird, but an at-best-halting appreciation of its historical significance; nonetheless, all three theorists offer useful pointers for what follows.

In his brief exploration of "Weird Fiction," Miéville foregrounds the weird's "obsession with numinosity under the everyday," and argues that over sixty years or so around 1910, it worked through versions—religious, materialist, spiritualist—of "estrangement from the supposedly quotidian" (2009: 510) that was, at heart, a response to the radically shifting conditions of capitalist modernity. As Miéville notes, weird fiction emerged in a "period of crisis" in which the "cruder nostrums of progressive bourgeois rationality [were] shattered." He stresses the importance of the First World War for this high period of weird fiction, suggesting that it "made claims of a 'rational' modern system a tasteless joke" (513). His take on the weird, brief and forceful, does two things: first, it historicizes weird fiction and contextualizes it as a response (whose relation to the historical events they mediate, however, is unexplored) to a crisis; second, he locates it historically, which is perhaps more problematical: ending with Lovecraft, Miéville does not explain how the contemporary upsurge of weird fiction may be explained, given that he has emphatically stressed the "constitutive relationship between the war and the Weird" (514). Miéville, I think, is very much on the right track in his effort to historicize, but somewhat too focused on World War I as the origin of the weird's concern with a larger modernist crisis, rather than itself the expression of that crisis. I will offer my own take on this later in the chapter, but let me segue into the next short theoretical section by stressing Miéville's argument that the weird's aesthetic response to the crisis it operates in is marked by its insistence on the appearance of the sublime—the Kantian admixture of beauty and fear—from "beyond" (511), an outside to the existing.

Fundamentally, then, the Weird is concerned with narratives that explore conceptions of inside and outside, suggesting that our perception of reality does not match what actually is real. Miéville's argument here tracks some other critics' arguments: Fisher proposes in *The Weird and the Eerie* that both of these concepts have a "preoccupation with the strange" and "a fascination for the outside, for that which lies beyond standard perception, cognition, and experience" (Fisher 2016: 8). But whereas the eerie, in Fisher's conceptualization, names a sensation of absent (expected) presences or present (expected) absences (61), the weird names an altogether more complicated problem, namely the realization that an "object is so strange that it makes us feel that it should not exist, or at least it should not exist here. Yet if the entity or object is here, then the categories which we have up until now to make sense of the world cannot be valid. The weird thing is not wrong, after all: it is our conceptions that must be inadequate" (15). Unlike Miéville, Fisher does not historicize this sense: indeed, in his later sections weird writers from H. G. Wells to Tim Powers are all addressed chiefly on aesthetic and formal terms.

The final theorist of the weird I want to discuss in this opening is Harman, best known as the most public of the philosophers of object-oriented ontology. Harman's discussion of the weird is restricted to Lovecraft, who figures in Harman's writing as the best literary expression of object-oriented ontology itself (what Hölderlin is for Heidegger, or Mallarmé for Badiou). Lovecraft represents an aesthetic access to the central tenets of object-oriented philosophy, and Harman's actual work on Lovecraft, his close reading of Lovecraft, is entirely aesthetical: he reads "individual passages" of Lovecraft's works in order to discover "what makes them effective" (2011: 51). For Harman, Lovecraft's chief trait as a writer, and by extension the chief definition of the weird, is the way his writing catches the "gap . . . between the world and our descriptions of it" (27). Harman's philosophy is, of course, fundamentally concerned with the reality of the world and our access to it—arguing that the relations between objects are inaccessible to us, but nonetheless real, in what is no doubt too short shorthand. Lovecraft, Harman argues, writes a "world in which (1) real objects are locked in impossible tension with the crippled descriptive powers of language, and (2) visible objects display unbearable seismic torsion with their own qualities" (27). This is altogether too tame for the outcome of this philosophical problem in Lovecraft's fiction, of course: what happens ultimately, Harman argues, is that we are confronted with the "tension between ourselves and our experiences. . . . [W]e need to endure a breakdown of the usual situation in which perceptions and meanings simply lie before us as obvious facts, or in which we stalk through life in quasi-robotic union with the empty words we utter and the learned habitual gestures that have come to seem like natural extensions of ourselves" (258).

Or, in other words, Lovecraft's prose—indeed largely what Miéville dubs his "adjectivalism" (Miéville 2009: 512)—produces an awareness of the intrusion into what is taken to be reality of things that belong just as much to reality, but are impossible to name.

What all three of these theorists share, then, is a belief in the way the weird indicates the existence of an outside to the perceivable that is, despite its trappings as externality, in fact a constitutive part of the real as we should acknowledge it to exist. In Fisher's words, the weird produces an "expanded sense of what the material cosmos contains" (2016: 18). But the point I would wish to emphasize here is that, against Fisher's argument that in Lovecraft, "there is an interplay, an exchange, a confrontation and indeed a conflict between this world and others" (19), the whole edifice of Lovecraftian Weird fiction (and then, by extension, the Weird in general) rests on the dissolution of the distinction, at least as far as this world's ontological status is concerned. Nothing in this world's constitution changes in Lovecraft's various descriptions of encounters with ancient and indifferent alien forces; all that happens is that characters, and sometimes the world at large, are made aware of their existence. That is to say: only when we take "this world" to mean that the idea of this world is Fisher fundamentally correct to say that the marker of the weird "is the irruption into this world of something from outside" (20).

The reason I spend so much time on what may appear to be nitpicky details of phrasing is that only one of these formulations names my proximate goal, namely to identify the relationship which the Weird names as fundamentally ideological. The specific relation between inside and outside in an epistemological, rather than ontological, sense is eminently ideological: we might even say that it names ideology itself. Ideology, after all, is one's "imaginary relationship to the real conditions of existence," as Althusser had it (2008: 36); it is the ability to define an inside that is not held to have an outside. When weird fiction then, in Fisher's phrasing, produces "ruptures in the very fabric of experience itself" (2016: 22), it offers an ideological challenge. Lovecraft himself only dimly— but at least dimly—grasped this: in his seminal introduction to *Supernatural Horror in Literature*, he argues that "few are free enough from the spell of the daily routine to respond to rappings from outside" (1973: 12), which may well be read as an untheoretical phrasing of the problem of ideology. Lovecraft's freedom to respond is then also a fundamental challenge to those who would rather not, and to the structures which have enabled the conception of reality in the first place. To envisage any outside is a radical challenge to the existing; and it is in the concrete ways in which weird fiction imagines this radical challenge as radical challenge that *weird* fiction becomes *Weird* fiction. The weird irruption becomes Weird when it names not just a moment of wonderment, bafflement, or strangeness, but when its weird nature becomes a fundamental challenge to our notions of reality—and, to nod to Fisher again, especially when what is invoked by reality is what Fisher calls "capitalist realism" (see Fisher 2009). What makes Lovecraft the go-to writer here is more than his acknowledged mastery of a particular style (something Miéville, Fisher, and Harman all agree on). Rather, it is the fact that "Lovecraft's stories frequently involve a catastrophic integration of the outside into an interior that is retrospectively revealed to be a delusive envelope, a sham" (Fisher 2016: 16)—something that merely weird fiction, whether M. R. James, Algernon Blackwood, Tim Powers, or Thomas Ligotti, does not. If all weird fiction, then, appears to perform something like ideological deconstruction, by representing the very way in which ideology erects boundaries of perceptibility and constitutes a reality that excludes large parts of what reality "actually" consists of, Lovecraft's fiction does something more: it asks us to consider the consequences of such a realization even if, as I will argue later, it often does not produce an intelligible, and certainly not progressive, answer to the challenges it poses. It is the specifics of this act that interest me: for, or so it seems to me, it is the historical specificity of the Weird to not just represent the possibility of an outside, but also to address itself to the consequences of this possibility, to speak to the way in which what is real changes, or does not, as we integrate the outside.

A spoiler: in what follows, I will not offer a narrative of Weird fiction's solving the crises of its times. Rather, I will suggest that even though both Lovecraft and VanderMeer register the specifics of their respective crisis moments and are invested in the question of what these crises may mean, indeed are even invested in the question of how we may cope with and perhaps overcome those crises, we need to understand them both to stagger under the weight of their discoveries. What happens in both texts is a historically specific, artistically and aesthetically challenging engagement that succeeds as Weird fiction despite—or, perhaps, exactly due to—failing to be what Fredric Jameson has famously called the "symbolic resolution" (2003: 27) of real systemic contradictions.

1930: The Lovecraft Event

"Any discussion of weird fiction," as Mark Fisher argues, "must begin with Lovecraft" (2016: 16). Fisher, of course, echoes a more general belief in the centrality of Lovecraft as both the most inventive and the most important of weird fiction authors, the progenitor of an entire mythos, and the most lasting influence from among a host of writers engaging with the weird. For my purposes here, though, Lovecraft must be the beginning because it is only with him that weird fiction becomes Weird fiction; perhaps it is even exclusively Lovecraft who produces the kind of registration which I am after here. Fisher, for all his perceptiveness, approaches Lovecraft from an almost entirely formalist angle, understanding the weird in the writer's work as an effect of prose style and narrative technique coupled with subjects that are beyond the bounds of the ordinary—and so, as I have pointed out earlier, does Harman, and to a lesser extent Miéville. Both see Lovecraft's specificity in his use of language, in the way he employs the (literally) inconceivable conjunctions possible only in language to open the bounds of reality itself. While I have no quibble with this, and indeed agree that it is constitutive of Lovecraft's appeal and also of his ideological challenge, I would like to expand from this formal and aesthetic point to read him as also writing against a historically specific background that is engaged in his texts. I want to focus here on what is Lovecraft's only long-form text, the novella *At the Mountains of Madness*.

At the Mountains of Madness is usefully understood to fall into two major parts. The first describes the genesis, plan, organization, and first discoveries of the Miskatonic University Expedition to the Antarctic. Narrated by the geologist and co-leader of the expedition, William Dyer, this first part starts out with the unexceptional findings initially made upon disembarkation in the Antarctic, but soon becomes more mysterious, as the expedition's biologist, Lake, makes independent discoveries which, as he soon reports to Dyer, "[w]ill mean to biology what Einstein has meant to mathematics and to physics" (Lovecraft 1999: 31), reported to Dyer via wireless. When Dyer and the rest of the expedition finally catch up with Lake, they find him and his entire team dead, his discoveries largely vanished, and a mystery before them. There, as Dyer notes, things might have rested, but for the central conceit of the story: Dyer is reporting events in detail now because a new expedition threatens to follow his and uncover what Lake had found—and what Dyer believes should now be left well alone. The second part of the story narrates Dyer's and his compatriot Danforth's exploration of an immense city, built long ago by ancient creatures, and now inhabited only by their fearful, shapeless workers, the shoggoths. Dyer's careful cataloguing of the architectural and historical past of this city, high on an Antarctic plateau, concludes with Danforth going insane from witnessing an unidentified terror.

The first section of the story, then, is largely concerned with mystery and discovery, with attempts to frame the unrepresentable; a doubly mediated suggestion of greater forces at work than reality has held present before, weird fiction. Through Dyer's narration of Lake's reports, the story suggests a grand ontological break, a break not so much with the means by which we know (Lake and Dyer are both committed to scientific explanations, and the story itself never commits itself to anything else) or the extent to which we can know, but rather with a fundamental reorientation of what is. The simplest version of this would be to say that Lovecraft's story insists on "something more out there," an outside of the kind of which Fisher speaks. But importantly, this outside is not outside the realm of reality as such: everything that happens within the story is based firmly in a commitment to integrating this outside into the world as we have known it before. The second half, by contrast, offers a deeper vision: not an ineffable outside, but an understandable, even if utterly strange, vision of the past. Graham Harman's belief that "the entire second half of the story seems like a very bad idea" is clearly natural, given Harman's insistence on Lovecraft as a writer primarily concerned with the construction of what Harman identifies as the "gap between objects and the power of language to describe them, or between objects and the qualities they possess" (2011: 3); but it is precisely Lovecraft's "overly detailed historical account" (148) that makes *At the Mountains of Madness* such a comprehensive statement of the modernist moment of crisis; or perhaps better, it is the combination of the essentially representational problem which the first section of the novella faces and the essentially historical problem of the second section that does it. In the first section, Lovecraft reproduces the fundamentally modernist problem of the capacity of language to represent reality itself; in the second, he confronts the equally as fundamental problem of historicization. The point here is very much then to integrate the lengthy, historical, and exploratory second section of the novella into the first. If the first, as Harman correctly points out, slowly builds toward a shocking irruption into the "normal, sane existence" (2011: 164) of humanity at large, the second immediately turns this irruption into a new form of normality, as it were.[3] The profoundly mundane political history which the second half of the story narrates—the Old One's arrival on earth, their creation of the shoggoths as slave workers, the war fought with the "Cthulhu spawn" (Lovecraft 1999: 90), and the Old One's eventual abandonment of the Antarctic plateau and retreat into the depths of the ocean—suggestively links to story's present (including Dyer's half-anxious note about the Old One's "evidently complex and probably Socialistic" (88) government). What emerges from this narrative is precisely not an ineffable outside, shadowing the real: rather, it is an extensive real which links the aesthetic response to the modernist crisis to a political one. As Stephen Shapiro and Philip Barnard point out, at least in part, this political response is inseparable from a history of American slavery (see 2017: 127); but I would suggest a slight change of emphasis, noting that the list of troubles which the Old Ones faced historically—slave rebellion (mass uprisings of the underprivileged), war, and a sense of dread emanating from yet further, still more alien settlements deeper in Antarctica—suggests an only slightly metaphorized version of Lovecraft's own time. Despite their differences from us, the Old Ones come to be readable as versions of humanity, facing concrete and material crises and persisting, only then to slowly succumb to the pull of transhistorical forces. It pays to insist, then, that the demise of the Old Ones takes place not in face of a shoggoth slave rebellion, as Shapiro and Barnard suggest, but rather in a slow, gradual decline spanning geological time. What *At the Mountains of Madness* appears to point out is that solutions to crises exist, but will remain momentary; its registration of the modernist moment suggests simply how natural decline is in the grander scheme of things, and the outside that is evoked by the novella holds no solutions. It simply reiterates that there is a history, a way to see one's moment embedded in a longer trajectory.

Lovecraft is not anything like a progressive, and his Weird fiction's invocation of outsides and what I take to be the constitutively ideological challenge of this action is not in any way an authorial criticism of, say, early late capitalism. *At the Mountains of Madness* understands how radical a challenge its outside would be, and successfully, if ambivalently, contains it, integrates it into its world. For Lovecraft, the outside which he invokes frequently the "darker and more maleficent side of cosmic mystery" (1973: 14)—such as socialism! This complicates his place as an uncanny observer of the crisis of his time. Lovecraft, as Shapiro and Barnard note, sits at a complicated nexus of self-fashioning, capitalist enterprise, and the registration of an overbearing social totality: he shapes himself an identity as "an ersatz eighteenth-century Anglo-Saxon gentleman of semipublic letters" (2017: 120), hardly the kind of figure which would have promised a utopian vision for the future at the best of times, but his fiction registers finely the larger anxieties of the age, most importantly the question of whether or not any kind of progress is still possible in the wake of so many political, social, and economic catastrophes. *At the Mountains of Madness* suggests that it is not: what is "out there" beyond the reality of everyday life turns out to be merely an extension of what we already know exists.

2010: The New Weird, Jeff VanderMeer's *Southern Reach* Trilogy, and the Breaking of the Neoliberal Order

Mark Fisher notes of Lovecraft's fiction that the "engine of fatality" in them is the "fascination that draws his bookish characters towards the dissolution, disintegration or degeneration that we, the readers, always foresee" (2016: 17). In Jeff VanderMeer's *Southern Reach*, it is precisely the promise of dissolution that drives the principal characters in their investigation of the weird phenomenon that has descended on a bit of land somewhere in the US South, dubbed "Area X." That area, bounded off by an invisible border that prevents most ingress and egress, presents itself as a pristine wilderness, a world out of time that is perhaps alien, a radical outside to the contemporary world that remains unexplained, and probably inexplicable, throughout the trilogy. Area X remains radically unknowable: it "has no leader to negotiate with, no stated goal of any kind" (335), and characters struggle to identify how to relate it to the world they know: "Incursion? Invasion? Infestation? What word worked" (154)? What becomes clear over the course of the novels, however, is that Area X will dissolve the existing, if the exact mechanism, means, and timing remain in doubt: we discover early on that it will assimilate members of expeditions sent to study it, replacing them (at best) with *doppelgängers* that struggle to cope with their own role in the world, and ultimately begins an expansion that, as the novel hints at the conclusion, may or may not have engulfed the whole world already.

There is no room here to examine in detail the complicated narrative which VanderMeer builds up over three novels. What I want to do instead is highlight how his Weird fiction, like Lovecraft's, binds its suggestive narrative of newly discovered radical outsides back onto a critique of the present. For the purposes of this chapter, I am less interested in the very overt environmentalism of VanderMeer's story, the way in which it emphasizes the cleansing effect of Area X. Area X has sprung into existence in a place where chemicals had been dumped previously—though it did not spawn because of that—and has transformed this area into a pristine, if weird, wilderness: "The most recent samples, taken six years ago and brought back by expedition eleven-D, showed no trace of human-created toxicity remained in Area X. Not a single trace. No heavy metals. No industrial runoff or agricultural runoff. No plastics. Which was impossible" (213). Area X, within which humans are transformed and adapted into creatures no longer human, is an explicitly post-human future—as we find out in due course, it literally is the future, a place in which time dilation stretches lifetimes.

But this overt message, even if it is complicated by the narrative details, is still less interesting than the novel's struggle with the ideological forces of its, our, time. What I am more interested in then is the way in which this depiction of a radical outside to the existing forms of life, and its overt engagement with the pressing political problem of the day, is both ultimately inert and produced through an overt hesitation about the possibility of thinking outsides that work suggestively in line with neoliberal capitalism.

There are a number of data points that I want to briefly mention here. The first of these is the constellation of military-governmental control of access to and memory of Area X, something that is presented as both structural and made: "The border had come down in the early morning, on a day, a date, that no one outside of the Southern Reach remembered or commemorated" (218). Over the thirty or so years of Area X's existence, the official narrative of an ecological catastrophe that requires the army to cordon off Area X has successfully quieted any interest anybody but the Southern Reach agency had in Area X. What's happening here, I would argue, is an enactment of the way in which the powers that be contain the alterity (indeed the knowledge of the existence) of the radical outside that VanderMeer's Area X constitutes—but also, in the way in which the Southern Reach agency is shown to be dilapidated, run down, and unsuccessful in coping with Area X, the fact that such containment is not predicated on there being secretive and powerful agencies with sinister motives for the possibility of an outside to be disregarded while the belief in the impossibility of an outside reigns undisturbed. The trilogy registers this complication: early on in the second novel, *Authority*, the novel's protagonist, Control, muses: "The Southern Reach had become a backward, backwater agency, guarding a dormant secret that no one seemed to care much about anymore, given the focus on terrorism and ecological collapse" (136). Area X, which initially is argued to be shielded from public interest precisely because it is presented as an ecological catastrophe, at the same time is held to be disregarded by people because of pressing ecological concerns: a paradox that names very well the apparent contemporary impasse to which Area X's outside is possible challenge. The institutional logic of the Southern Reach agency not only suggests a fairly limited number of possible names for what Area X is (invasion, incursion, infestation—all negatively connoted, all bound up in the idea of a challenge to the better status quo), but in fact understands Area X within an economic paradigm that seems inescapable. At one point, a character suggests, looking at satellite photos of Area X, that these were "[g]lamour shots of an inexhaustible resource" (448), immediately and fully coopting the pristine wilderness of the area. These moments do not, of course, exhaust the novel, and to focus on them may well be to read the novel against the grain; but I would suggest that they are more illustrative of the complicated relationship the text has with its contemporary than the surface narrative. Part of the point here is that the moment of VanderMeer's novel is a radically different one from Lovecraft's. As Lovecraft's reference of the "socialism" of the Old Ones already suggests, the existence of systemic outsides to the capitalist West and its crises was still a persistent feature in Lovecraft's time; today, in Dietmar Dath and Barbara Kirchner's terms, "globalization has produced a world with no outside" (2012: 18, my translation), and so the reaction to new outsides are perhaps even more of a challenge than they were earlier. To be sure: the reading of Area X as a source of economic resources remains a one-off of sorts, but we should nonetheless note the reflexive way in which the novel sees characters understanding the radical outside of Area X as simply another space to be integrated into an economic regime that permits no outsides even as, as critics from Rosa Luxemburg to David Harvey have consistently pointed out, it requires them constitutively. The Southern Reach trilogy in this way registers the struggle which the very idea of an outside as a place of utopian hope has to undergo in the present: something also indicated by the way the novel insists on how people can survive in Area X. From the beginning of the trilogy, VanderMeer's novel avoids names and rather designates its characters by their functions—Control, for one, but also the first novel's protagonist, the Biologist. In Area X, we discover, names are dangerous: they allow whatever inhabits Area X easier access to people, and thus are exchanged for merely formal descriptions of functions. Indeed, much of whatever success the Southern Reach agency has is predicated on its "making people into their functions" (389). Here as before, there is a certain theoretical ambivalence present: if the radical outside of Area X requires making people into their functions, such an action also rings all too forcefully of our own economic system, in which "human resources," rather than individuals, are made to work.

Alison Sperling suggests that the Southern Reach trilogy "presents an unnerving world in which the fixity of the laws of nature no longer seem to hold" (2017: 215)—where, as one might say, "things fall apart / the center cannot hold," as Yeats had it, a call back to the modernist crisis which we already saw registered in Lovecraft's writing. But the more problematical point to raise here is that if the laws of nature no longer seem to hold, the laws of the neoliberal world order constantly press against the realization of the radical challenge which Area X poses, and are effectively irreducible from them. What I take then from this is the somewhat complicated conclusion that VanderMeer's novel speaks at the same time to the need to imagine a radically unknowable outside to neoliberal reality and to the difficulty of imagining this outside as effective in doing something about the here and now, as ever being able to provide a genuine space of hope. What makes VanderMeer's novel Weird, rather than merely weird, is the way in which it is affirmatively interested in thinking about the world and its possible outsides in precisely these terms: not, that is, in producing uncanny effects and the idea of a meaningless intrusion, but in the way it understands the outside to be a radical challenge, in which it thinks it systemically. But like Lovecraft, it is strikingly—formally and thematically—ambivalent about the consequences that the realization of the existence of an outside would have. The Weird's inherent promise of a destabilization of capitalist realism collides with the inability to imagine it lastingly in anything but capitalist realist terms: and this, I would contend, is the chief lesson we can draw about the Weird from VanderMeer's novel.

Conclusion: Opening Weird Spaces in Weird Times

I have suggested two things earlier: first, that not all things weird are Weird; second, that the two examples of genuinely Weird fiction I have offered are Weird because they related their weird moments historically, to a socioeconomic moment in which the imagination of an outside always also names the possibility of a systemic outside and a thinking of such an outside's consequences—a specifically Marxist analysis, to my understanding. Neither Lovecraft nor VanderMeer, in the final analysis, is an uncomplicated advocate of the utopian possibilities inherent in establishing the existence of an outside: in fact, in the final analysis both texts end up producing outsides that do not remain outsides at all, that in different ways cannot offer solace to readers anxious about their respective crises. They realize the necessity to imagine an outside, that is, without imagining that outside to be particularly effective; and, in both cases, this failure of the imagination, if you want to call it that, is itself symptomatic of the historical moment in which they are writing: and, we might say, of the Weird as a form in the first place. But we should not miss the weirdness of the return of the Weird in this sense or of the return of Lovecraft in particular. In the simplest terms, Lovecraft's fiction produced no way forward in 1930; it did not inaugurate a form which was capable of responding positively to its moment of crisis. The use of the Weird in the conditions of a similar-but-different "foundational underlying crisis" (Miéville 2009: 513) must immediately appear insufficient. If nothing else, it must immediately be understood to represent a failure of the present to produce its own (actual) symbolic resolutions to its foundational contradictions, to pick up from Fredric Jameson. How curious is that? The Weird, as a form, in its bodily, eerie return in Lovecraft reprints, Lovecraft films, Lovecraft comics, but also in its contemporary version in VanderMeer, both signal the contemporary desire to somehow resolve the momentary crisis of capitalism—in its very imagination of an outside—but, perhaps, also signal the way this crisis appears to elude even symbolic resolution twice over, in both the form in which outsides are integrable, indeed ultimately do not remain outsides at all, and that signal no possibility of change, and the repetition of this form from an earlier historical moment. The Weird's attractiveness as a form lies, paradoxically, in a surface awareness of the fact that it does imagine an outside—in the memory of Lovecraft—and its complexity and fundamental ambivalence in the problem that such outsides themselves are insufficient, and easily integrated into the oppressive and crisis-inflected insides that Weird fiction registers.

Perhaps the most meaningful difference in this parsing of Lovecraft's moment versus our own moment is the different relationship which we have to the outside that the Weird brings in. When Lovecraft suggests that the "time has come when the normal revolt against time, space and matter must assume a form not overtly incompatible with what is known of reality—when it must be gratified by images forming supplements rather than contradictions of the visible and measurable universe" (Lovecraft 1968: 295–6), it may be precisely the refusal to think the "overtly incompatible" that suggests the complexity of the Weird's resurgence at the time of neoliberal crisis. After all, the inescapable fact that neoliberalism would like us all to believe is that neoliberalism is inescapable, that all we can ever hope for are "supplements" (see also Fisher 2009). In negotiating a complicated inside-outside relationship, the Weird produces what Fisher calls a "hypernaturalism—an expanded sense of what the material cosmos contains" (2016: 18). Such a version of the outside, which is now only the outside of immediate experience and everyday imagination, is, then, at least by neoliberalism's own logics, also fully an inside: as yet perhaps untouched, but always capable of integration. The logic of neoliberalism must ultimately rationalize Cthulhu away by cost-benefit analysis, or conceive of Shoggoths as merely the next set of laborers to be (again) exploited.

What is different from Lovecraft to VanderMeer, then, is also historically specific, and not only in the specific anxieties that are registered in either writer's work. The contemporary Weird evokes a far greater sense of wonder, and the possibilities inherent in the encounter with an outside, than Lovecraft's fiction ever did, suggesting, perhaps, the way in which our squabble with the reality we live in is more acute than it was for Lovecraft. The contemporary systemic crisis may be far more a crisis for which we desire an outside than Lovecraft's ever was, or perhaps differently put: to us, "outside" signals a broader and deeper political perspective than it would have to Lovecraft, and not simply because, in the specific instance of Lovecraft, personal conservativism, indeed recidivism, would more likely have made the author himself unreceptive to the idea of a radical challenge to the existing. The greater point may be that the entire idea of an outside has come to be more radically curtailed in contemporary neoliberal capitalism than it was in Lovecraft's time, when concrete systemic alternatives were only being tried out. But even as our imagination appears more ready to conceive of an outside, so the resistance from the prevailing ideologies is more forceful—so neoliberalism's hegemony presses in on the possibility of making the outside work for a change on the inside. As Alison Shonkwiler and Leigh Claire LaBerge summarize, according to Fisher the "content of fantastic imagination is ceaselessly metabolized by capitalist realism" (2014: 6). Shifting from the sociocultural context of modernist liberal capitalism and the early New Deal to that of post-postmodern neoliberal capitalist realism shifts signally the system of possibilities in imagination, and imagination's valences. And with it, if not the form and sociocultural function of the Weird, certainly its stakes. VanderMeer's outside makes nothing readily available that isn't dissolution tout court (here, too, it is easier to imagine the end of the world than the end of capitalism); but we may hope that if the Weird is here to stay, its engagement with the present may yet lead to useful outsides and visions of the future.

Notes

1 Readers interested in an alternative history of the weird might refer to Joshi (2003), but it should be noted that Joshi's conception of a canon resting specifically on "aesthetic legitimacy" (2003: 334) is both theoretically suspect and contrary to the argument I am raising here.
2 History, with a capital H, here merely designates something like the totality in which human life occurs. Various versions of it trace back to Hegel's idea of Universal History, Marx's belief in the primacy of class struggle as a historical force, simplified versions of Marx's argument in naïve teleologies of human development towards communism, and Francis Fukuyama's idea of the "end of History." For a not-at-all brief, but inexhaustibly edifying discussion of this, see Jameson (2009).
3 This normality is, of course, complicated: Dyer's narrative, while revelatory of much that is shocking, also hides much that may be even more so, such as the ultimate reason of Danforth's madness; and in its attempt to stop the Starkweather-Moore Expedition from exploring the same region of Antarctica, hints that there may yet be much that cannot be spoken about and should be left alone.

References

Althusser, L. (2008), *On Ideology*, London: Verso.

Dath, D., and B. Kirchner (2012), *Der Implex. Sozialer Fortschritt: Geschichte und Idee*, Frankfurt: Suhrkamp.

Fisher, M. (2009), *Capitalist Realism: Is There No Alternative?* Winchester: Zero Books.

Fisher, M. (2016), *The Weird and the Eerie*, London: Repeater.

Harman, G. (2011), *Weird Realism: Lovecraft and Philosophy*, Winchester: Zero Books.

Jameson, F. (2003), *The Political Unconscious: Narrative as a Socially Symbolic Act*, London: Routledge.

Jameson, F. (2009), *Valences of the Dialectic*, London: Verso.

Joshi, S. T. (2003), "Establishing the Canon of Weird Fiction," *Journal of the Fantastic in the Arts*, 14 (3): 333–41.

Lovecraft, H. P. (1968), *Selected Letters, 1925–1929*, ed. A. Derleth and D. Waudrel, Sauk City: Arkham House.

Lovecraft, H. P. (1973), *Supernatural Horror in Literature*, New York: Dover.

Lovecraft, H. P. (1999), *H. P. Lovecraft Omnibus 1: At the Mountains of Madness*, New York: Voyager.

Miéville, C. (2009), "Weird Fiction," in M. Bould et al. (eds.), *The Routledge Companion to Science Fiction*, 510–15, London: Routledge.

Noys, B. (2007), "The Lovecraft 'Event.'" Available online: https://www.academia.edu/548596/The_Lovecraft_Event (accessed October 31, 2019).

Shapiro, S., and P. Barnard (2017), *Pentecostal Modernism: Lovecraft, Los Angeles, and World-Systems Culture*, London: Bloomsbury.

Shonkwiler, A., and L. C. LaBerge (2014), "Introduction: A Theory of Capitalist Realism," in A. Shonkwiler and L. C. LaBerge (eds.), *Reading Capitalist Realism*, 1–25, Iowa City: University of Iowa Press.

Sperling, A. (2017), "Second Skins: A Body-Ecology of Jeff VanderMeer's *The Southern Reach Trilogy*," *Paradox*, 28: 214–39.

VanderMeer, J. (2014), *Area X: The Southern Reach Trilogy*, New York: Farrar, Straus and Giroux.

Wegner, P. (2009), *Life Between Two Deaths, 1989–2001: U.S. Culture in the Long Nineties*, Durham and London: Duke University Press.

Wilde, A. (1979), "Modernism and the Aesthetics of Crisis," *Contemporary Literature*, 20 (1): 13–50.

7

After Weird

Harman, Deleuze, and the American "Thing"

Daniel D. Fineman

"The brain is wider than the sky,
For, put them side by side,
The one the other will include
With ease, and you beside."

—Emily Dickinson, "CXXVI-The brain is wider than the sky"[1]

This chapter will quickly engage in a too-brief and abrupt treatment of the first stanza (as this is all time will allow) of the abovementioned Dickinson poem—one of her more famous philosophical poems. This analysis is given to immediately supply a working example of a different weirdness in American literature than the one supplied by Graham Harman's interesting and broadly influential work, *Weird Realism: Lovecraft and Philosophy* (2012). Dickinson's strange perspective illustrates not only her own peculiarity but what was a more general reaction in the mid-nineteenth century to the paradoxical demands of an American national version of romanticism. Their paradoxical obligation was to instill, through the artificiality of reading, an original, unmediated, and nonrepresentational experience that challenged commonsensical entification broadly, whether of the subject or object. Such an impossible goal led to great literary creativity and some metaphysical torsion. This was accomplished through what I would deem an *intensive* weirdness as opposed to Harman's, which I view as *extensive*. Further, Dickinson's lyric immediately engages the metaphysical issues that are this chapter's concerns in a way that I believe is supportive of a counterperspective to that of Harman's ontology—namely, the philosophy of Gilles Deleuze. However, the primary point of this chapter is not to decide between the ontologies of Deleuze and Harman but to briefly reflect on what each can uncover in the unpacking of American literature. While I think Harman's orientation is well suited to decoding his early twentieth-century target author, H. P. Lovecraft, my introductory reading of Dickinson should hint that I believe a more Deleuzian orientation more fully captures the incipient ontology of mid-century American Romanticism. Together, these two creative authors (Dickinson and Lovecraft) and two philosophers (Deleuze and Harman) supply, in the end, perspectives that are complementary even though their ontological commitments are almost enantiomorphic.

For Deleuze, as for Dickinson, objects are not to be taken for granted but rather interrogated about their mode of genesis. Following Gilbert Simondon, Deleuze repeatedly showed that what is the case is not individuals per se but intensive interactivities. Therefore, he rejected the Cartesian criterion of definitive, objective intuition, the "clear and distinct." His ontology replaces what typically are called things with space-time dynamisms without fixed essences. While the density of his thought makes its brief exposition difficult, he provides the most succinct effort in his defense of his positions delivered to the *Société française de Philosophie* on January 28, 1967:

> [W]hen we examine the history of philosophy as a whole, we will have a tough time discovering any philosopher whose research was guided by the question *What is this?* . . . The question *What is this?* prematurely judges the Idea as simplicity of the essence; from then on, it is inevitable that the simple essence includes the inessential, and includes it in essence, and thus contradicts itself. Another way of going about . . . [that] must be completely distinguished from contradiction, is to have the inessential include the essential. But the inessential includes the essential only in case. This subsumption under "the case" constitutes an original language of properties and events. This procedure is totally different from that of contra-diction and can be called vice-diction. It is a way of approaching the Idea as a multiplicity. It is no longer a question of knowing whether the Idea is one or multiple, or even both at once; "multiplicity," when used as a substantive, designates a domain where the Idea, of itself, is much closer to the accident than to the abstract essence, and can be determined only with the questions *who? how? how much? where and when? in which case?*—forms that sketch the genuine spatio-temporal coordinates of the Idea. (Deleuze 2004: 95–6)

In this transcript of what was an actual conversation with many of the great figures of French philosophy, Deleuze was previewing the two amazingly original and complex works he was about to publish. These two, *Difference and Repetition* and *The Logic of Sense*, unlike the more historical works that preceded them, were to reveal the full originality of his thought. What is, dynamically, "the case" for Deleuze takes the *place* (one of the meanings of *vice*-diction comes from the Latin: vice, ablative of *vicis* [genitive singular], to change or turn) of the thing. Cases are particular, motile, and primary. What appears, that which Deleuze labels the *actual*, comes out of "its" multiplicity, what he labels the *virtual*. This vocabulary merits some fuller introduction.

Deleuze acquired, with differences, his virtual/actual concepts from one of his major influences, Henri Bergson. As in so many central concepts of Deleuze, his preferred image of thought is almost antithetical to "common sense." Thus, Deleuze writes about the difficulty of understanding Bergson's *Matter and Memory*:

> We have . . . confused Being with being-present. Nevertheless, the present is not; rather, it is pure becoming, always outside itself. It is not; but it acts. Its proper element is not being but the active or useful. The past, on the other hand, has ceased to act or be useful. But it has not ceased to be. Useless and inactive, impassive, it IS, in the full sense of the word: it is identical with being in itself. (Deleuze 1988a: 55)

The present is not presented: the virtual is that pure motility of becoming out of which that which presents itself comes. What is manifestly given—the actual—is not that which gives the virtual: here we might say, "The thing is not the thing." The virtual is the mobile matrix that presents its intensity, the actual, that is its non-coordinate consequent. Thus, the actual and virtual exist in "a double process of reciprocal determination and complete determination" (Deleuze 1994: 209).

So, what takes the place of a thing, for Deleuze, is a "mobile haecceity." He borrows this term from Medieval philosophy. A brief note in *A Thousand Plateaus* clarifies: "This is sometimes written 'ecceity,' deriving from the word 'ecce,' 'here is.' This is an error, since Duns Scotus created the word from 'haec,' 'this thing.' But it is a fruitful error because it suggests a mode of individuation that is distinct from that of a thing or subject" (Deleuze and Guattari 1988: 540–1). This mode is one of differencing rather than being per se. One should note that these instantiations are unique because they are aleatory: they are irredeemable haecceities and, as such, are the ground of any essences with which they participate.

Every actual is a symptomatic sign of the forces that are its agencies. However, each intensity is a "pure difference": the case that appears is neither itself nor is it that which is now making it: the actual is radically asymmetric from its virtual. Deleuze's refusal of the doxa of things requires his verbal originality as the noun/verb separation of language itself antagonizes his concept. Thus, he turned long and often to literature—and most especially American literature—as a medium less prejudicial to his insight. In nineteenth-century American creative writing, he found an important foreshadowing of his philosophy. In mobilizing literary practices for philosophical ends, he engages a technique practiced by many from Plato to Nietzsche and on to Harman and his primary source, Heidegger. Perhaps now the stage is better set to read the stanza that fronted this chapter.

The Dickinson Example

Dickinson's poem, partially quoted in the beginning of this chapter (see Dickinson 1924: 67), is intentionally and weirdly perverse. It conflates those two essences, thought and extension, which traditional dualism presents as necessarily unmixed. Thus, the lyric violently antagonizes the typical demand for the separation of subject and object and instead puts them into a mutually constitutive play without valorization or available taxonomy: it is a vice-diction. The ambiguous antecedent of the indefinite pronoun, "one," comically refuses the valorization of either ideational idealism or naïve realism alone. This interference between the usually discrete—often represented as immiscible—constituents of experience is not a vacillation nor is it presented as error. The poem does not express doubt or indecision but enacts an ineluctably reciprocal and dynamic interactivity without resolution or even conclusive adequation. This stuttering orientation is not that of the inarticulate but rather the presentation of that which the literal disallows when confined to its own doxa.

Thus, the poem suggests sense[2] but disallows fixed literal meaning. This metaphysical dissonance, echoed in the staccato caesuras, is not the detour of metaphor but a commitment to nonrepresentation[3] as the grounding of being. The oxymoronic interplay is a modality of differential production, the creation of a singularity and not an instance. The poem refuses traditional assignment as representational fiction or as a thing-in-itself. Instead, it anticipates, without the possibility of firm preordering or definitive teleology, readings that can be no longer purely intelligible and must be existentially productive. While the poem expresses what Deleuze would call a heterogenesis by and through activity that engages the human, the portrait is not of or for the human as such. The personal is undone, depersonalized, and so too is the object: this presentation not only opposes the typical and facile counterpoint of the subjective to the objective but disables those usually antithetical categories and so preempts them as explanatory positions.

The personal, for Dickinson, is impersonal. Thus, the lines provide a material site—every time—for the relational constructions that arises from differential conjunction without correlation. Hers is the combinatorial realm of the felt, not thought alone: "If I read a book and it makes my whole body so cold no fire can warm me, I know that is poetry. If I feel physically as if the top of my head were taken off, I know that is poetry. These are the only ways I know it. Is there any other way?" (Dickinson 1958 II: 473–4). This affective criterion is not the language of designation, manifestation, or signification but of intensity in a world with both infinite variety and univocity. The poem presents the complexity of a turbulent fluid dynamics in which what is the case is always not an "in itself" but the differential output of forces otherwise inarticulate.

In short, the poem presents a weird ontology unseen in most theorists and quite different from that variety of object-oriented philosophy (abbreviated as OOP) that has been quite influential recently. This chapter intends to place these two versions in some preliminary dialog and to suggest their different philosophical commitments by mobilizing the somewhat antagonistic perspectives of Deleuze and Harman in their interpretations of American literature. While Deleuze's work came first, this chapter will also emphasize Harman as his renditions of speculative realism have recently been more influential especially in regard to that variety of the gothic known as the "weird." As both philosophers are wide, deep, and hugely productive and as the American literature that served both as a medium of philosophical exemplification is complex and variegated, this short chapter can only be indicative and not definitive.

Harman's Weird

While its genealogy is complex and its antecedents voluminous, the recent rise of interest in the so-called weird can be traced in large part to one article and the book that sprang from it. The article "On the Horror of Phenomenology:

Lovecraft and Husserl" came out in 2008 in *Collapse IV*. The book is Graham Harman's aforementioned *Weird Realism: Lovecraft and Philosophy*, which appeared in 2012. The two versions differ not only in length but to a degree in philosophy: from an emphasis on Husserl in the article to Heidegger in the book. Nonetheless, the basic commitments of the two are quite consistent. Both the journal and the author are important because of the philosophical perspectives they display.

The just previous volume of *Collapse*, number III, featured four essays taken from a seminar at Goldsmith's. These essays form the epicenter of what has become known under various banners but most prominently as "speculative realism" (SR) or, as I have mentioned earlier, "object-oriented philosophy" (OOP). Harman was one of these original fathers of SR and his notions of weirdness—he is quite happy to admit—spring from his philosophical position. This metaphysics has grown quickly popular and finds echoes in widely varied corners of the academy. However, each of the four philosophers engaged at Goldsmith's brought somewhat different traditions and vocabularies to the party and that diversity has replicated itself in subsequent versions.[4] Harman's position is largely a broadened and generalized version of tool-being (see his text of 2002 book, in fact called *Tool-Being*) especially as it appeared in Heidegger's *Being and Time* (see Heidegger 1962). Iain Hamilton Grant was vested in German idealism, especially Schelling's nature philosophy. Ray Brassier was the most eclectic of the lot, and so hardest to label, but he seems a French-fried nihilist. In Quentin Meillassoux, we find someone in the tradition of Alain Badiou. While many Deleuzians view Badiou's "take" on Deleuze—in *Deleuze: The Clamor of Being* (1999)—as problematic, Meillassoux's interests in Deleuze is shared by all the figures associated with SR. It is sincere and deep as demonstrated in their writings and bibliographies. In some later SR practitioners, such as Levi Bryant, we find those whose background was thoroughly and brilliantly Deleuzian. Therefore, the linkage here is not without antecedent or purchase (see Bryant 2008).

Certainly, Harman has, to some extent, interacted with and commented on Deleuze's ontology. Bruno Latour is one of Harman's seminal influences and his engagement with Latour's actor-network theory (ANT) is necessarily a secondary engagement with Deleuze as Latour regularly admits his indebtedness to Deleuze. Again, Harman obliquely engages Deleuze in his commentaries on Manuel DeLanda and, in so doing, invited the present text. In a brief essay, "DeLanda's Ontology: Assemblage and Realism," Harman expresses some doubt about DeLanda's claim that Deleuze is also a realist (Harman 2008a: 368). More importantly, he takes issue with DeLanda's rendition of an assemblage portrayal of becoming. While Harman himself profited intellectually from a somewhat similar notion to assemblage (roughly, the virtual multiplicity that realizes its dynamic differences in an actual intensity)—inherent in Latour's ANT (Latour compares the relations of his networks to Deleuzian rhizomes)—he here rejects the notion that DeLanda's portrayal is an adequate realism. Whether Harman's reading of DeLanda is definitive or not, it does not fully reflect Deleuze's own position, but it does supply some basis for comparison. Their incipient counterpoint is revealed in Harman's synopsis:

> DeLanda's shift toward the virtual, much like Deleuze's own, seems motivated by an underestimation of individual actual things. But realism is already guaranteed as soon as we deny that a thing can be reduced to its relations, since this gives us a world of obstinate individuals that cannot be dissolved into anything else. It is not required that we shun the actuality of these individuals. What is required is that we develop a new theory of specific objects: withdrawn from their constituent parts and environmental wholes, yet somehow managing to engage in causal interactions with those neighbors anyway. (Harman 2008a: 380)

All the assumptions registered here are crucial, but they are not of Deleuze. They point to the central dehiscence between the Deleuzian notion of the "real" and that which Harman depends upon. Throughout his many works, Harman begins almost each time as if the commonsense notion of the object is a given.[3] He does this in the abovementioned quotation ("as soon as we deny. . ."). Thus too, at the start of the centerpiece investigated here, *Weird Realism: Lovecraft and Philosophy*, he sets up the phenomenological problematic as if it were apparent and necessary: "Once we note that the world contains both withdrawn real objects with both real and sensual qualities" (Harman 2012: 5). This verges on a structural circularity. Who is this "we"? How do we "note"—it seems paradoxical—that which is withdrawn? How do we determine what "real qualities" are? How do disambiguate them from "sensual qualities"? Or, in the abovementioned quotation, is the "underestimate" based upon granting definitional self-evidence? Harman does not—as he might—fully defend the givenness of the object through an interaction with the text most seemingly on point, Heidegger's book-length treatment, *What is a Thing?* (see Heidegger 1967). This absence is likely because Harman's elaboration of tool-being here has—while derived from Heidegger—distinguishes itself from that textual origin. Further, in his various texts, Harman defends well the elaboration of his thought, his version of realism, but the point here is still basic and essential in the comparison with Deleuze.

Deleuze's Weird

From the start to the end of his career, Deleuze concerned himself with the question; "How is the given given?" The arc of this career is foreshadowed in his early lectures (1956–7) published now as *What Is Grounding?* (see Deleuze 2015). There, he quickly covers the seminal figures in the history of philosophy who would form the targets for his early books until he found his own voice in *Difference and Repetition* (1968). Even in these embryonic lectures, however, his incipient positions and commitments are becoming clear. He has antipathy to Descartes and is drawn most strongly to Spinoza, Leibniz, and Bergson, figures largely absent in Harman's discursive frame. It is from them that Deleuze's even weirder notion of weird realism springs, a realism of intensities that cannot withdraw or phenomenally hide as they exist not as separable entities but only as forceful interactivities.

Even at the start of his career, Deleuze saw Descartes as philosopher of equivocity, one who mistook the representational demands of dualism for becoming itself. By contrast, in Leibniz Deleuze found someone who understands extension, the usual sine qua non of objecthood, as the expression of force not as a dimension that can exist in itself: "Force is expressed in extension" (Deleuze 2015: 97). Thus, Deleuze makes his early but never surrendered commitment to "the desubstantiation of extension" (98). What then is left? No "simple things" remain: "It is the critique of atomism, which had claimed to find the simple on the level of the composed. Sure, there are simple elements, but these are dynamic unities, not material ones. Force is the real reason of extension" (98). As shown before, Deleuze does not believe in things as usually understood but sees differential dynamism as the only reality of a chaotic world. What this leads to is a new notion of what a "thing" is. This understanding entails a displacement not unlike the paradigm shift in physics from the notion of a discrete particle to the kinetic notion of the waves, plural.

One wave for Deleuze would be unintelligible for as itself it would not be communicating its force to any other and could not, therefore, present an existence at all. As a homogenous and separate impulse, no sole wave could exist in any sense until it met another. One might say that for Deleuze being is haptic. The real is constituted, then, of interference. An object for Deleuze is a gerund, not a body speculatively separable from its motion. Thus, Deleuze's ontology is predicated on the inversion of the "thing itself" that was basic to Kant and has remained philosophically relevant even though this idea almost immediately drew withering fire from Jacobi and Hamann. However, a version of this idea underwrites Harman's version of the thing. Here is the conclusion of his criticism of DeLanda/Deleuze in which he uses an exemplary object to instantiate his theory:

> What are the properties of *the tree in its own right*, apart from its capacity to serve as material for larger aggregates, to unify and supervene upon smaller ones, or its dual propensity to close off from the environment while also bleeding into it? It is not clear where we find *the tree itself* in the DeLandian model, since it is registered only through its effects on other assemblages—which in turn have properties only in relation to still other assemblages, with the hot potato of reality passed down the line, and nothing actual taking any final credit for being real. In this way, the tree becomes a specific, relational state of affairs rather than an autonomous object . . . this strikes me as the very deadlock that motivates present-day philosophies of the virtual, which sense correctly that "events" or "states of affairs" are not adequate to account for the whole of reality, and realize well enough that potentiality is always a form of relationality, yet also assume that individual objects can only be defined in relational terms. But *if we define objects as inherently deeper* than all the states of affairs in which they ever become involved, then no recourse to a disembodied virtual is needed. (Harman 2008a: 382, emphases added)

Whether this is fair to DeLanda or not, I believe it misrepresents Deleuze's position. There is no "in itself" of trees or anything for Deleuze. All things are intensities that exist not as parts apart as in some Apollonian dream of taxonomic mereology or as in the set relations favored by analytic perspectives. Intensive things, dynamic cases, which are the "objects" of Deleuze's weirder realism are the productions of the ongoing, concurrent, interactivity of the virtual forces that motivate their becoming. They are material but not definitive, real but not separable; they are immanently caused haecceities.

However, the image of "relations among relations" that Harman and others in SR criticize does deserve emendation as this phrase can be misleading. It implies distance, the gaps that are essential to Harman, between specific nodes. Instead, Deleuze often uses the better terms "fluxes" or "flows": these are material currents among currents that produce effects but all outside the convenience of fixed embodiment. This materialism is like the very weird world of fluid dynamics, one that modern physics can only handle in its least complex cases. These actualized intensive beings not only do not but also cannot resemble their constituting multiplicities, their virtual assemblages, any more than the turbulence at the intersection of two rivers resembles its differential inputs. They cannot be closed "off from the environment" as they are not just context sensitive but context constituted: they are ecological expressions. Further, there is never—as the aforementioned passage implies—assemblages "themselves." Nor can there be a knowing or even sense of assemblages interactive with other assemblages since this is to portray them as already-Newtonian objects. Assemblages have no separable activity from that produced by what Deleuze registers as their singularity. They have a radical haecceity, a "thisness" which is not subject to regulation or transportation. To give them a discrete, passive, and continuing agency, a fixed character, is to cast them into the role of SR objects which is exactly what they are not: they are concurrent actualizations, emergent intensities.

This character of the distinction, the haecceity, of intensive things does not spring from their essences as they are never themselves out of themselves. They are in their very heterogenesis nonidentical to their composition: every intensive thing is the literal effulgent of its vice-dictory constitution, which is why they lend themselves to problematics in philosophy and inconclusion in literature. Again, they are interference phenomena without noumena. Examples may help a bit to make this seem realistic: consider the standing wave, the beat frequency, or the moiré. It may seem that each of these can be parsed into discrete and intelligible parts but that appearance is only insofar as one enters the symbolic. Such a transcription is not innocent but entails the concomitant insertion of the phenomenon into the common-sensible image of objects. Certainly, Deleuze never doubted symbolic signs present themselves—albeit falsely—as adequations of description. This is the nominal "closure" of the Saussurean structure. But every trace functions, as Jacques Derrida was at some pains to point out, through the sublated interference between its physical and semiotic facets. Each seeming instance then of disaggregation, of what Harman deems gap production, occurs only in a representation. This is quite ironic, as SR prides itself on having moved past "the linguistic turn." Every word is in fact a shifter and, as such, examples the obscurity incipient and inherent in acts of deixis.

Such ineluctable obscurity is also Harman's milieu and method. The utility of his method in the paradoxical activity of analyzing the necessary obscurity of reference is especially evident in regard to Lovecraft's many techniques—well studied and elucidated in the middle chapter of Harman's book—of expressing the inexpressibility, the ineffability, of the object. Even though the "reason" for this inadequacy is almost inverted between Deleuze and Harman, their basic results remain comparable. While the incomprehensibility of intensive things in Deleuze derives from their differential and unresolvable oppositional production and while the equally inadequate availability of Harman's objects is due to their "withdrawal," both present a world whose lack of intelligibility is constitutive. Further, while I believe that Deleuze's ontology suits Dickinson and the many other authors of the longer American Renaissance (Whitman, Poe, Thoreau, and Melville), I think that Lovecraft himself had an incipient ontology close to that which Harman theorizes. Thus, Lovecraft's weird tales lend themselves to an SR diagnosis. Let us quickly review Harman's insights.

Harman and Lovecraft

While his references to the gothic tradition that preceded his central author, H. P. Lovecraft, are slight, Harman's philosophical scope is itself strikingly ambitious. He states "philosophy's sole mission is *weird realism!*" (Harman 2008b: 334). Mobilizing quickly both Husserl, in the early version, and Heidegger, in the later, Harman invokes the concept of the object, albeit with a "torsion" (363), as that which necessarily evades full characterization. Thus, he declares that "real objects hide" (356). While the current Anglo-American school might well bristle at this claim, Harman sees it as the necessary consequence of any realist ontology. This limitation is, in short, because any "real" object evades comprehensive characterization. To explain this stipulation, he gives us a very quick introduction to his version of SR: "Let any 'object' refer to any reality with an autonomous life deeper than its qualities, and deeper than its relations with other things" (348). This vocabulary may presume more than it defines. The definition seemingly suffers from a degree of vagueness, generalization, and circularity. However, are these nominal weaknesses bugs or features?

In part, these definitional difficulties reflect the attributes of the post-Kantian system that Harman builds though he is not a Kantian. In the *Critiques*, things are presented as both that which one seeks and that which can never appear in their presumed totality. Thus, the object functions as both goal and impossibility. This constitutive conceptual dehiscence appears in Harman as the basis of his insight: "My thesis is that objects and weirdness go hand in hand. An object partial evades all announcement through its qualities, resisting or subverting efforts to identify it with any surface" (346). The vocabulary here is, again, somewhat loose, vaguely metaphorized, and personified, but Harman has already made it clear that to attempt precision in description is a fool's errand as for both him and Lovecraft. He states: "The meaning of being might even be defined as *untranslatability*. Language (and everything else) is obliged to become an art of allusion or indirect speech, a metaphorical bond with a reality that cannot possible be made present" (Harman 2012: 16). This is the ontological version of the literary critical principle of which he is fond, the heresy of paraphrase. As to be clear and distinct violates his central concept that all objects withdraw from all others (including the human subject) he can explain his indefiniteness as necessary.

While this effect of obscurity is superficially similar to that in Deleuze, it is from opposing reasons. The intensive thing is obscure not by its absence but its mode of presentation: "the idea . . . is not the clear and distinct but rather, as Leibniz sensed, the distinct-obscure" (Deleuze 2004: 94). The actualization supplied is the interference of its constituting forces, which in that combination, that conjunction, lose any possibility of disaggregation into constituents. The obscurity, then, is not that of failed representation but combinatorial presentation. The actual results from its virtual but cannot resemble it: the obscurity is radically affirmative, an additive result, like harmony was for Poe, that produces an effect not directly attributable to any of its parts. This is the synergy of an inseparable symbiosis.

By contrast, Harman's world affirms absence: the object is, but it is largely unavailable. Still, Harman rejects a skeptical solipsism. How so? This seems like having your ontological cake and eating it too. Therefore, Harman should be plagued completely by Humean questions of direct interactive causation since Harman's extensive things, unlike Newton's, cannot touch in principle. Therefore, he invents the concept of "vicarious causation" where "the absent thing-in-itself can have gravitational effects on the internal content of knowledge" (Harman 2012: 17) and so he adopts the more harmonious Newtonian model, not of direct contact, but of the planets, of action at a distance. Thus, he gets as an additional nice serendipity a way out of Hume's questions that so "woke" Kant. While this is not at all the immanent causation Deleuze borrows from "the prince of philosophers," Spinoza, it shares an impossibility of disaggregation into explanatory parts.

Conclusion

The broad point here is that Harman's model suits Lovecraft's practice, while Deleuze's suits that aesthetic practiced by Dickinson and some other American romantics. Similar parallels, born out of opposing reasons, can be found in the importance both philosophers give to style over content and in the inadequacy of common sense. So, while Harman is a philosopher of discontinuity—believing in *productive* "gaps" (Harman 2012: 2–3)—and Deleuze espouses heterogenetic continuity and miscibility, both are able to find reflection in American literature in their respective authorial foci. Why is that?

With the tiny space still available in this perforce short chapter, I can only unsubstantially hint at a resolution to the issues raised. Dickinson and Lovecraft are products of their respective environs, historical and material. Dickinson's life in Amherst was one of what Levi-Strauss deemed *bricolage*, the adaptation of ideas to available materials, a proletariat and female orientation in a largely preindustrial setting. For her, the idea constantly had to surrender to the demands of the available intensities of life. She lived in constant and appreciative conjunction with the available people, plants, and animals around her. The fluidity of the seasons presented to man's then weak technology insurmountable demands that liquified standardization. To each of these challenges, she brought an intensive engagement still required in the largely rural and natural environs of Amherst in the mid-nineteenth century. Hers then was a life and poetry of constantly revisionary appreciation and application over representation, of the need to be in contact with one's surroundings, social and material. This was a world—compatible with and embodying Deleuze's flows—that was without break, without standardization. Hers was a world of insistent haecceities.

By contrast, Lovecraft was a twentieth-century urban dweller who lived in an industrial city of regulation and regularity. His was a synthetic ambiance where law and *engineering* codes—the opposite of bricolage—pretended rather inadequately to master the objects they dictated as if they were manifestations of their blueprint renderings. In that pretended adequacy of rules to things, they crushed the very sublime wonder that was Dickinson's ambiance and Lovecraft's deepest longing. It is hardly surprising then that his literary practice is one of withdrawal to a world of wonder and deregulation that would lend itself to Harman's ontology. Lovecraft wished for the life she had and Deleuze theorizes. While she was oriented toward what the late Louis Althusser presented as the aleatory demands of the "encounter" (see Althusser 2006), he was crushed by financial poverty, lack of recognition, and an alienating city setting. Surrounded by objects of banality and mechanical reproduction, he sought and found their hidden mystery, their withdrawn character. If there was sublimity, it could only be in a speculative realism.

To summarize: Deleuze's and Harman's ontologies are almost polar opposites, one being inclusive and combinatorial and the other separatist and hermetic. However, they weirdly share a number of traits: rejection of paraphrase, emphasis on the tension of between content and style (what Deleuze calls "the stutter"), a new post-human orientation, a rejection of correlationism, a distrust of literal language, and a complete rejection of the commonsensical renditions of objects. That both philosophers have explanatory power is because of these shared aspects of their mutual problematic, the enigma which is the thing.

Notes

1 Usually, in Dickinson scholarship, more recent editions are being used. However, due to copyright restrictions, this 1924 edition has been quoted, instead.
2 The term *sense* for Deleuze is almost the opposite of that famously propounded by Frege as his "solution" to the ambiguities of reference and meaning. Frege enacts a continuation of a dualistic attitude toward objecthood—as does Harman's ontology—and so remains trapped—as is much of the analytic tradition following Russell's "On Denoting"—in a duplicity rather than, as in Deleuze, an existential conjunction.
3 Representation, whether scientific or informal, is for Deleuze an expression of the "Dogmatic Image of Thought" that insists upon assigning different cases at different times sameness under the concept of identity and thus never escaping Leibniz's question about the indiscernibility of identicals. What is the case, in contrast, does not represent or resemble the inputs—the ordinal, not cardinal, "series" of conjunction without coordination—nor, as interference, is it itself itself. What is the case is unrepresentable except as produced difference: a diaphora.
4 SR has generated a huge reaction both in the philosophical community and, as in this volume, in those who wish to employ its structures to examine other fields from the arts to ecology. Still, SR is not one consistent position nor is it an approach without critics. Even between its branches, SR has severe dissonance. Those who do not have the time or will to attempt to master this polymath area can find some idea of its huge variety in the freely available collection, *The Speculative Turn*, listed in the bibliography (see Harman et al. 2011). Those who wish to encounter the most severe, extended, and, indeed, vituperative attack on Harman's OOP can read Peter Wolfendale's *Object-Oriented Philosophy: The Noumenon's New Clothes* (2014). That volume also contains a scathing review by one of SR's other fathers, Ray Brassier, that well illustrates some of the massive antipathies that have quickly opened in the field. Perhaps a more balanced and amusing revelation of a friendly difference between Harman's OOP and one of his most important antecedents, Bruno Latour, is found in their dialog that appears in *The Prince and the Wolf*.
5 When Harman does try to define what or how a thing may be, his presentation is often more stipulation than explanation. Take this version from the "Horror of

Phenomenology" article: "Let 'object' refer to any reality with an autonomous life deeper than its qualities, and deeper than its relations with other things" ("Horror" 348). Not only are we not given a reason why we should "let" this definition stand, all the elements of the definition are themselves unclear and in need of definition. This regress, however, reflects Harman's basic conviction of exactly the axiomatic withdrawal of objects: "For we are never really sure just what an object is" ("Horror" 365).

References

Althusser, L. (2006), *Philosophy of the Encounter: Later Writings, 1978–1987*, London: Verso.
Brassier, R., I. H. Grant, G. Harman, and Q. Meillassoux (2007), "Speculative Realism," *Collapse III*: 307–435.
Bryant, L. R. (2008), *Difference and Givenness: Deleuze's Transcendental Empiricism and the Ontology of Immanence*, Evanston: Northwestern University Press.
Deleuze, G. (1983), *Nietzsche and Philosophy*, Minneapolis: U Minnesota Press.
Deleuze, G. (1988a), *Bergsonism*, New York: Zone Books.
Deleuze, G. (1994), *Difference and Repetition*, New York: Columbia UP.
Deleuze, G. (1997), *Essays Critical and Clinical*, Minneapolis: U Minnesota Press, 1997.
Deleuze, G. (2004) "The Method of Dramatization," in *Desert Islands and Other Texts: 1953–1974*, 94–116, New York: Semiotext(e).
Deleuze, G. (2015), *What Is Grounding?*, Grand Rapids: &&& Publishing.
Deleuze, G., and F. Guattari (1988), *A Thousand Plateaus: Capitalism and Schizophrenia*, London: The Athlone Press.
Dickinson, E. (1958), *The Letters of Emily Dickinson, in three volumes*, Cambridge, MA: Harvard University Press.
Dickinson, E. (1924), "CXXVI-The brain is wider than the sky," in *The Complete Poems of Emily Dickinson*, edited by Alfred Leete Hampson, introduction by Martha Dickinson Bianchi, 67, Boston: Little, Brown, and Co.
Harman, G. (2002), *Tool-Being: Heidegger and the Metaphysics of Objects*, Chicago: Open Court.
Harman, G. (2005), *Guerrilla Metaphysics: Phenomenology and the Carpentry of Things*, Chicago: Open Court.
Harman, G. (2007), *Heidegger Explained: From Phenomenon to Thing*, Chicago: Open Court.
Harman, G. (2008a), "DeLanda's Ontology: Assemblage and Realism," *Continental Philosophy Review*, 41 (3): 367–83.
Harman, G. (2008b), "On the Horror of Phenomenology: Lovecraft and Husserl," *Collapse IV*: 333–65.

Harman, G. (2011a), *Quentin Meillassoux: Philosophy in the Making*, Edinburgh: Edinburgh UP.

Harman, G. (2011b), *The Quadruple Object*, Winchester: Zero Books.

Harman, G. (2012), *Weird Realism: Lovecraft and Philosophy*, Winchester: Zero Books.

Harman, G. (2013), *Bells and Whistles: More Speculative Realism*, Winchester: Zero Books.

Harman, G., L. R. Bryant, and N. Srnicek, eds. (2011), *The Speculative Turn: Continental Materialism and Realism*, Melbourne: re.press.

Heidegger, M. (1962), *Being and Time*, New York: Harper & Row Publishers

Heidegger, M. (1967), *What Is a Thing?*, Chicago: Henry Regnery Company.

Houellebecq, M. (2006), *H. P. Lovecraft: Against the World, Against Life*, London: Weidenfeld & Nicolson.

Hull, T. (2006), "H.P. Lovecraft: A Horror in Higher Dimensions," *Math Horizons*, 13 (3): 10–12.

Joshi, S. T. (1980), *H. P. Lovecraft: Four Decades of Criticism*, Athens: Ohio University Press.

Joshi, S. T. (1990), *The Weird Tale: Arthur Machen, Lord Dunsany, Algernon Blackwood, M.R. James, Ambrose Bierce, H.P. Lovecraft*, Austin: University of Texas Press.

Kant, I. (1965), *Critique of Pure Reason*, New York: St Martin's Press, 1965.

Kant, I. (1987), *The Critique of Judgment*, Indianapolis: Hackett.

Koryé, A. (1968), *Metaphysics and Measurement: Essays in Scientific Evolution*, Cambridge, MA: Harvard University Press.

Latour, B. (1996), "Actor-Network Theory: A Few Clarifications," *Soziale Welt*, 47: 369–81.

Latour, B., G. Harman, and Peter E. (2011), *The Prince and the Wolf: Latour and Harman at the LSE*, Winchester: Zero Books.

Lovecraft, H. P. (2005), *H. P. Lovecraft: Tales*, Library of America.

Lovecraft, H. P. (2006), *Collected Essays of H. P. Lovecraft: Philosophy, Autobiography and Miscellany*, New York: Hippocampus Press.

Lyotard, J.-F. (1994), *Lessons on the Analytic of the Sublime*, Stanford University Press.

Zourabichvili, F. (2012), *Deleuze: The Philosophy of the Event and The Vocabulary of Deleuze*, Edinburgh: Edinburgh University Press

8

Concerning a Deleuzean Weird
A Response to Dan Fineman
Graham Harman

The first thing the reader will have noticed about Dan Fineman's critique of my work on H. P. Lovecraft is that he is not very harsh (see Harman 2008b, 2012a). The only moments when I felt inspired to self-defense were during his occasional complaints about my lack of precision or definiteness in language. That much, I think, is untrue: though I do at times try to write poetically, few readers have complained about a lack of clarity in my books or articles. I daresay they are much clearer than the works of such Francophone heroes as Jacques Derrida or Jacques Lacan, whose best insights are often clothed in linguistic "experimentation" of a sort that can tax the reader's patience.

Otherwise, Fineman has positive things to say amid what might otherwise have been the most conflictual moments in his article. In the first place, I wrongly expected that he would contest my interpretation of Lovecraft. Instead, he more or less grants my reading of that author, and simply couples it with what he considers to be a parallel match between Gilles Deleuze and Emily Dickinson. As Fineman admits near the end of his essay: "Further, while I believe that Deleuze's ontology suits Dickinson and the many other authors of the longer American Renaissance (Whitman, Poe, Thoreau, and Melville), I think that Lovecraft himself had an incipient ontology close to that which Harman theorizes. Thus, Lovecraft's weird tales lend themselves to an SR diagnosis" (Fineman, 99). A friendly dispute indeed! I would also agree that Deleuze provides excellent resources for interpreting Whitman, Thoreau, and Melville: though I am not as convinced with regard to Poe, who seems awfully close to Object-Oriented Ontology (OOO), as argued in my recently published article "Poe's Black Cat" (see Harman 2019). In the second place, once I saw the first mention of Deleuze in Fineman's article, I was expecting to be roasted in a furnace of Deleuzo-Guattarian vengeance. But while Fineman does defend Deleuze's ontology against my own, he also states that "both philosophers are wide, deep, and hugely productive" (Fineman, 93). It is hard to be annoyed by a critic who speaks this generously even in his most critical moments. Thus, all we are really left with is a dispute over whether Deleuze's philosophy or OOO is the more fertile theoretical current, and this is a conversation I am happy to have. But first, let's touch briefly on a pair of minor disagreements.

Two Minor Disagreements

A central conception of Fineman's piece—one that never quite reaches full development—is his distinction between Deleuze and Dickinson's "intensive" weirdness and my own "extensive" kind. What is puzzling here is not the link between Deleuze and intensity, which goes without saying, but that between Dickinson and weirdness. The poem Fineman has in mind is the one that begins: "The Brain—is wider than the Sky—." He tells us that this verse "is intentionally and weirdly perverse." I follow Fineman's argument that a sort of perversity results from this image, insofar as Dickinson "conflates those two essences, thought and extension, which traditional dualism presents as necessarily unmixed. Thus, the lyric violently antagonizes the typical demand for the separation of subject and object" (Fineman, 92). Inserting the brain and the sky into the same space of comparison feels to me, just as it does to Fineman, like a deliberate perversion of modernity's post-Cartesian rift between thought and physical extension. Where I have a harder time following him is when he calls Dickinson's poem *weirdly* perverse. I must confess that Dickinson does not strike me as an author of the weird in any important sense—certainly not as much as Lovecraft or Poe, and I would say not even as much as Hawthorne or Melville. At least as concerns Lovecraft I have tried to give a precise, technical definition of weirdness: the separation between a withdrawn real object (RO) and its tangible sensual qualities (SQ). Fineman never assesses this definition; much less does he criticize it or give an alternative formula for the weird that might encompass Dickinson better than my own. It is worth noting that I would make exactly the same point about Deleuze: although various perversities abound in his writings, it is hard for me to see Deleuze as in any sense a philosopher of the weird. Indeed, if weirdness requires the uncanny absence of things unseen that somehow still have a vague and unsettling effect, it would be hard to imagine a philosopher *less* weird than Deleuze. For although his virtual is never actually present in any given instant, it certainly does not hide in the manner of Kant's thing-in-itself or Heidegger's *Sein*, both of which have a sort of MacBethian weirdness that is hard to find anywhere in the droll and affable atmosphere of Deleuze's works. To summarize, since I was never convinced by Fineman's classification of either Deleuze or Dickinson as "weird" in the first place, I was unable to grasp his central distinction between intensive and extensive weirdness.

A second minor disagreement is also worth mentioning, if only because it comes up so frequently in recent philosophical discussion. I speak of the following passage by Fineman: "Certainly, Harman has, to some extent, interacted with and commented on Deleuze's ontology. Bruno Latour is one of Harman's seminal influences and his engagement with Latour's actor-network theory (ANT) is necessarily a secondary engagement with Deleuze as Latour regularly admits his indebtedness to Deleuze" (Fineman, 94). No footnote is made to any passage in Latour that would justify this claim, though certainly I have heard Latour speak of his youthful fascination with *Anti-Oedipus* (see Deleuze and Guattari 2004). Nonetheless, it does not seem to me that Latour is a Deleuzean in any important sense, whatever the apparent similarities between rhizomes and networks. This point is argued in my book *Prince of Networks*, and I will return to it later in this chapter (see Harman 2009). There is similar cause for quibble when Fineman asserts that

> Meillassoux's interest in Deleuze is shared by all the figures associated with SR. It is sincere and deep as demonstrated in their writings and bibliographies. In some later SR practitioners, such as Levi Bryant, we find those whose background was thoroughly and brilliantly Deleuzian.... Certainly, Harman has, to some extent, interacted with and commented on Deleuze's ontology. (Fineman, 94)

Though Fineman is right that all of the figures associated with Speculative Realism and OOO admire Deleuze on some level, the depth and nature of the admiration vary significantly from one of us to another (see Bryant et al. 2011). Thus, I stand by my oft-stated claim that the four original Speculative Realists have no shared philosophical heroes (Harman 2018: 91). For on the one side we have Iain Hamilton Grant and a OOO parallel in Levi R. Bryant, whose abiding debts to Deleuze are visible even in their most recent work (see Grant 2006; Bryant 2008, 2014). A little further away on the spectrum is Ray Brassier, who at one time—like Grant—was awash in Deleuze as a doctoral student at Warwick University, but whose more recent views on the French thinker are far more critical (see chapter 6 of Brassier 2007). Next on the scale would be Quentin Meillassoux, whose references to Deleuze and Deleuzians are not exactly disrespectful, but do display a degree of puzzled irony (see Meillassoux 2007). As for my own case, what I responded to most positively in Deleuze—when first reading him in 1990—was the irreverent *tone* of his work rather than any specific philosophical idea. What I mean to say with these remarks is that Deleuze's link with SR and OOO is more tortuous and less uniform than Fineman suggests.

Against Mining and Continua

Toward the end of his essay, Fineman identifies what he says are surprising points in common between me and Deleuze: "rejection of paraphrase, emphasis on the tension between content and style (what Deleuze calls 'the stutter'), a new post-human orientation, a rejection of correlationism, a distrust of literal language, and a complete rejection of the commonsensical renditions of objects" (Fineman, 101–2). A discussion of these purportedly shared features could itself make for an interesting article. But Fineman wisely devotes his energies instead to the more obvious points of *conflict* between Deleuze and OOO. In the following passage, he already gets to the heart of the matter: "For Deleuze, as for Dickinson, objects are not to be taken for granted but rather interrogated about their mode of genesis. Following Gilbert Simondon, Deleuze repeatedly showed that what is the case is not individuals per se but intensive interactivities" (Fineman, 90). It is true that OOO emphasizes fully formed individuals, as opposed to the Deleuze/Simondon focus on genesis and the *process* of individuation (see Deleuze 2004; Simondon 2005). Whether Dickinson is equally committed to the reign of flux and flow is a question I leave for others to determine; when it comes to her poetry, I have interest without expertise. I would simply reject Fineman's view that objects in OOO are "taken for granted," a charge too often heard from Deleuzean and Simondonian quarters. To explain why will require a brief detour into the three forms of reduction I have called undermining, overmining, and duomining (Harman 2013; see also Harman 2011).

If someone asks us what something is, there are really just two kinds of answers we can give: we either tell them what it is made of (whether causally or compositionally) or tell them what it does (whether to our minds or to something else). These are the only two kinds of knowledge that exist; I challenge my readers to find another. The first of these strategies can be called *undermining*, since it subverts the object by claiming it is too shallow. For the underminer, the world does not really contain the familiar entities we encounter in everyday life; instead, these must be reduced to some more primal element. At the dawn of

Western thinking in Archaic Greece, the pre-Socratics all either sought a root physical element of which everything is built—water, air, water/earth/air/fire combined, atoms—or else they viewed even these as too specific, and placed their bets instead on a formless *apeiron* from which everything emerges and back into which it eventually passes. The problem with this strategy, which lives on especially in contemporary physics, is that it cannot account for what is called emergence: incidentally a pivotal concept for DeLanda, whom Fineman esteems as highly as I do (see DeLanda 2011). Emergence means, among other things, that entities have a self-contained reality over and above their constituent parts or histories. To take a simple example, children are emergent beyond their parents, even though the parents must certainly count as one of the most important causes of their children. Numerous traces of my parents' character and genetics can no doubt be found in me, but such important biographical features as my philosophy career and incessant world travel are nowhere to be found in my parents' personal histories. In short, once I am causally set free from the humans who generated me, I take on a life of my own that becomes increasingly independent of my origins. I say this in response to undermining philosophers of the "pre-individual" such as Deleuze and Simondon, and to their defenders such as Fineman. The fact that all entities emerge from a specific causal background does not entail that they are nothing more than that background. Any object—including human beings—rises to some extent above the conditions that produced it, and any object might have been produced in several different ways other than the one in which it was actually produced.

I should also mention the contrary strategy called *overmining*, since Fineman's Deleuze ends up dabbling in this as well. If undermining considers objects as too shallow to be real, overmining views them as too deep. If entities are nothing more than their effect on my mind or on other entities—as overmining holds—then why naively posit the existence of real things outside these effects? In the British Empiricism of the seventeenth and eighteenth centuries, especially in the writings of George Berkeley, real things vanish altogether in favor of their perceivable attributes (see Berkeley 1982). In the Actor-Network Theory of Bruno Latour, things vanish in favor of their sum total of relations: "there is no other way to define an actor but through its action, and there is no other way to define an action but by asking what other actors are modified, transformed, perturbed, or created by the character that is the focus of attention" (Latour 1999: 122). For the Agential Realist position of Karen Barad (2007), thought and world do not even preexist each other, but arise only through their mutual relation. Whereas undermining is haunted by an inability to explain emergence, overmining paints itself into a corner in which change is simply impossible. Consider Aristotle's response to the Megarian philosophers in the *Metaphysics*. Whereas the Megarians held that no one is a house-builder unless they are building a house here and now, Aristotle realized that a sleeping house-builder is still a builder in a way that I am not, even when I am fully awake and make bumbling, abortive efforts to build a house (see Book Theta, chapter 3 of Aristotle 2016). In other words, overmining is an "actualist" philosophy in which everything is fully expressed in any given moment, with nothing held in reserve, and this makes it impossible to explain why anything would ever change from its current state. Now, it may seem that Deleuze cannot possibly be placed in such a box; after all, he—along with Henri Bergson—is the great thinker of the *virtual*, and the virtual has nothing to do with the actual. Indeed, the virtual seems like the very unactualized surplus that is needed in the cosmos for change to occur; moreover, it is more sophisticated on several counts than Aristotle's own alternative of *potential*. Nevertheless, Fineman's relationist interpretation of Deleuze also treats him, in part, as an overminer: "[Things] cannot be closed 'off from the environment' as they are not just context sensitive but context constituted: they are ecological expressions. Further, there is never—as the passage above implies—assemblages 'themselves'" (Fineman, 97-98).

That is to say, in Fineman's hands the undermining Deleuze of preindividual virtualities is shadowed by an overmining Deleuze whose entities "are not just context sensitive but context constituted." I am not accusing Fineman of a contradiction, since his twofold strategy is common enough in the history of philosophy. Given that overmining and undermining strategies both have obvious weaknesses, it is often the case that both are combined in an effort to pool their strengths. Consider Arthur Stanley Eddington's parable of the "two tables," one of them made of tiny physical particles and the other defined by its effect on me, the room, and the pens and pencils it supports (see Eddington 1929). What this misses is the table as a real entity emergent beyond its components and "submergent" beneath its current uses (Harman 2012b). Or consider Wilfrid Sellars's talk of a difference between the "scientific image" and the "manifest image" of any given thing (see Sellars 2007). Much like Eddington, Sellars is left with a theory of two kinds of *images*, with no ability to account for the real thing that differs from them. This is a textbook case of *duomining*, which, in attempting to combine the strengths of undermining and overmining, unwittingly signs up for the frailties of both as well. To defend *both* a virtual beneath all actual contexts *and* a heightened context-sensitivity of reality—as

Fineman does—is not just to land squarely on the horns of a dilemma, but to boast loudly about being impaled by them.

Like most others who defend Deleuze's position against that of OOO, Fineman lists the greater *dynamism* of Deleuzean ontology as a selling point that should lead one to prefer it to object-oriented approaches. To give just one example, Fineman accurately proclaims that "an object for Deleuze is a gerund, not a body speculatively separable from its motion" (Fineman, 96). It is in these sorts of ideas that we find the strong Bergsonian root of Deleuze's thinking, which few observers would wish to downplay (see Bergson 1998; Deleuze 1988). Arjen Kleinherenbrink's *Against Continuity*, which gives a full-blown object-oriented reading of Deleuze, is the remarkable exception that proves the rule (see Kleinherenbrink 2019), though even Kleinherenbrink only makes this case for the period beginning with *Anti-Oedipus*. More importantly, the Bergson/Deleuze emphasis on the dynamic or mobile continuity of being needs to be placed in a wider context stretching back to ancient Greek philosophy.

The most thorough ancient discussion of the continuum is in Aristotle's *Physics*, just as that period's supreme discussion of discreteness can be found in his *Metaphysics*. Any system of human thought in any discipline must find a way to account for both gradual transitions and quantum leaps, even if only by subordinating one completely to the other. Aristotle's preferred solution is a division of labor. As he relates in the *Physics*, time, space, number, and development are examples of continua, since none of these consists of any *definite* number of pieces. The experience of reading (or writing) the present article can be sliced up into either three parts, or seven, or ten thousand, or five billion, depending on our arbitrary decision. For Aristotle, there is no natural way to quantize time, and the same holds for space, development, and number. Among other things, this doctrine puts Aristotle in a position to refute several of Zeno's famous paradoxes, insofar as they rely on the notion that time can be divided in discrete ways (see Aristotle 2018).

But things are very different in the *Metaphysics*, where Aristotle is focused primarily on the status of individual substances. With Aristotelian substance, we have a good example of something that *is not* an infinitely divisible continuum. I write these words while on a weekend trip to Chicago, and however many people are currently located within its city limits, it is some definite number of people, not a blob-like mass of humanity that can be carved up as the observer sees fit.

Now, in Bergson's philosophy we find the bold attempt to claim that even *individuals* are carved out of a continuous mass according to the needs of human practical activity, just like the imaginary units of time or space into which we carve up those well-known continua. This Bergsonian notion of the arbitrariness of individual things leaves deep traces on Deleuzean philosophy as well—again, unless we accept Kleinherenbrink's maverick vision of an object-oriented Deleuze. So then, how are we to adjudicate between two apparently equal models: one in which entities are real individuals, and another in which the world of things is itself a continuum carved up by human fiat? The answer is that they are not equal, since Bergson's version contains a contradiction not found in the Aristotelian theory of substance. Namely, if we join Bergson in saying that human practical needs are what split the world up into chunks, this means that the human agent is already sufficiently distinct from the world-continuum to be able to carve it up, which means that the human being is being treated in advance as a genuine individual entity. For how could the human carve itself out of the continuum if it were not carved out beforehand in order to do the carving? I have made a similar critique of the analytic philosophers James Ladyman and Don Ross (see Ladyman and Ross 2007; Harman 2010b).

An additional point is worth making. Given that the Bergson/Deleuze/Simondon line of thinkers is rightly characterized as a group concerned with flux, flow, becoming, and continuous change as opposed to the supposed static petrification of Aristotle and his heirs, all three are often linked with the self-described "process philosopher" Alfred North Whitehead and another, closely related "philosopher of change," Bruno Latour (see Whitehead 1985; Latour 1993). But in fact a great rift separates Bergson, Deleuze, and Simondon on the one side from Whitehead and Latour on the other, as I have argued elsewhere (see Harman 2014b). They differ precisely on the topic of the continuum, since the just-mentioned Bergsonian trio celebrates the continuous while Whitehead and Latour give us philosophies in which any relation must bridge a gap between its relata by way of some mediator (God for Whitehead, a local mediator for Latour) and in which there is also a gap between any two instants of time, which is the most un-Bergsonian idea imaginable. On that note, we have covered the two major points on which I think OOO is superior to the Deleuzean ontology. The first is Deleuze's unfortunate tendency to undermine (and sometimes duomine) objects, and the second is that no theory of the continuum is able to account for those aspects of reality that are discrete or quantized, whereas the reverse does not hold: OOO treats objects as discrete but their qualities as continuous, and thus accounts for *both* aspects of reality rather than indulging in a crude feat of explaining one of them away. In the remaining portion of this chapter, I will address some of Fineman's less central charges against OOO.

Loose Ends

Along with Fineman's Deleuzean commitment to the continuous over the discrete, we find a closely related partiality for "difference," a term favored as much by Derrideans as Deleuzeans. Three specific passages in Fineman's article come to mind. Early on, we find this: "Every actual is a symptomatic sign of the forces that are its agencies. However, each intensity is a 'pure difference': the case that appears is neither itself nor is it that which is now making it: the actual is radically asymmetric from its virtual" (Fineman, 92). Fineman revisits the topic halfway through his piece: "This character of the distinction, the haecceity, of intensive things does not spring from their essences as they are never themselves themselves. They are in their very heterogenesis non-identical to their composition" (Fineman, 98). And directly before that: "To give them a discrete, passive, and continuing agency, a fixed character, is to cast them into the role of SR objects which is exactly what they are not: they are concurrent actualizations, emergent intensities" (Fineman, 98). Perhaps the weakest aspect of Fineman's article is that no reasons are given as to why one should prefer this vision of the world to OOO's. Passages like this appear throughout in a spirit of assertion, as if a veteran club member were laying down the law to an incoming novice. This makes it difficult to mount a counterattack, since it is always possible that Fineman would give different arguments from whichever ones I might imagine on his behalf. But it is clear that, like many of the recent stars of French philosophy, he has little tolerance for the concepts of essence or identity, though OOO—at least in my version— defends both to the hilt.

As for essence, it seems that two different issues are conflated by Fineman under the banner of "essentialism": (a) the question of whether or not a thing *has* an essence and (b) the question of whether or not the essence of a thing can be *known*. Edward Said is frequently guilty of mixing the two (see Said 1979; Harman 2014a). The political problems with essence actually arise only with (b), when someone makes a sweeping declaration such as "the Arab peoples are essentially incapable of democracy." But for OOO, of course, no one can ever be sure what the essence of anything is, which is an entirely different issue from whether or not something *has* one. The term "essence" is actually harmless, as long as we use it only to mean that which makes a thing be what it is, apart from any of the relations in which it is currently involved, without positing this essence as eternal. The issue of identity is similar, as I once argued in a critique of Jacques Derrida's "White Mythology" (see Derrida 1982; Harman 2005:

110–16). For even if we consider an apple and banana as pure becomings of self-differentiation rather than static chunks of reality, the apple and banana are both *specific* becomings, and for this very reason they are identities. The only way to get around identity would be to say that "everything is everything else," and in that case we are left face to face with Aristotle's deserved mockery that "if contradictory things are all true of the same thing at the same time, it is obvious that all things will be one. For the same thing would be a battleship and a wall and a human being.... And so the claim of Anaxagoras comes true, that all things are mixed together, so that nothing is truly any one thing" (Aristotle 2016: 1007b19–1007b21, 1007b24–1007b26), a passage against which Derrida's counterpunch misses wildly.

Another way Fineman expresses the concept of difference is to speak of singularities: "The oxymoronic interplay is a modality of differential production, the creation of a singularity and not an instance" (Fineman, 92). This is immediately reminiscent of DeLanda's interpretation of Deleuze, as developed in his *Intensive Science and Virtual Philosophy*, one of the early classics of twenty-first-century continental philosophy. As I have stressed in three different places, the main difference between DeLanda's position and OOO is that he wants to look deeper than individual entities toward such notions as singularities, attractors, and phase spaces (see Harman 2008a; chapter 10 of Harman 2010a; Delanda 2002; Delanda and Harman 2017). The intuition guiding DeLanda's standpoint seems to be as follows. Any individual entity always occupies some actual point in space and time and manifests some actual set of qualities. Therefore, in order to attain the virtual as something deeper than the actual, we need to steer clear of individuals as well. Yet from a OOO standpoint there is nothing wrong with an interest in singularities, attractors, or phase spaces, as long as it is recognized that these are objects in their own right: after all, if they are to be considered real, then they must have a definite reality that is reducible neither downward to their components nor upward to their effects. And if DeLanda were to argue—as he sometimes seems to do—that the attractor of a marble as it rolls around a sink is *more* real than the actual marble, he would run afoul of his own insistence on emergence, since the marble's motion must be something over and above its attractor.

It is easy to see why Fineman would find the notion of such disembodied mathematical structures appealing. For he openly celebrates at least one of its results in citing Deleuze: "No 'simple things' remain: 'It is the critique of atomism, which had claimed to find the simple on the level of the composed. Sure, there are simple elements, but these are dynamic unities, not material ones.

Force is the real reason of extension'" (Fineman, 96). But if he means to critique OOO as a form of atomism, then he is simply wrong. Although no OOO object is reducible to its components, all OOO objects are compound; the object-oriented school is no friend of simples. Nor does OOO defend "extension" in the least, since the notion of physical entities as occupying a definite point in space and time may well be true, yet it also relationizes these entities; and of all philosophies, OOO is the one *least* satisfied with understanding anything in terms of its relations. The sense I get is that Fineman is mistaking OOO for a kind of materialism, which is actually its greatest enemy—at least in my own version of OOO. This becomes further evident when he praises Deleuze's fluxes and flows for existing "outside the convenience of fixed embodiment." Whatever work is being done here by the word "fixed," to posit that everything is constantly in motion and thus has no specific character at any given instant is to cruise the troubled waters of a continuum theory of reality, whose defects we have already considered.

Concluding Remarks

I will close by responding briefly to two of Fineman's more puzzling criticisms. The first runs as follows: "Each seeming instance then of disaggregation, of what Harman deems gap production, occurs only in a representation. This is quite ironic, as SR prides itself on having moved past 'the linguistic turn'" (Fineman, 98). There are two problems here. The first is that the notion that "gap production occurs only in a representation" is true only for Deleuze, who tends to treat actuality as a surface filled with sterile and discrete productions while the productive depth is not made up of numerous individuals. It is not true in the least for OOO, which does not accept the existence of a gap-free continuum, since in that case it would be impossible to jump from the one to the many: even if the impossible proviso were added—and Deleuzeans often add it—that the virtual is "both heterogeneous and continuous." The second problem is the reference to the linguistic turn. It is unclear what Fineman hopes to accomplish with this critique, since OOO never claims anywhere that either human language or any sort of human "representation" is required for gaps to be produced at the level of the sensual. Quite the contrary, which is why so many misguided critics have accused us of "panpsychism."

Finally, there is the following head-scratcher: "and so [Harman] adopts the more harmonious Newtonian model, not of direct contact, but of the planets, of action at a distance. Thus, he gets as an additional nice serendipity a way out of Hume's questions that so 'woke' Kant" (Fineman, 100). Where to begin with this? OOO recognizes no action at a distance whatsoever. It is true that we sympathize with the occasionalists and their view that direct interaction is impossible: but only in the way they set up the problem, not in the nature of their solution. The view of OOO is that every interaction needs a mediator capable of touching both relata in any relation: vicarious causation, as we call it (Harman 2007). But in no way does this occur in the manner of "action at a distance." For it requires that two real objects be mediated by a sensual one that touches both directly: or conversely, that two sensual objects be mediated by a real one in direct contact with both. The reason we call such objects "sensual"—and not "sensible," as some misreadings continue to state—is to bring in the connotation of immediate carnal contact between one entity and another. Finally, it is also unclear what Fineman thinks OOO is "dodging" in Hume. I would say instead that Hume and Kant both dodge in advance the central challenge faced by OOO: how to account or causation *without* positing some privileged type of entity as the global causal medium. For whereas the occasionalists simply posit God as the universal mediator of things incapable of relating in their own right, Hume and Kant merely secularize this God by relocating all causation to the human mind. Indeed, this is perhaps the one respect in which OOO is more "woke" than any other approach to causation.

In closing, it remains unclear to me what Fineman means when he says of Dickinson that "[her] poem refuses traditional assignment as representational fiction or as a thing-in-itself. Instead, it anticipates, without the possibility of firm preordering or definitive teleology, readings that can be no longer purely intelligible and must be existentially productive" (Fineman, 92–3). Here again, there are at least two problems. First, it is unclear how there can be anything like the "weird" without a thing-in-itself; aside from which, this is the least of one's problems if an effort is being made to call the poetry of Emily Dickinson "weird." However such an effort might run, we cannot prove an author to be "weird" simply by noting that their work is "existentially productive." Any number of poets are capable of transforming our relation to the world without being weird at all: Sappho, St. John of the Cross, even Robert Frost—none of them is remotely Lovecraftian in their gifts or their tone. And furthermore, OOO has argued passionately for a *theatrical* account of aesthetics, and thus for a notion of all art as existentially productive (Harman 2020). We rest the case here until Fineman and I cross paths again.

References

Aristotle (2016), *Metaphysics*, trans. C. D. C. Reeve, Indianapolis: Hackett.

Aristotle (2018), *Physics*, trans. C. D. C. Reeve, Indianapolis: Hackett.

Barad, K. (2007), *Meeting the Universe Halfway: Quantum Physics and the Entanglement of Matter and Meaning*, Durham, NC: Duke University Press.

Bergson, H. (1998), *Creative Evolution*, trans. A. Mitchell, New York: Dover.

Berkeley, G. (1982), *A Treatise Concerning the Principles of Human Knowledge*, Indianapolis: Hackett.

Brassier, R. (2007), *Nihil Unbound: Enlightenment and Extinction*, London: Palgrave Macmillan.

Bryant, L. R. (2008), *Difference and Givenness: Deleuze's Transcendental Empiricism and the Ontology of Immanence*, Evanston, IL: Northwestern University Press.

Bryant, L. R. (2014), *Onto-Cartography: An Ontology of Machines and Media*, Edinburgh: Edinburgh University Press.

Bryant, L. R., N. Srnicek, and G. Harman, eds. (2011), *The Speculative Turn: Continental Materialism and Realism*, Melbourne: re.press.

DeLanda, M. (2002), *Intensive Science and Virtual Philosophy*, London: Continuum.

DeLanda, M. (2011), "Emergence, Causality, and Realism," in L. R. Bryant, N. Srnicek, and G. Harman (eds.), *The Speculative Turn: Continental Materialism and Realism*, 381–92, Melbourne: re.press.

DeLanda, M., and G. Harman (2017), *The Rise of Realism*, Cambridge, UK: Polity.

Deleuze, G. (1988), *Bergsonism*, trans. H. Tomlinson and B. Habberjam, New York: Zone.

Deleuze, G. (2004), *Difference and Repetition*, trans. P. Patton, London: Continuum.

Deleuze, G., and F. Guattari (2004), *Anti-Oedipus: Capitalism and Schizophrenia*, trans. R. Hurley, M. Seem, and H. Lane, London: Continuum.

Derrida, J. (1982), "White Mythology," in *Margins of Philosophy*, trans. A. Bass, 207–71, Chicago: University of Chicago Press.

Eddington, A. S. (1929), *The Nature of the Physical World*, New York: MacMillan.

Grant, I. H. (2006), *Philosophies of Nature after Schelling*, London: Continuum.

Harman, G. (2005), *Guerrilla Metaphysics: Phenomenology and the Carpentry of Things*, Chicago: Open Court.

Harman, G. (2007), "On Vicarious Causation," *Collapse* II, 171–205.

Harman, G. (2008a), "DeLanda's Ontology: Assemblage and Realism," *Continental Philosophy Review*, 41 (3): 367–83.

Harman, G. (2008b), "On the Horror of Phenomenology: Lovecraft and Husserl," *Collapse* IV, 333–64.

Harman, G. (2009), *Prince of Networks: Bruno Latour and Metaphysics*, Melbourne: re.press.

Harman, G. (2010a), *Towards Speculative Realism: Essays and Lectures*, Winchester, UK: Zero Books.

Harman, G. (2010b), "I Am Also of the Opinion that Materialism Must Be Destroyed," *Environment and Planning D: Society and Space*, 28 (5): 772–90.

Harman, G. (2011), "On the Undermining of Objects: Grant, Bruno, and Radical Philosophy," in L. Bryant, N. Srnicek, and G. Harman (eds.), *The Speculative Turn: Continental Materialism and Realism*, 21–40, Melbourne: re.press.

Harman, G. (2012a), *Weird Realism: Lovecraft and Philosophy*, Winchester, UK: Zero Books.

Harman, G. (2012b), "The Third Table," in C. Christov-Bakargiev (ed.), *The Book of Books*, 540–2, Ostfildern, Germany: Hatje Cantz Verlag.

Harman, G. (2013), "Undermining, Overmining, and Duomining: A Critique," in Jenna Sutela (ed.), *ADD Metaphysics*, 40–51, Aalto, Finland: Aalto University Design Research Laboratory.

Harman, G. (2014a), "Objects and Orientalism," in M. Xie (ed.), *The Agon of Interpretations: Towards a Critical Intercultural Hermeneutics*, 123–39, Toronto: Univ. of Toronto Press.

Harman, G. (2014b), "Whitehead and Schools X, Y, and Z," in N. Gaskill and A. Nocek (eds.), *The Lure of Whitehead*, 231–48, Minneapolis: University of Minnesota Press.

Harman, G. (2018), *Speculative Realism: An Introduction*, Cambridge, UK: Polity.

Harman, G. (2019), "Poe's Black Cat," in C. Washington and A. C. McCarthy (eds.), *Romanticism and Speculative Realism*, 217–35, London: Bloomsbury.

Harman, G. (2020), *Art and Objects*, Cambridge, UK: Polity.

Kleinherenbrink, A. (2019), *Against Continuity: Gilles Deleuze's Speculative Realism*, Edinburgh: Edinburgh University Press.

Ladyman, J., and D. Ross, with D. Spurrett and J. Collier (2007), *Every Thing Must Go: Metaphysics Naturalized*, Oxford: Oxford University Press.

Latour, B. (1993), *The Pasteurization of France*, trans. A. Sheridan, Cambridge, MS: Harvard University Press.

Latour, B. (1999), *Pandora's Hope: An Essay on the Reality of Science Studies*, Cambridge, MA: Harvard University Press.

Meillassoux, Q. (2007), "Subtraction and Contraction," *Collapse* III, 63–107.

Said, E. (1979), *Orientalism*, New York: Vintage.

Sellars, W. (2007), "Philosophy and the Scientific Image of Man," in *In the Space of Reasons: Selected Essays of Wilfrid Sellars*, ed. K. Scharp and R. B. Brandom, 369–408, Cambridge, MA: Harvard University Press.

Simondon, G. (2005), *L'individuation à la lumière des notions de forme et d'information*, Grenoble: Jérôme Millon.

Whitehead, A. N., (1985), *Process and Reality: An Essay in Cosmology*, New York: The Free Press.

Part Two

Medium

Untitled (ink on paper 17" x 11") by Keith Tilford © 2010.

9

Get Out, Race, and Formal Destiny (On Common Weirdness)

Eugenie Brinkema

"*Heimlich* thus becomes increasingly ambivalent, until it finally merges with its antonym *unheimlich*.
—Sigmund Freud, "The 'Uncanny'"

"weird, *adj.*
2 a. Partaking of or suggestive of the supernatural; of a mysterious or unearthly character; unaccountably or uncomfortably strange; uncanny.
4 a. Out of the ordinary course, strange, unusual; hence, odd, fantastic.
weird, *n.*
1a. The principle, power, or agency by which events are predetermined; fate, destiny.
3a. That which is destined or fated to happen to a particular person, etc.; what one will do or suffer; one's appointed lot or fortune, destiny."
—From the *Oxford English Dictionary*

Recognition, Misrecognition, Appropriation

We have to talk about Boogie.

Immediately following the title credits to Jordan Peele's critically and popularly lauded *Get Out* (2017), which themselves appear only after a two-minute, *Halloween*-citing set piece in which a black man wandering dark suburban streets is stalked, brutalized, and captured by a masked figure in a white car, dragged away to its waiting trunk, his limp body swollen with the uncatalogably large membership of a robust historical archive of other limp—lynched, broken, beaten, dragged—black men, inverting any presumptions of which bodies are to be regarded as public threat and which threatened, followed by a rushing tracking shot of forest landscape, the film arrives in a well-appointed urban apartment. *Get Out* thus begins having trespassed suburban, rural, and urban places, signaling a promiscuous geography in its navigation of the American imaginary. That apartment is given, *announced*, in a sequence of five shots of enlarged black-and-white photographs hung on the wall, set to Childish Gambino's "Redbone," with its tellingly warning refrain, "must stay woke." The photographs are framed in a peculiar and distinct manner: each image is slightly tilted, the top of each cut off by the cinematic frame, while a thin vertical strip of a neighboring photograph remains visible, as is the blank wall that separates each image. This framing, in addition to emphasizing the incommensurability of the photographic and cinematic frames—reasserting their difference and the difference between cinematic frame and some phenomenological portion of reality (unconcealing the very logic of mediation)—renders each image simultaneously visible and occluded, excises some component of the central image while including a supplementary, illegible portion of another. This cinematic display evokes the formal quality of a series with its attendant conceptual terms of repetition, membership, and formal commonality, while also suggesting juxtaposed frames of celluloid, graphic panels, the pages of a book, or any number of other inter- and transmedial image types.

The first of the five shots is a static partial image of a photograph of a black man in an empty urban space holding a plume of white balloons, supplemented by a dark column from the adjoining image; the second is of that adjoining image in full, its previously indistinct form revealing now a photograph (top and bottom borders excised) of a gloriously pregnant black body intruding into the frame from the left. Between these first two shots is a hard cut, when, of course, formally, nothing prevented a seamless tracking revelation of their proximity. The third image, also after an abrupt cut, contains an overlapping sliver of that second image, now a vertical band on the left, and a new image, again its top border cut off by the cinematic frame, of a white leaping dog and its owner pulling in opposite lines of force. The fourth image introduces movement, tracking slowly into the space of the apartment, attending to two more enlarged photographs on the wall, one of street lights at night, the other of a backlit bird in flight; the final of the five introductory shots pulls back, this time from the other side of the apartment, to an image of a child wearing a mask (echoing the one worn by the assailant in the opening minutes). If there is a question about whether these are purchased décor, the images are recast and recontextualized within minutes when the film's protagonist, Chris, is seen scrolling through similarly styled black-and-white pictures on his camera's LCD screen, each focusing on contingent lyrical details of the urban landscape (a plant growing between concrete ridges, a shadowy dog on two legs in the moonlight), revealing him to be the photographer of these opening images. This avowal is never a problem for *Get Out* nor for the mass of critical and popular writing on the film. Such a summation is typical: "Before we even see Chris, we're shown black-and-white prints of his work on the walls of his Brooklyn apartment. . . . It's the kind of collection that could be reasonably described as 'raw' and 'honest,'—unpretentious snapshots of New York streets and the diverse range of people who spend time there" (Cruz 2017).

But these particular images pose great difficulty for the critic. Or, rather, despite going completely unremarked in that sizable mass of criticism, the *provenance* of these images *ought* to pose great difficulty for any commentary on *Get Out*. And so: we have to talk about Boogie, born Vladimir Milivojevich and the creator of all of the photographs—each part of an existing catalog; each already titled, for example "Mother-to-be; Bed Stuy BK 2004"—in both Chris's apartment and camera. (This is no uncredited secret: Boogie is listed as providing photographs under the auspices of the film's Art Department.) Milivojevich is a white Central-Eastern European, hails from Belgrade, and has multiple projects documenting the war-torn history of Serbia, including the 2009 monograph *Belgrade Belongs to Me*; since the late 1990s, he is best known for extensive work in his adopted home of Brooklyn, most famously in stark images documenting gang, gun, and drug culture. The photographs in Chris's apartment are drawn from an early 2000s series from the then-infamous neighborhoods of Bushwick, Bedford-Stuyvesant, and Queensbridge—before gentrification (in other words: before Chris's adult time, from the era when he was a child, and, in 2017, an anachronistic vision of the city). Several (though not all) appeared in Boogie's first monograph, the 2006 *It's All Good*.

Boogie is one of the most prolific and influential street photographers working today, with a robust artistic and commercial catalog by the date of *Get Out*, and the point of difficulty for any starting treatment of the question of the image—dynamics of sight and blindness; visibility (hyper-/over-/in); fetishization; objectification—which is central to any thinking of micro- and macro-aggressivity, antiblack racism, and the possibility of forms of resistance in this film—is the spectator's uncomplicated attribution of these images to Chris in his diegetic work as a photographer. For Boogie's images are so well known that Peele's film solicits (or at least admits) the possibility of a prior recognition of these photographs as exterior to the narrative world of the film. The works of a lesser-known artist or previously unpublished work by a known artist might have been chosen in their stead, but that they were not solicits (or at least admits) a frisson of the *this seems familiar am I seeing what I think I'm seeing*. After all, Boogie's credited street photographs are also images any other woke urban couple might acquire for the mise-en-scène of their apartment. But this possibility (solicitation; admission) immediately collapses when spectators see the scroll of formally similar images on Chris's camera and are retroactively asked to disavow any sense of extra-diegetic *familiarity* with the earlier images and to regard them *unfamiliarly*, as belonging to the artistic practice of the film's protagonist, a diegetic practice with which other characters already are, and with which the spectator will be asked to become, aesthetically *familiar*. These photographic images, that is, are shown in order to be possibly read one way and then reframed in order to be read another way. This teasing hermeneutic dance opens up the chance for a spectatorial progression that follows the structure of a misrecognition that is experienced and then incompletely refused, disavowal's "I know very well and yet . . . ." But if Boogie's images are not recognized, they never need be disavowed. Thus, not unlike the famously ambiguous ending of Michael Haneke's *Caché* (2005)—in which empirical viewers may fail to see amid a crowd of children the brief and hidden (per the title) encounter between the two sons of the film's protagonists, a meeting that by narrative conceit should not be able to happen and yet happens nonetheless, introducing epistemological problems just as the film ends—*Get Out* formally solicits the possibility of an aesthetic recognition of Boogie's corpus (prior, external, and with an extensive catalog *not* invoked in the film) that is impossible to fully accept and it simultaneously solicits the possibility of its failure to be recognized, in which case that frisson would not require a paradoxical affirmation and disavowal. Although it has been widely claimed that the two audiences the film solicits—whose experiences of the film do not align, like the mismatched photographic and cinematic borders of the opening montage—are black against white audiences, an equally fundamental rupture exists between two audiences divided by their possible or impossible recognition of the sign of this other photographer and other archive.

Why dwell on this possibility that the form of the film admits, if not solicits? One reason is the choice of which of Boogie's photographs the film engages and repurposes. There is a mismatch, an asymmetry between the photographs we see that are attributed to Chris and the broader corpus for which Boogie is known. The images Peele chose are particularly atypical in Boogie's corpus precisely for their avoidance of two themes central in other ways to *Get Out*: the question of violence and the question of race. Chris's putative "signature style" is built on stylistic exceptions in the larger body of work from which it is drawn, a gesture of archival selection not irrelevant in a film about the violence of token exceptionalism. In soliciting the possibility of the recognition of Boogie's work, the images evoke the trace of this missing archive. Not unlike the Freudian formalism of the *unheimlich* (displayed in the first epigraph) and its signature return of the (inadequately) repressed, such that repression is the failure of a logic of totalization, there is a return of the (inadequately) repressed corpus of Boogie, which creates, textually, the trace of a missing archive that the film spectrally suggests must also belong to Chris. The incomplete framing of the opening images homologizes the incomplete provision of the archive: while something is unconcealed, it is not fully revealed, it is slightly wrong, something is askew, awry, absent, and one is literally not getting the whole picture, even though one is also, almost, nearly getting the whole picture. This is complicated further by particular aspects of that missing archive, not all of which can be missing from Chris's portfolio (at least according to the logics of antiblack racism)—in particular, Boogie's well-known series with skinheads, a project to which Chris would not seem to have access, not by virtue of aesthetic talent, but by virtue of structural logics that govern which (embodied) eye has contingent aesthetic access to which subjects. In an oft-retold origin story of his first New York City street photographs, Boogie cites his European whiteness as what enabled aesthetic access:

> I remember the first time I went to Bed-Stuy, just walking around, a white guy with a camera and my photo bag. I'm walking around and these guys from across the street were like, *Hey, man, come over here*, and we started talking. I guess it was my accent—I don't sound like anyone they hate—and ten days later they're like, *Hey, Boogie, would you like to take some photos of us with guns?* (qtd. in Ferranti 2016, emphasis in the original)

Chris, however, sounds and signs *precisely* like the anyone that white supremacists definitionally hate, and thus there is a nonreciprocity to the extradiegetic fantasy logic by which outsiders will be granted a particular privilege to travel among and document an unfamiliar community. That difference in forms of racial privilege also leaves its mark on the film, but solely to the extent that the viewer recognizes the images as not-quite-only-Chris's. In other words, to mount a critique of this nonreciprocity of aesthetic privilege requires refusing sole authorship of the images to Chris—he must be disallowed full ownership over his diegetic aesthetic practice *in order that* a critique of racial asymmetry be admitted to the film.

This is an especial problem for *Get Out* because the film marks Chris's artistic practice as a virtuosity intimately bonded to his blackness, which must narratively be his and his alone, and which is the occasion for his vulnerability to violence. The switch from micro- to macro-aggression in the film occurs during a bidding auction for Chris's body, won by Jim Hudson, a blind art dealer whose preying on Chris turns on wordplay: "I want your eye," he says to Chris, sliding from literal organ to metaphorical-aesthetic sensibility and discernment, thus wanting the totality of the corpus of Chris's work both shown and not shown at the cost of wanting the consciousness-voiding and body-brutalizing appropriation of his physical organ of sight.

(Boogie is not a black photographer. Does that matter? It matters a great deal that Jim Hudson is not a black photographer. Am I asking after the same matter here? And, if not, what, in the repetition, is failing to faithfully repeat?)

Get Out is haunted from the very beginning by a confusion between the corpus of photographic work the viewer is directly shown and the broader archive recognized alongside/beneath/haunting those enlarged photographs and these images on the camera. Those works of Boogie's that do not appear in the film— needles entering overused veins; slumped abandoned children; street-strewn bodies in indifferent urban landscapes; a whole missing archive that suggests a parallel world in which Chris is tarrying with junkies in dilapidated houses and going on gang raids—leave their textual trace as a resistant something that is simultaneously not visibly and narratively present in or overtly admissible by the film but nevertheless is *not unknown to it*. The *I know but I can't acknowledge it yet*. The *somehow this is already familiar I've seen this all somewhere* that gives form to the experience of microaggression's *somehow I knew this was coming am I hearing what I think I'm hearing I've been through this all before*, which Claudia Rankine words thusly in *Citizen: An American Lyric*, her paean to the lived anguish of racist language: "Each moment is like this—before it can be known, categorized as similar to another thing and dismissed, it has to be experienced, it has to be seen. What did he just say? Did she really just say that? Did I hear what I think I heard? Did that just come out of my mouth, his mouth, your mouth?" (2014: 9).

Ordinary and Shared by All

Uncertainty about that which one is simultaneously certain names a formal structure, one predicated on an ambiguity at the heart of the central concern of this volume. The *weird*, for all that one strand of its etymology (given in the second epigraph) and one privileged modern aesthetic deployment of its sense suggests an unfamiliar, strange, odd, unpredictable occurrence, is also etymologically what is destined and fated, the determinism of what is absolutely going to come about—an overwhelming and overruling necessity. Not unlike the double attributions of the intimately related figure of the uncanny, made famous by Freud's etymological and citational unpacking, in which the homely and unhomely turn over into each other, the weird is marked by a strangeness to what was always already certain to come about, an at-oddsness and peculiarity to what is fated, destined: the brute happening of what happens. The linguistic archaeology of the term from Shakespeare's use of it in *Macbeth*—and I am glossing here—traces how that play's infamous sisters are given as both *weyard* and *weyward*, such that the weird names both the expected (fated, predestined, predicted) and the unexpected (what is unusual, odd, goes awry, runs wayward) (see Shamas 2007: 14–17). But what distinguishes the weird in part from Freud's *unheimlich* is a thrownness to the scope. As opposed to Freud's resolute lodging of the uncanny in the home (the home of the family, the home of the maternal body), the weird, with its bond to questions of the numinous and larger forces of fate and destiny, takes on a cosmic scale. Its vastness and abstraction—beyond the individual, familial, cultural, earthly, human-comprehensible—suggests that weirdness involves structures beyond any one individual's or race's or species' control.

However, the corrective that *Get Out* makes to Lovecraft's famous definition of "weird fiction" in *Supernatural Horror in Literature*—"[a] certain atmosphere of breathless and unexplainable dread of outer, unknown forces" (1927: 15)—is that Chris and spectator experience a *breathless and yet entirely explainable dread of outer, known forces*. This mode is what I want to call *common weirdness*—common, as in prevalent, ordinary, predictable; common, as in public, as in shared alike by many. *Common weirdness* names the fated, destined, seen-to-certainly-be-coming of the terrible—the expected bad occurrence, the anticipated horrible event—and simultaneously the weirdness of those things (bodies, images, forms) that appear to have and be *in common*. Part of what is strange in *common weirdness* is precisely and paradoxically its obviousness, what exists on the surface: an interior respectively revealed to be entirely what a subject thought it was all along, an outside that breaks in and confirms instead of surprises—*a weird that is not at all strange*. The film's title plays on the same ambiguity or doubleness: *Get Out* signals both incredulity in an epistemic register (Get out of here) and a warning and imperative signaling an urgent drive away from a state or threat (Get out of here!)—in the former case, one does not believe what has been presented to the ear or eye; in the latter, one believes so surely that one warns and gives notice of impending danger to others.

Zadie Smith formulates this logic of confirmation in an exhaustive detailing of the film's compendium of "black fears about white folk":

> White women who date black men. Waspy families. Waspy family garden parties. Ukuleles. Crazy younger brothers. Crazy younger brothers who play ukuleles. Sexual psychopaths, hunting, guns, cannibalism, mind control, well-meaning conversations about Obama. The police. Well-meaning conversations about basketball. Spontaneous roughhousing, spontaneous touching of one's biceps or hair. Lifestyle cults, actual cults. Houses with no other houses anywhere near them. Fondness for woods. The game bingo. Servile household staff, sexual enslavement, nostalgia for slavery—slavery itself. (2018: 213–14)

Smith's conclusion about the textual effect of this imported archive is telling: "Every one of these reversals 'lands'—just like a good joke—simultaneously describing and interpreting the situation at hand, and this, I think, is what accounts for the homogeneity of reactions to *Get Out*: It is a film that contains its own commentary." Thus, black viewers regard the film as "vindication"—confirmation of an always-already-known set of real and irrational fears—and white viewers feel "a cringe of recognition" (214). The film operates not only at the surface—containing its own commentary; interpreting as it presents its conceit—it also functions as confirmation and recognition, two epistemological strategies of sufficiency that would seem to exclude *Get Out* from the epistemologically compromised realm of the weird. As though translating one of the most famous accounts of the ludic nature of post-1970s horror from Philip Brophy's essay "Horrality"—"The contemporary Horror film knows that you've seen it before; it knows that you know what is about to happen; and it knows that you know it knows you know" (1986: 5)—*Get Out* shifts from an emphasis on oversaturated, predictable cinematic-generic conventions to oversaturated, predictable ideological-cultural conventions. Chris and black viewer alike have seen this all before, and even if they don't really know what is about happen, they also, kind of, admittedly, do.

Thus, for all that *Get Out* traffics in signs of the conventional aesthetic affectivity of the weird—strangeness, apprehension, dread, a sense of something being off, perhaps never more than in those black bodies whose subjectivity is sunken while their bodies are possessed by white subjects, as in the famous admixture of Georgina's brilliant smile all while a tear rolls down her face—and for all that the violent machinery of *Get Out* literalizes in its coagula procedure

Mark Fisher's privileged form of the weird, "montage—the conjoining of *two or more things which do not belong together*" (2016: 11)—the *common weirdness* of *Get Out* disentangles weirdness from the shock of the set (outside, outer, unknown, different, new) and reorients it toward the shock of a confirmation of what is (inside, intimate, known, the certain and wholly predictable). The *wrongness* that Fisher locates in his study of the weird—which he aligns with "the presence of the new" and "a signal that the concepts and frameworks which we have previously employed are now obsolete" (13)—is thus reencountered as the wrongness of what is nevertheless on the surface: sure, familiar, seen to be coming, and not at all obsolete. After all, the unexpected and dreadful affects of the conventional weird are hard-pressed to account for Chris's friend Rod's insistence *from the very beginning of the film*, "Don't go to a white girl's parent's house"; "They got you on display now, huh?"; "You ain't getting in my head"; [on the hypnosis] "How you not scared of this, man? . . . White people love making people sex slaves"; [on the strange affect of the black people Chris meets at the Armitages], "It's because they probably hypnotized. Look bro, all I'm doing is connecting the dots. I'm taking what you presented to me, okay?" If Rod's interpretation seems outlandish, by the end of the film it is elevated to a perfectly accurate description of the situation at hand, rendering him a reliable narrator as the film is unfolding (and despite his sexualization of a broader regime of use, in some of the couples at the Armitages, a sex slave is precisely what the appropriated black body has become).[1]

Grappling with common weirdness and the weirdness of what forms are shared in common requires one further step. Despite—indeed, precisely *because*—that common weirdness is so resolutely linked to occurrences that take place on and at the surface, it also constitutes an imperative for its form to be *read*.[2] The common does not move us past the impasse of what Althusser dubbed "the illusion of immediate reading" or naive calls for a reading *without* distance, *without* dislocation, *with* a false promise of transparency (Althusser and Balibar 2009: 17). Indeed, common weirdness must be read for it is not only that racial animus and fetishization is what is to be wholly expected—seen to be coming—but that Chris's photographs perform the very same formal operation of coagulation that the film criticizes as the most horrific violations of its villains. If one aspect of the surprisingly homogeneous critical agreement on the meaning of *Get Out* is that it is about a fetishization of black virtuosity (athletic, artistic, sexual) devoid of the particularity of black consciousness, history, experience, people—the film repeats this structure, deploying an Eastern European's photographic corpus excised of the particularity of Serbian wars, history, violence, and people. Visual form and the photographic archive trouble the conventional critical description of the film and suggest that *Get Out* is far more ambivalent about appropriation, regarding it as a kind of *common* formal destiny of aesthetic objects, and that appropriation, citation, coagulation is not a predictable one-to-one register of violence, but the movement of the interplay of bodies and forms, which can go in multiple directions at once. If one attends to it, there are countless further references to representational reflexivity in *Get Out*; as just one example, take Jeremy's references to Chris's *frame* ("With your frame and genetic makeup . . ."), a word that compounds formal allusions, from frame as in support to frame as in what gives a parergonal border to Chris's photographs, that term for something impossible to detach without revealing internal lack, and thus a limit that lends form to any system by inscribing something exterior which intervenes, as Derrida words it, "in the inside only to the extent that the inside is lacking" (1987: 56).

The film's archive of meta-formal remarks suggests that something in any paraphrase of the film will miss the complexity and polyvocality of the critique that is worked out on the level of its own grappling with form. Thus, for all that *Get Out* is a horror film, for all that it is a critique of America's limousine liberalism and faux post-racial harmony, it is also unquestionably a film obsessed with the double meaning imputable to the term *representation*: the act by which sensual properties are mediated in an aesthetic object and the political act of one figure standing in the place of another, the latter sense literalized in *Get Out* and shown to be a form of brutality that sinks and disappears certain figures for the express gain of others. What remains unknown is any *singular* reading method that could (ever) come to terms with the ordinary, unhidden, common weirdness that is American racism. Instead of constituting an effortlessly describable summation of a critique (*any* critique), *Get Out* deploys its formal language and the language of form (photographic, cinematic, rhetorical) in order to insist on the interpretive imperative of the ordinary, unhidden, common weirdness of black life in contemporary America, one that ultimately regards reading as a practice of survival.

The Blindness of Description

The conceit of *Get Out*, with its mash-up of *Guess Who's Coming to Dinner*, Eddie Murphy's famous routine about a black family in a haunted house, and the original 1974 *Stepford Wives* (with a good measure of *Rosemary's Baby* body-borrowing paranoia thrown in), is easily summarized: the film's protagonist Chris warily travels to his girlfriend Rose's house to meet her parents, only to encounter a series of both expected and odd—

What, reader, is the difference between a summary and a description? The former is a gesture of condensation, a winnowing and economizing, a paring down to essential traits or points or aspects. *Summarius*, pertaining to the whole or a totality, is what is made brief or abbreviated in relation to that whole or totality by containing, naming, articulating substance. A summary pertains, always, to a question of quantity. A description, by contrast, is a flat de-hierarchized recounting of details, without the hierarchical valuation of aspects that would synthesize or prioritize component parts. It also, however, is a second gesture: *descriven*, mid-thirteenth century, means to interpret or explain or represent, from roots for writing (*scribere*). It also means "to form or trace by motion"—to (literally: by pen, by hand) *outline the form* of something. If a summary abbreviates totality by essentializing substance as problem of content, description outlines the local and particular form of something. This question of their difference is central to any thinking of form in *Get Out*, a film that is obsessed with summation, description, totality, particularity, and the relation of content to form.

Where were we? Yes: the conceit of *Get Out* is easily summarized. Protagonist Chris warily travels to his girlfriend Rose's house to meet her parents, Missy and Dean Armitage, only to encounter a series of expected and odd behaviors—a black housekeeper and gardener displaying oversolicitous and yet hostile affect; Missy's hypnosis of Chris, ostensibly to help his smoking addiction; Rose's aggressive and competitive brother, Jeremy; awkward conversations about black culture with elderly white guests at the Armitages' estate; and so on—which the film ultimately reveals is part of an elaborate multigenerational conspiracy that transplants the brains of white people into black bodies now rendered pure media, leaving the barest traces of consciousness at a distant remove from perceptual reality, lodging black subjectivity in what the film dubs The Sunken Place.

Summary is easy, if also aggressively empty. Description is more complicated. If easily summarized, the film is not so easily described—or, rather, the film makes clear that one ought to be wary of claims for the value of (any) description. As with the description of Boogie's photographs—no, Chris's photographs (but, really, Boogie's photographs [while also resolutely being Chris's photographs])— such that whose images one is thereby describing, whose eye (literal and metaphorical-aesthetic) is put into question in the very act of writing such a description—is simultaneously a description of the images that are provided while necessarily detailing a description of the totality of images from the larger archive from which those images are taken and which are not made visible—images themselves that are incompletely diegetically shown (fragmented, canted, partitioned)—description is no simple matter. Indeed, one might say that relying on description to provide an accurate vision of anything would itself be a form of critical blindness. This is a stance the film overtly takes.

When the art dealer Jim Hudson and Chris first meet, before the auction, before the preparations for surgery, Hudson praises Chris's work, insisting his aesthetic judgment is sound despite his blindness, saying of his method: "My assistant describes the work to me in great detail. . . . The images you capture: so brutal, so melancholic. Powerful stuff; I think." Everything hinges on that final "I think"—a qualification that marks the limits of description to be adequate to a phenomenal perception of a thing. The description of Boogie-cum-Chris's work, however, is no simple matter: in the critical account quoted earlier, Chris's work is "described as 'raw' and 'honest,'" while, based on Hudson's assistant's description, the blind art dealer concludes that Chris's work is "brutal" and "melancholic." Without adjudicating either valuation, it is worth noting the antipathetic regimes to which each set of terms belongs: "raw" and "honest" refer to frankness, invoking an epistemological claim about the evidentiary value of photographs as documents related to debates about realism; "brutal" and "melancholic" refer to affect and questions of aesthetic reception related to sensation. In a film that slides between the literal and metaphorical (those two *eyes* of Chris's that are preyed upon), the alignment of description with literal blindness suggests a bond between description and critical blindness.

Hudson's theory of the adequacy of description relies on an unspoken importation of the classical rhetorical figure of *hypotyposis*, a vivid description of a scene or event, a sketch so detailed it puts the image of a scene or event directly in the mind, a figure that, Roland Barthes writes, "institutionalized the fantasmatic"—its function being to "put things before the hearer's eyes," not in a "neutral, constative manner, but by imparting to representation all the luster of desire" (1986: 145-6). Setting aside the relation of ear to eye and sound to image in *Get Out*, about which one might write much—including of the relation between amplified sound and diminished visual and transformational capacity of The Sunken Place, itself evocative of the broader regime of the acroamatic—forms of oral teaching intended only for select disciples and thus a secreting of forms of knowledge in a concealed, sunken space—and, relatedly, the role of (maternal) voice and rhythmic sound in hypnosis; anachronistic sounds and their medial correlatives, including the 1939 "Run rabbit run," which plays in the car in the opening of the film, yet crackles as if it were being listened to on an LP; the relation of blindness to strategic deafness in Chris's inverted Odysseus-with-the-sirens move (the ur-heroic gesture) of stuffing cotton (née wax) in his ears in order not to be vulnerable to manipulative sound in the film's violent climax—at stake in the assistant's description of Chris's photographs to the blind art dealer is a broader question of the relation between word and image, speech and sight, and ideologies of sufficiency or insufficiency that govern each relation. The hedge of "I think" names the epistemic instability of description. Given that what is described—to put the image in the mind's eye—is the mass of textual details of which there can always be more, any description also performs its own constitutive incompleteness. Not unlike the discordance between the photographic and cinematic frame in the opening montage of photographs in Chris's apartment, which fail to align and thus positively show their partiality, the aesthetic-affective evaluations of "brutal" and "melancholic" are shown to be readings (partial ones; ones to be interrogated), which if offered as fixed truths are linked to literal blindness.

And so: is the evaluation based on the assistant's description interpretively plausible? Persuasive? The photographs that the viewer of *Get Out* are shown, if anything, display a counterarchive to black pain, urban brutality, raced melancholia: the joy of a pregnant belly; the formal surge of floating balloons; a leaping dog not at bodies but into the frame itself. An interpretation of Chris's work as brutal and melancholic either is accurate and persuasive, but of an archive the spectator has not and will never diegetically see, or it is not descriptive but prescriptive—a description that, in images of black joy, can read (into them) only brutality and melancholia. (Perhaps the affects it always knew it would find when a white eye looks on black life.) Description is not merely one way of getting images wrong, finding in them what one expected to find all along and thus failing to encounter either their particular form or the surprises and wayward digressions that reading uniquely unconceals—one can also find in description the very violence of racist logic, as in Rankine's account of carceral repetition, "And you are not the guy and still you fit the description because there is only one guy who is always the guy fitting the description" (2014: 105). Peele's film equally disavows and disqualifies any taking of Chris's photographs as documentary and evidentiary objects that require no description, while simultaneously disavowing and disqualifying any definitive readings of the photographs—that "I think" recalling that *all* images have form, that they all require interpretation, that any *final* declarative reading would itself be a form of *failing to see*.[3]

What *does* take on definitive power in the formal logic of *Get Out* is an alternative visual regime—the cell phone's flash as the pure capacity for unconcealing the condition of possibility for visibility. The flash is delinked from individual subjectivity and aesthetic vision (from the eye and from an eye) as raw presencing of light. After all, when Chris takes the flash picture of Andre, which brutally pulls him out of The Sunken Place, Chris does not hold the camera in front of his eye but down by his waist: the camera eye fails to align with either his literal or metaphorical one, and its mechanistic function is linked to automatic processes of the medium itself. Unlike images that require interpretation—a regime that includes Chris's professional photographs; the archival catalogs of Rose's previous black lovers, which themselves are reminiscent of catalogs of lynching souvenirs and thus suggest interpretive linkages to other trophies in the Armitage house, such as the hunted buck; the photograph of Chris displayed at auction, an image that objectifies while fetishizing—the flash is marked by its immediacy, uncomplicated by its relation to (any specific) image: without form, the pure flash of light is the inverse of The Sunken Place with its lightless surround. The pure flash of light signals the purity of light, its efficacy, and its condition of visibility *without an image*, a trigger that pulls back into presence sunken consciousness but at the expense of containing no form that would enable interpretation. This condition of possibility for representation, in announcing only ever an undetermined image to come, also fails to radically transform the structures in which that representation is situated and from which it emerges. It produces only shock, figured in Andre's nose-bleeding charge and bellowing warn: "Get out!"

In its grappling with these meta-representational figures, *Get Out* thus demonstrates one of the central theoretical dilemmas of any discussion of form. For a film that is obsessed with the question of what kind of form the black body is for white culture, it is equally formophilic and formophobic. *Get Out* is wholly aware of one robust tradition of a philosophical thinking of form that emphasizes the bond between visible form and the logic of racism, perhaps best articulated in Derrida's "La forme et la façon," his preface to Alain David's 2001 *Racisme et antisemitisme*. There, Derrida reads David as suggesting that the "originary crime" of racism and anti-Semitism is "privileging form and cultivating formal limits" (2001: 11), that the violence of racism is given directly in an investment in a limitation by form and that the motor of catastrophic violence is an obsession with a purity of form which posits within its own thinking a threatening contamination of that purity—all derived from form's quality of being identified with the metaphysical canon of appearance, sense, presence, evidence. This is the logic of visible shape in play in the cringing avowal of a golf-loving white party guest that he knows Tiger Woods and his admonition to Chris, "Let's see your form." But another regime of form is also in play in Chris's actual practice of survival: the urgency he ascribes to a *reading* of form, given in an almost technical definition when, of Walter the gardener, Chris insists, "It's not what he says, but how he says it," reasserting a textual dimension that does not announce itself in visible shape but via forms of language that signal the necessity of interpretation. Black survival is figured as what requires infinite reading, ultimately requiring Rod's suspicious accounting of signs—not ones that are hidden, but precisely the register of what is certain, on the surface, and seen to be happening. The Sunken Place is formally given as a form of retreat and distancing from a perceptible frame of reality that is metonymized in a framed aspect ratio; what it also demonstrates is the violence of a retreat from an interpretable portion of the world. What sinks in The Sunken Place is not only capacities for action and the self-presence of consciousness but also the scope of the world available for interpretation.

Common weirdness thus demands a revision of conventional accounts of formalism. Against the Russian formalist demand for an artistic practice and interpretive disposition that would make the familiar newly unfamiliar—*ostranenie* being nothing but a strategy of making every text *weird*—the *common weirdness* of Get Out suggests that a futurity for black life requires a stance of infinite interpretation of the ordinary, not to make the familiar unfamiliar, but to come to terms with the familiar that is common and given and shared by all. This mode of survival involves reading signs not because they are unknown (strange, unpredictable, hidden) but precisely *because* they are so insistently on the order of the necessary, what is fated, what is destined. Infinite and open reading by way of accounting for one's *appointed lot*. If summary and description are put under pressure by the film, and an ongoing reading of form is what is linked to possibilities for survival, then the homogeneous critical agreement on a description of the film's post-racial ideological critique is precisely beside the point. Get Out demonstrates the infinite readability of black life *tout court* and ought not be summarized for any purported single final reading that would evade further interpretation. Disqualified are all metalanguages (appropriation, structural violence, microaggression) as adequate to account for the atmosphere of dread, the body count littering the ground, the indescribable trauma and tear-pouring eyes. If *common weirdness* does not tarry with the noumenal or cosmic realm, it traffics in something far darker: a formal destiny of indescribable hurt that was nevertheless seen to be coming all along.

Notes

1 For a fine reading of *Get Out* in relation to *horror vérité*, in which "the terrifying nightmare is everyday reality," see Landsberg 2018.
2 An alignment of the weird with the question of form is not without precedent. Graham Harman begins his extensive study of Lovecraft in *Weird Realism: Lovecraft and Philosophy* with what seems like a study of precisely this question—describing Lovecraft as often lamenting "the inability of mere language to depict the deep horrors his narrators confront, to the point that he is often reduced to hints and allusions at the terrors inhabiting his stories" (2012: 4). Harman thus emphasizes that literal linguistic summation, paraphrase, or description will constitutively fail to account for Lovecraft's horror. Defining "paraphrase" as "our technical term for the attempt to give literal form to any statement, artwork, or anything else," Harman invokes Cleanth Brooks and his "heresy of paraphrase" from his 1947 *The Well-Wrought Urn* by way of insisting on the priority of some other strategy of approaching Lovecraft's literature (2012: 9). Harman, however, in collapsing paraphrasing with literalizing, confuses the question of form: to literalize is to take words in their natural meaning; to paraphrase is to tell in other words—the latter is a strategy of difference (changing words, retelling in one's own words, summarizing by way of accounting), while the former is a strategy of refusing difference (presuming words mean precisely and only what they say, refusing figuration and metaphoricity). Brooks's famous heresy targeted not a literal approach to language, but an anti-interpretive approach to *form* that would reassert paraphrased thematics (or content) as the work of reading. Because of speculative realism's own blindness toward the linguistic turn, Harman cannot bring himself to actually speak to form, and thus in place of form or formalism, he writes of Lovecraft's *style* and, paradoxically, ends up relying on literal descriptions of stylistic traits like "Chiaroscuro Gone Awry" or "The Accursed Buzzing" *as though* they were themes. Even the "Worse than Formless" is treated not as a problem of form but as a theme that Harman himself *literalizes* by looking at literal formlessness as a trope in Lovecraft's writing.

Harman ends by mis-describing formalism and accusations against it—that it turns "criticism into an empty intellectual game" as a result of "downplaying the content of literature so severely in favor of structural irony and paradox" (2012: 246)—and in so confusing *formalism* with a description (and a not very accurate one at that) of *deconstruction*, he concludes that "we can only agree with the general spirit of [Brooks'] attack on paraphrase" (2012: 247). "The similarities and differences between object-oriented philosophy and the 'formalism' of Brooks' New Criticism can be summed up as follows," he concludes, "We agree with the point that nothing can be paraphrased," but "we cannot support formalism, which holds that the specific content of any experience is relatively unimportant. But neither can we support materialism, which grants privilege to the original soil from which anything grows. . . . Instead we can only support *objects*. The reason objects are not formalizable is because they cannot be reduced to their conditions of knowability, whether mathematical or otherwise" (2012: 253). However, of course, Brooks doesn't say that nothing *can* be paraphrased, but that paraphrase does not exhaust the meaning of a poem and that it is a "heresy." Harman thereby confuses interpretive strategy with mere possibility. Although his straw man formalism that "belittles content, since it treats content as mere fodder for larger structural relations" sounds a great deal more like the criticism of a straw man historicism, one merely wants to point out that a vision of objects as "not formalizable" because "they cannot be reduced to their conditions of knowability" belies treatments of form that emphasize its impenetrability, unknowability, and difficulty from Leibniz to Derrida, seeming purposefully ignorant of the metamorphological unfoldings of meaning in any act of reading advanced by post-structuralism: the shared insistence that reading does not ever exhaust its object, that reading is not recuperative but is generative. In *Positions*, just to take one example, Derrida argues that a hermeneutical reading ought not (and does not) "seek out a finished signified beneath a textual surface," but that "reading is transformational" (1981: 63). If Harman wants a nonexhausted object, he has chosen the wrong enemies. Reading for form names the *energia* of nonexhaustability itself.

3 The question of finality notates the failure (ideological and formal) of the alternative ending of *Get Out,* released with the DVD and circulated broadly online, in which Chris, finally having freed himself from the brutality of the Armitages, is surrounded by street-strewn corpses when the police arrive and he is taken into the carceral system for good (as a kind of black male destiny), but says to Rod with stoic resignation, "I ended it." What rings false in this ending is not an affective failure (despite Peele's insistence that it would have been too depressing to modern audiences to have that hopeless realism) but its declaration of *telos*. In the film's actual ending, Rod and Chris drive away, corpses remain strewn, absolutely nothing has ended—one cycle of a structure that is on the surface has merely played out. It would be far weirder to suggest racialized violence was singularly end-able.

References

Althusser, L., and É. Balibar (2009), *Reading Capital*, New York: Verso.
Barthes, R. (1986), "The Reality Effect," in *The Rustle of Language*, trans. Richard Howard, 141–8, Berkeley: University of California Press.
Boogie (Milivojevich, V.) (2006), *It's All Good*, Brooklyn, NY: powerHouse Books.

Boogie (Milivojevich, V.) (2009), *Belgrade Belongs to Me*, Brooklyn, NY: powerHouse Books.
Brophy, P. (1986), "Horrality: The Textuality of Contemporary Horror Films," *Screen* 27 (1): 2–13.
Cruz, L. (2017), "In *Get Out*, the Eyes Have It," *The Atlantic*, https://www.theatlantic.com/entertainment/archive/2017/03/in-get-out-the-eyes-have-it/518370/ (accessed October 28, 2019).
Derrida, J. (1981), *Positions*, trans. Alan Bass, Chicago: University of Chicago Press.
Derrida, J. (1987), *The Truth in Painting*, trans. Geoff Bennington and Ian McLeod, Chicago: University of Chicago Press.
Derrida, J. (2001), "La forme et la façon," preface to Alain David, *Racisme et Antisemitisme: Essai de philosophie sur l'envers des concepts*, Paris: Ellipses.
Ferranti, S. (2016), "Grim Photos of Gang Life in Brooklyn from the Early 2000s," *Vice*, https://www.vice.com/en_us/article/jm54wx/boogie-its-all-good-photo-book-anniversary-interview (accessed October 28, 2019).
Fisher, M. (2016), *The Weird and the Eerie*, London: Repeater Books.
Freud, S. (2003), *The Uncanny*, trans. David McLintock, intro. Hugh Haughton, New York: Penguin.
Harman, G. (2012), *Weird Realism: Lovecraft and Philosophy*, Winchester, UK: Zero Books.
Landsberg, A. (2018), "Horror vérité: Politics and History in Jordan Peele's *Get Out* (2017)," *Continuum*, 32 (5): 629–42.
Lovecraft, H. P. (1973 [1927]), *Supernatural Horror in Literature*, New York: Dover Publications.
Oxford English Dictionary (1989), 2nd edn, 20 vols, Oxford: Oxford University Press.
Rankine, C. (2014), *Citizen: An American Lyric*, Minneapolis, MN: Graywolf Press.
Shamas, L. (2007), *"We Three": The Mythology of Shakespeare's Weird Sisters*, New York: Peter Lang.
Smith, Z. (2018), "Getting In and Out," in *Feel Free: Essays*, London: Penguin, 212–23.

10

From a Heap of Broken Images Toward a Postcolonial Weird

Ana Lily Amirpour's Western Landscapes

Maryam Aras

"I watched the 'Making of Michael Jackson's *Thriller*' video thousands of times. It taught me how to be an American" (Rizov 2014), filmmaker Ana Lily Amirpour said during an interview for the promotion of her first feature film *A Girl Walks Home Alone at Night* (2014). The behind-the-scenes documentary from 1983 accounts for all the hard work and dedication the best among makeup artists, choreographers, and costume designers put into the short music film that was to become one of the most iconic pop products of its time (MTV 1983).

"Why Michael wanted to make *Thriller* the most—he wanted to change into a monster," makeup artist (credited as "monster maker") Rick Baker explains in the making of. A few moments later, Jackson repeats: "You put this thing on and you slowly metamorphosize into this whole other person." How to create "the perfect illusion" is certainly not what young Ana Lily Amirpour, child of Iranian immigrants, born 1980 in the UK, took away from watching the documentary "thousands of times." Her films do, however, speak the language of American pop culture, of citation, pastiche, a fascination for the weird, of intermediality. What the filmmaker-to-be seemed to have learned from it is the very meaning of US pop culture—the space it occupies in US society and in people's lives, the transformational power it contains, and the ways in which fiction and reality are so often intertwined. And, after all, that its products *can be* for everybody—as the scenes of fan crowds consisting of mainly black and latino/latina teenagers cheering Michael Jackson from afar suggest (MTV 1983).

In her two feature films, *A Girl Walks Home Alone at Night* (2014) and *The Bad Batch* (2016), Amirpour consequently rearranges classic American genres as the Western and the gothic movie, and she does it in a weirded fashion. Building upon long-established and postmodern imagery alike, she creates new meaning by resignifying and hybridizing those proto-American traditions. How does the weird in her work correlate with her stance of becoming American through watching the *Making of Michael Jackson's Thriller* documentary? This chapter takes Amirpour's self-placement as a starting point to discuss her understanding of Americanness which is—as argued here—fundamentally tied to the weird in her to-date two full-length movies. Characterizing her first movie as an "Iranian vampire spaghetti western" and setting her second film in an outdoor prison across the Texas desert inhabited by followers of a grotesque cult, Amirpour creates the western landscape as a "thematic space" (Bal 2009: 139) that acts through resignification and hybridization of long-established US-American imagery. In this chapter, I argue that both films make use of the weird as a basic principle of Amirpour's vision of America.

The weird in Amirpour's films takes (at least) two different shapes: It creates an aesthetic surface of a creative interplay of filmic citations, allusions, and symbols that are weird by means of hybridization and *verfremdung*. Here, she plays the keys of postmodern cinema coming from the position of her own Iranian Americana. Although formally, Mark Fisher's definition of the weird as "the conjoining of two or more things which do not belong together" (2016: 22) might serve as a straightforward way to approach her work, Amirpour's positionality already blurs the boundary to the second way in which the weird acts in her films—it operates as a strategy of decolonialization of pop culture. In *A Girl* it does so as a creator of a visually complex symbolic matrix of a hyphenated Americana that is readable only for Persian speakers and, therefore, reallocates the agency of audiences. This strategy continues in *The Bad Batch* in form of a weirding of the white Christian founding myth. Amirpour's visual storytelling not only deconstructs the loaded imagery of the chosen people in a wasteland (or the American gothic), but takes it further toward a Postcolonial Weird that creates its own myth of an Americana of misfit agency and culture.

In *A Girl*, the auteur realizes the American Weird as such a basic American principle in her *imaginative geography* (see Said 1978: 46–63) of Bad City as well as in the figure of a female vampire who wears a chador instead of the prototypical cape and who kills abject male characters. While the weird functions here as a definitional feature of a thematic space that draws on Iranian-America and the American idea of Iran alike, in *The Bad Batch* it is based on a proto-American western wasteland reconceptualized as place of expatriation.

Through her visual play with these iconic images of pop mythology, Amirpour follows a strategy of "symbolic resistance"[1] that exposes the character of the mainstream American self-image as fundamentally weird. This chapter aims at identifying those strategies, which emanate from Said's concept of *imaginative geographies* but work here not as ideological instruments of domination but as performatively powerful tools in subverting that very proto-American imagery.

First, this chapter highlights Amirpour's strategies as a weirding of Iranian-America through a close reading of *Bad City*, the *thematic space* in *A Girl*. As an "acting place rather than a place of action" (Bal 2009: 139), it structures the interplay of plot and characters as a kind of matrix. I elucidate how the frequently mentioned noir-like aesthetics of the film misleads a non-Persian-speaking audience over what Amirpour is subverting with her imagery, by pinpointing parody of Iranian diaspora, its nostalgia for the prerevolutionary era of the second Pahlavi Shah Mohammad Reza, and motifs of Khomeinism alike. In inscribing a semantic level of Iranianness in the landscape that escapes the English subtitles of the Persian dialogue, Amirpour challenges the interpretative authority of Western audiences and reallocates the cultural agency of her imaginative geographies.

Furthermore, the same matrix of a weird American landscape, a network of archetype-characters, and a religious imagery are employed in *The Bad Batch*. Amirpour uses the weird hereby in various ways: it is a substantial part of the film's thematic space whose grotesque imagery is inspired by motifs of Puritan Eschatology. As a strategy of symbolic resistance, it is also present in the figure of Arlen who embodies the ultimate blonde amazon fighting her way through the wasteland—similar to the Girl, both functioning as anthropological as well as mythological demons. As metaphors for the human world (what Thacker describes as the anthropological side of demons), the characters work as female avengers of womanhood or an oppressed people (Thacker 2011: 26–31). On a semiotic/mythological level, they are signifiers whose relations to their signified systems—to America and the image of the Islamic Republic in the West—become deconstructed. Ultimately, I will show how both films make use of the weird as a continuum, an evolving category that builds upon existing traditions of white Puritan imagery and the American gothic moving toward a weird of postcolonial cultural production and agency.

Background of *A Girl Walks Home Alone at Night*

Amirpour developed *A Girl Walks Home Alone at Night* based on a short film by the same name, which won the award for best short at the Noor Iranian Film

Festival in Los Angeles in 2012. The seven-minute feature stars actress Nazanin Boniadi as the vampire girl and Marshall Manesh as "The Man" who is following her. Both of them were already well-known actors at the time and had guest roles and supporting roles in the sitcom *How I Met Your Mother* (Boniadi as Ted Mosby's love interest Nora and Manesh as "Ranjit" the taxi driver). For the movie, however, Amirpour decided to cast Sheila Vand as "The Girl." They had worked together before on Amirpour's short *Pashmaloo [Hairy]* (2011) in which Vand plays Farah, an Iranian-American woman coming back to Iran where she climbs up a hill outside Tehran with her friend Nilou and lectures her about why she should remove her facial hair. In *Pashmaloo*, Amirpour already developed certain elements of irony that refer to the Iranian-American diaspora in California, most famously Westwood, Los Angeles, where a huge number of (mainly but not exclusively) monarchist exiles settled down after the Revolution of 1979 (nicknamed Tehrangeles for that reason). Amirpour's casting practice contributes significantly to the weirdness of her characters. She preferably casts actresses and actors in roles that somehow run contrarily to their established images or previous roles (as Manesh, who—especially during the running time of *HIMYM* from 2005 until 2014—was famous for his funny performance as Ranjit or as Jim Carry in a—however central—textless supporting role in *The Bad Batch*).

After she won the award for best short film, Amirpour was able to secure a budget for her first full-length feature through crowdfunding. *Vice Film* and *Kino Lorber* joined the project later. The shooting took place in Bakersfield, California, which Amirpour and her team transformed into Bad City:

> Once we'd decided we would make Bad City, we made everything [ourselves]. We made the street signs, we made the newspaper, we made the currency, we made the money, the posters on the wall, the commercials in the TV. It was very much like Frank Miller's *Sin City*, a complete full-blown graphic world. (The Vilcek Foundation 2014)

The Weird and the Eerie in the Landscape of Bad City

Bad City, at a first glance, is an eerie place. The black-and-white aesthetics of the film have been compared to Iranian New Wave or Italian Neorealism (St. Art Magazine 2017)—an association that can easily come to mind considering the long shots of the few characters in front of rundown buildings and ancient oil pumps. The whole scenery of the city seems dilapidated: apart from the characters, there are no people on the streets; the oil pumps and a huge illuminated refinery seem to run on their own. This is, as Mark Fisher notes, a characteristic of the eerie as "we find it more readily in landscapes partially emptied of the human" (Fisher 2016: 11). The origins of this wasteland—the reason for the transformation of the City into "Bad" City—remain unknown to the viewer. The eerie is, in Fisher's words, "fundamentally tied up with questions of agency. What kind of agent is acting here? Is there an agent at all?" (Fisher 2016: 11).

While we might think of human (or even demonic) agency that remains undisclosed, Fisher also points to the eerily absent forces of capitalism, "conjured out of nothing, capital nevertheless exerts more influence than any allegedly substantial entity" (Fisher 2016: 11). What will be suggested here, however, is a more specific reading of "a system" running Bad City and the metaphorical use of the eerie later on.

Amirpour herself characterizes *A Girl* as an "Iranian Vampire Spaghetti Western" (Vice 2014). Consequently, the very basic definition of the weird by Fisher of "what does not belong" is here as concise as his observation that "[t]he form that is perhaps most appropriate to the weird is montage—the conjoining of two or more things which do not belong together" (Fisher 2016: 22). This montage of an Iranian-Vampire-Spaghetti-Western already signals how Amirpour's play is actively weirding each of those genres.

Apart from this formally visible montage, there are semantic layers of Iranianness inscribed into the matrix of landscape and characters whose weirdness are only comprehensible to Persian speakers: all things connected to language are Persian in Bad City—the traffic signs, the graffiti, the characters speak Persian—but with a heavy American accent at times. All female characters are veiled when outside—apart from the Girl—in the usual urban Iranian fashion, wearing a pulled-back headscarf. The corpse pit surrounding the city is probably the most obvious link to the Islamic Republic, a reference to the political mass murders of the 1980s. Amirpour herself, however, always denied that she created Bad City is a metaphor for the Islamic Republic. "It's an Iranian fairytale. It's an Iranian Story with Iranian characters," she told *The New Republic* (Breger 2014). However, asked for a possible connection of shooting location in Bakersfield and the dialogue in Farsi, she answered: "A film is a place of the mind. So, I just see this as my soundstage where I'm putting my play on. I'm modeling it after a lawless, nameless ghost town from like, a Sergio Leone western. Or *Rumblefish*, which is also a stylized American town, or Gotham or Sin City" (Breger 2014). Bad City is an interstitial imaginary space. Its landscape itself is a montage of eerie, monstrous, machinic elements, and suburban neighborhoods, looking like a materialization of an Edward Hopper painting (for a further discussion of the aesthetics of the landscape, see subchapter "Decoding the Eerie"). During a traveling shot in the beginning of the film, one of the rare scenes shot by daylight, Persian-speaking audiences can read the term "naft-e aziz" ("dear oil"), on the doorplate of the refinery—an ironic allusion to either/both Iranian and US politics. The reallocation of cultural agency—first and foremost through Iranian metaphors—that Amirpour hides behind the often-mentioned stylishness of the eerie will be discussed in more length in the section "Decoding the Eerie."

Parody and Weirdness of the Characters in *A Girl*

Apart from the Girl, all characters are archetypes, mere placeholder figures, which fulfill a function in a metaphorical network. This does not mean that they are not compelling characters, on the contrary. Amirpour is also not very subtle about this conception—the characters have their roles attributed to their names: there are Hossein "The Junkie," Atti "The Prostitute," Saeed "The Pimp," and Shayda "The Princess." Arash—the Girl's pretty love interest—does not have such an attribute. He is a James Dean lookalike who, coming from a costume party, is dressed up as Dracula when he and the Girl meet for the first time. He is the son of Hossein "The Junkie," and, before meeting the Girl, works to pay for his father's addiction, fostered by Saeed "The Pimp." Arash seems lost and alone, an exception from the other male characters. The placeholder names all relate to the setting in a certain way: Hossein is the name of the highest Shi'ite martyr and son-in-law of the prophet Mohammad, Imam Hossein. Therefore, Hossein is a very common name in Iran. Also prevalent and well documented is heroin consumption and addiction in Iranian society, making the compound of "Hossein 'The Junkie'" all the more an element of irony while the character itself provokes merely abjection. The figure of Saeed "The Pimp" fits as much into the realm of diaspora as into certain Iranian milieus. He is the parody of a Tehrangeles yob, living in a kitsch-ed apartment, where he listens to badly produced dance music. His body is inscribed with a number of Persian scripture tattoos and a Faravahar, the symbol for the Zoroastrian God Ahura Mazda, often used and displayed in the diaspora as a means of ancient-Iranian (and sometimes anti-Islamic) identification. On his neck, right above the Faravahar on his chest, he sports the word "sex" tattooed into his skin. Interestingly, the word "sex" is the only writing that occurs in Latin scripture, also among the street graffities across Bad City—we could read this as a comment on how sexuality as desire is unspeakable in official Iranian discourse.

In his final scene, Hossein "The Junkie" drugs Atti "The Prostitute" against her will and makes her dance for him to a well-known melancholic tune of Dariush, a prerevolutionary superstar—a scene reminiscent of 1950s and 1960s Tehran's so-called Kafe-Cabareh bars. The female dancers and singers in these establishments were often accused of being high-paid prostitutes, regardless of their art.[2] On point in this scene is also Amirpour's choice of music. Dariush's "Cheshm-e man" ("My Eyes") is a ballad full of longing and nostalgia. First published in 1973, it is still immensely popular since it captures the pain over the lost homeland among exile communities in a very emotional manner. As argued elsewhere, the sheer irony of this highly stylized scene is only comprehensible to audiences who can read the metaphoric fabric of it: "Amirpour deconstructs notions of diasporic nostalgia by using this iconic tune to be danced to by a beautiful woman in back light, for a man by the name of the highest Shi'i martyr. However, the dancing beauty is a prostitute and the man with the holy name is a junkie" (Aras 2018: 298). This scene is in fact one of only two scenes in the film in which Amirpour's camera adopts a male gaze—a perspective that will be undercut by the events that follow (Goodwin 2016). The Girl comes to Atti's rescue, and kills and feeds on Hossein. Atti confides in the Girl afterward, telling her she only wanted to make quick money in order to leave Bad City forever but forgot where to go along the way. Ironically, Atti is short for the name Atieh, meaning "future" in Persian. The motif of leaving, and of exile, is ubiquitous in contemporary Iranian culture since the 1979 revolution (as it was to a smaller extent already under the Pahlavi regime before). The best-known example for that motif is probably Asghar Farhadi's film *A Separation* (2011) in which the plot enfolds around the initial wish of the female protagonist to leave the country.

The Fascination of the Weird: The Girl

"The first thing really was the chador. I had one . . . and I put it on and I felt like a creature. I felt like a bat or a stingray, and I just instantly saw that this was an Iranian vampire" (Breger 2014), Amirpour recalls her initial inspiration for the film. It is the metaphor of the female vampire in her chador that ultimately carries the weird essence of the movie.

To unpack this metaphor, it is helpful to read the Girl's character and her relation to Bad City through the lens of Thacker's conception of demons.

According to him, the anthropological demon is a metaphor for the human world, a way of thinking about a human in relation to a group, and the mythological demon refers to a reaching outside the human sphere (Thacker 2011: 26–31). The anthropological side of the Girl's twofold nature works on the metaphorical level of the film—in the vampire girl, Amirpour condenses what it takes to go about one's life as a woman in a world inherently hostile to women, a system that is designed to govern and control the female body. The Girl is the average female between "the Prostitute" and "the Princess," who becomes an avenger of womanhood. On a semiotic level, however, she is what Thacker calls a mythological demon, an allegorical link that connects the human with the nonhuman sphere. Although Mark Fisher disavows the vampire to provoke any sensation of weirdness due to a "generic recognizability" and a "pre-existing set of protocols for interpreting and placing the vampire" (Fisher 2016: 15), the creature of the Girl seems unknown and weird to the other inhabitants of Bad City. "Are you religious or something?" Atti asks her, referring to her chador. The Girl denies and Attie asks, "So *what* are you?" (emphasis added). The Girl, therefore, transgresses religious biopolitics, which also claim the veiled female body as "their" symbol. The nature of the Girl, however, is captured most graphically in the sequence when she is skateboarding over a lit street in the night, the chador floating around her body, giving it an almost sensual look-and-feel (Aras 2018: 298). I argue that by creating this new kind of vampire image, Amirpour plays with the major signifier of the Islamic Republic in the West—the veiled female body. Reclaiming this Orientalist image, she deconstructs the relation between signifier and signified. In resignifiying and hybridizing the symbol of the Girl in her chador, Amirpour employs a strategy of symbolic resistance that, very playfully, creates something weird, something new. "A veiled body can mean anything." (Aras 2018: 298).

Decoding the Eerie

The stylish eeriness of Bad City not only dreads its inhabitants and fascinates audiences and critics but also (almost) covers up the symbols and allusions of agency in the landscape. "What kind of agent is acting here? Is there an agent at all?" (Fisher 2016: 11).

Throughout Bad City, there are signs scattered which allude to an uncanny system behind it all: election posters with the term "ra'is" (Persian for "leader," "head of"), graffiti of the word "vahshat" ("horror"), the corpse pit surrounding

Bad City, the oil pumps which seem to run on their own, and so on. Amirpour has created Bad City as a thematic space, as an "object of presentation itself, for its own sake," as Bal puts it. "Space thus becomes an acting place rather than a place of action" (2009: 139). While these allusions either add to the eerie stylishness of the film's black-and-white look for non-Persian-speaking audiences, or go unnoticed, they create meaning and a certain background story for Persian speakers. Where they can sense or read the signs of a political regime and an order that is designed to control the public space, agency is not only signaled through those signs but is also reallocated to audiences who are actually able to make sense of the film's symbolical matrix. Ideological Shiism is not directly mentioned, but the allusions to an order that kills people, leaves a town in decay and tries to control the female body are part of the acting place.

Ultimately, Amirpour takes up the schizophrenia of the public/private realm split of the Islamic Republic. The pop culturally branded teen-like bedroom of the Girl is a private (thematic) space, a safe haven of its own. It is littered with posters and fan merchandise that seem to come from the 1980s and 1990s but, looking closely, in some cases turn out to be references to the Iranian indie bands that make up a large part of *A Girl*'s soundtrack.

The Symbolical Matrix of *The Bad Batch*

The Bad Batch is a straightforward vision of America, having been described as "postapocalyptic" or "dystopian." In many interviews, Amirpour stated that it was actually a depiction of how she sees the United States today (Karpan 2017). She shapes a barren outlaw wasteland inhabited by cannibal bodybuilders and followers of a grotesque cult across the Texas desert. Here, convicts are deported to, after receiving a number tattoo behind the ear. After the fence gate, there is a notice board, which reads in English and Spanish:

WARNING

BEYOND THIS FENCE IS NO LONGER THE TERRITORY OF TEXAS. THAT HEREAFTER NO PERSON WITHIN THE TERRITORY BEYOND THIS FENCE IS A RESIDENT OF THE UNITED STATES OF AMERICA OR SHALL BE ACKNOWLEDGED, RECOGNIZED OR GOVERNED BY THE LAWS AND GOVERNING BODIES THEREIN. GOOD LUCK.

As in *A Girl*, the characters in *The Bad Batch* are symbolic figures. We follow Amirpour's outcast antiheroine Arlen (played by former fashion model Suki Waterhouse) who, equipped with a hamburger, has to make her way through the desert prison. We watch her in terror, losing two limbs to the cannibal bodybuilders. Their leader is called Miami Man—an illegal Cuban immigrant who wears nothing but white pinstriped tango pants. She is able to escape, transporting her mutilated body on a skateboard. She loses consciousness and is saved by "The Hermit," a bag person roaming the desert with his packed shopping cart. Played by an almost unrecognizable Jim Carrey, his character is an outcast among the outcasts, at the same time a weird wise man who does not speak.

Arlen then arrives at Comfort, a makeshift settlement ruled by a grotesque cult guru named "The Dream," played by Keanu Reeves, who throws occasional parties with free drugs for his followers. Somehow, she has managed to obtain an ancient prosthetic leg and starts to settle in. She is almost wooed to join The Dream's harem-like bodyguard squad of pregnant women but escapes once more. Trying to survive in the desert, Arlen encounters a black woman with her child at a garbage dump and recognizes her as one of the cannibals. She shoots the woman. The little girl, seemingly aware of her non-existing chance of survival on her own, joins Arlen and follows her back to Comfort. Later, the child ends up in The Dream's palace, and in an alliance of emergency, Arlen and Miami Man together search for his daughter. A love story against all odds begins.

The symbolic figure of Arlen could be interpreted as yet another "avenging angel figure wielding a gun, fighting a righteous war," as Dan O'Hara analyzes this American millennialist imagery of apocalyptic Hollywood films in his chapter of this volume (O'Hara, 21). And indeed, Amirpour condenses many characteristics of millennialist imagery in her main figure: The depiction of how Arlen's body is mutilated by the cannibal bodybuilders follows a tradition of apocalyptic comedies in American fiction, a "logic of humor-in-horror of the mutated, displaced, tainted, broken, deformed, or 'different' body" (25), as O'Hara points out. "It is an excision of the taint the earliest Puritans feared they had brought with them to America from Europe—the deformity of the body, being via maternal impression the outward sign of spiritual corruption " (25).

However, building upon this established imagery, Amirpour, as in *A Girl*, also breaks with the traditions she is alluding to. There is no "righteous war" to fight for her "avenging angel." When Arlen takes up a gun, she kills, however hesitantly, out of dirty revenge. She also stays partially disabled, only equipped with a prosthetic leg and forced to deal with the flawed beauty of her maimed torso, as a scene in which she tries to replace her missing arm visually in a mirror suggests.

From a Heap of Biblical Imagery: World-Building in *The Bad Batch*

As in her first film, Amirpour employs an approach of strong visual storytelling that relies mainly on what she calls "world-building"—a to-detail furnishing of the setting as well as of the characters (Tiffany 2017). The thematic spaces of the outdoor prison and the settlement of Comfort seem to blur the lines between fiction and reality: the village of the cannibal bodybuilders is filmed at an airplane junkyard in Lancaster, the Californian desert. "I had this idea that there would be weird, leftover parts of America from the '80s and '90s, just left to waste" (Tiffany 2017), she explains in an interview. The filmset for Comfort is built around a cast-off community in Salton Sea, in the Californian desert as well: "There's 10,000 to 20,000 people living off the grid. They just live there, in the desert, outside of the system.... It's weird, you get to build this world, and it's amplified surreal shit, but it's the real DNA of stuff that's here" (Tiffany 2017).

While the weird in *A Girl* was partly accompanied by (or hidden behind) the eerie, in her second film Amirpour makes use of the weird, the grotesque and the absurd as a means to present, simply speaking, a dog-eat-dog world. First, she furnishes the sheer brutality of the cannibal bodybuilders in a 1980s, 1990s trashy fashion (with the according soundtrack by *Ace of Base*). Second, she builds a slum village led by a playboy-guru—a grotesque metaphor for an ideology of the chosen people, here embodied by The Dream messiah, who preaches a lazar-like community. These characters Amirpour puts in the midst of a biblical desert.

For the scene of a drug party in the desert out of Comfort, she hired the people who live in Salton Sea to play the party crowd. Keanu Reeves is standing on a massive neon-lit boom box that also serves as booth for DJ Jimmy. Surrounded by his pregnant bodyguards, The Dream gives following speech, cheered by the party crowd:

> Lemme tell you something about Jimmy. You know why Jimmy's here? He's Bad Batch. Non-functioning member of society, that's what they told me.
> That's right—all of us here. We weren't good enough, smart enough, young enough, healthy enough, wealthy enough, sane enough...
>
> Freaks.
> Parasites.
> This here is the bad batch.
> We ain't good.
> We're bad.

In this absurd, meaningless populism, Amirpour forebodes Trump's "we-against-them" rhetoric (she wrote the film script during 2013 and 2014). While the fence and the text of the warning billboard that separate the desert prison from the rest of the country already allude to "the wall" discourse of Trump's anti-immigration policy, the metaphor of the community of outcasts reaches into the past of white American history. In Amirpour's portrayal, The Dream shapes the prison inmates into his flock of the chosen people—a fundamentally weird version of "the errand into the wilderness," historicized as the fulfillment of the Old Testament by preachers of the New England Puritans (Lowance Jr. 1980: 128).

Although cast in different lights, there is a common ground of Amirpour's two films, a "world-building" of thematic spaces/acting places based on religious ideologies that share the same origin of eschatological fundamentalism. In the case of Bad City, there is obviously a hidden system at work which "runs" things—the killings, the machines, the oil refinery, women's veils, the election posters. In *The Bad Batch*, there is a grotesquely weird representation of a "New Jerusalem" in a biblical desert—a playboy messiah who drugs his people—a weird American Pastoral.

The archaeologist and cultural theorist Jan Assmann identifies a shared origin of language of violence in Christianity and Islam. In his short book *Totale Religion—Ursprung und Formen puritanischer Verschärfung*, he argues that this language of violence against former neighbors, now marked as "unbelievers"—and ultimately ideas of apocalypticism—derive from a "monotheism of exclusive loyalty" that is founded in the Book of Deuteronomy (2016: 128–31). According to Assmann, Deuteronomy has been quoted in order to legitimize forced divorces of interreligious marriages in early Judaism and therefore, enforce the law of one specific God as state law (2016: 128–31).

In Amirpour's work, the eerie and the grotesque are used to mask religious ideologies from which her protagonists try to escape. In the case of *A Girl*, it is Khomeini's version of Shiism that is created to establish the rule of the twelfth Imam al-Mahdi on earth. It is meant to govern almost all aspects of human life, especially that of women. In the case of *The Bad Batch*, we encounter a populist, absurd form of Evangelical Puritanism.

Within Iranian Studies, the merging of populist rhetoric and apocalyptic symbolism sounds all too familiar. The parallels to the Islamic Revolution of 1979 are obvious here, as Khomeini not only played on—for Iranian Shiism—an invented tradition of political Islam and the creation of the righteous rule of al-Mahdi in the present, but also based his religious movement within the revolution on the notion of "the oppressed" (*mostaz'afin*)—a term that spread after Fanon's *The Wretched of the Earth* was translated into Persian with this exact term (*mostaz'afin-e zamin*) (Abrahamian 1993: 47).

In the end of both films, the weird also functions as a tool of human connection against these ideologies: together the Girl and Arash leave Bad City and the mutilated amazon Arlen and Miami Man share a kind of ritual meal with Miami Man's child and thus form a new family in the midst of the desert. In Amirpour's words: "Any kind of (human) connection feels like a relief in life" (Tiffany 2017). Through her weird play of symbolic resistance, Amirpour creates a New American Weird from a heap of images that were broken to begin with, toward a Postcolonial Weird.

Conclusion: Toward a Postcolonial Weird

This contribution discussed the ambiguous nature of the American Weird in terms of its problematic historical roots as well as in its capacity to be used as a creative category as Ana Lily Amirpour represents it in her films. The weird is, as argued, already present in white Evangelical Millennialism, in the doctrine of the settlers as the chosen people who were to establish a New Jerusalem in the "New World." Amirpour uses the imagery of the American Pastoral to create the settlement of Comfort in the midst of an outdoor prison in her second feature, *The Bad Batch*. By means of the grotesque, she exposes the weird character of the white Christian founding myth. In the same film, she takes up the weird as a powerful tool of symbolic resistance to create a love story between a mutilated white-trash amazon and an illegal Cuban cannibal bodybuilder, a romance against all odds. The same strategies are at work in *A Girl Walks Home Alone at Night*. Here, Amirpour wraps notions of ideological Shiism and Iranian diasporic nostalgia in the eerie black-and-white thematic space of Bad City. As analyzed in this chapter, the weird is also employed in its creative capacity, as a strategy of symbolic resistance, weirding genre-related motifs as the vampire, the avenger in the name of the oppressed and the black chador as a Western symbol for Islamic Iran toward new meaning. Thus, Amirpour transforms ur-American imagery and its postmodern shapes into art that has the potential to redefine the status quo of today's Americana. When used in this fashion, the weird cannot only be a category but a strategy of postcolonial cultural production and agency.

Notes

1 Brosseau discusses the potential of "symbolic resistance" as an expression of Said's "imaginative geographies" cultural agency against hegemony (Brosseau 2017: 13–14).
2 Or, rather, for a misconception of their art as morally dubious. See Meftahi (2016) and Breyley and Fatemi (2015).

References

Abrahmian, E. (1993), *Khomeinism: Essays on the Islamic Republic*, Berkeley and Los Angeles: University of California Press.
A Girl Walks Home Alone at Night (2014), [Film], Dir. Ana Lily Amirpour, USA: Vice/Lorber.
Aras, M. (2018), "Vampires, Veils and the Western Gaze—Gender Images and the Notion of Beauty from Qajar to Postrevolutionary Iran," in M. Whiskin and D. Bagot (eds.), *Iran and the West: Cultural Perceptions from the Sasanian Empire to the Islamic Republic*, 286–304, London: I.B. Tauris.
Assmann, J. (2016), *Totale Religion: Ursprung und Formen puritanischer Verschärfung*, Wien: Picus.
Bal, M. (2009), *Narratology: Introduction to the Theory of Narrative*, Toronto: University of Toronto Press.
Breger, E. (2014), "We Like Vampires Because We Hate Death," *The New Republic*, 24 November. Available online: https://newrepublic.com/article/120376/interview-ana-lily-amirpour-director-iranian-vampire-movie (accessed February 25, 2019).
Breyley, G. J., and S. Fatemi, (2015), *Iranian Music and Popular Entertainment: From Motrebi to Losanjelesi and Beyond*, London and New York: Routledge.
Brosseau, M. (2017), "In, Of, Out, With and Through: New Perspectives in Literary Geography," in R. Tally Jr. (ed.), *The Routledge Handbook of Literature and Space*, 9–27, London and New York: Routledge.
Fisher, M. (2016), *The Weird and the Eerie*, London: Repeater Books.
Goodwin, M. (2016), "When the Vampire Looks: Gender and Surveillance in A Girl Walks Home Alone at Night," *Mizan: Journal for the Study of Muslim Societies and Civilizations*, 18 April. Available online: https://mizanproject.org/pop-post/when-the-vampire-looks (accessed February 20, 2019).
Karpan, A. (2017), "The Bad Batch Is How I See America," *Film School Rejects*, 25 June. Available online: https://filmschoolrejects.com/ana-lily-amirpour-interview-the-bad-batch/ (accessed February 20, 2019).
Lowance Jr., M. I. (1980), *The Language of Canaan: Metaphor and Symbol in New England from the Puritans to the Transcendentalists*, Cambridge: Harvard UP.

Making Michael Jackson's Thriller (1983), [TV documentary] MTV, 2 December.

Meftahi, I. (2016), *Gender and Dance in Modern Iran: Biopolitics on Stage*, London and New York: Routledge.

Rizov, V. (2014), "Ana Lily Amirpour," *Filmmaker Magazine*, 17 July. Available online: https://filmmakermagazine.com/people/ana-lily-amirpour/#.XGwWLOhKg2w (accessed February 19, 2019).

Said, E. (1978), *Orientalism*, New York: Pantheon.

St. Art Mag. (2017), "A Girl Walks Home Alone at Night: Contesting Cultural Expectations," *St. Art Magazine*, 6 October. Available online: https://www.st-artmagazine.com/film/2017/10/6/a-girl-walks-home-alone-at-night-contesting-cultural-expectations (accessed February 21, 2019).

Thacker, E. (2011), *In the Dust of This Planet (Horror of Philosophy Vol. 1)*, London: Zero Books.

The Bad Batch (2016), [Film], Dir. Ana Lily Amirpour, USA: Vice/Annapurna.

The Vilcek Found. (2014), "Interview with Ana Lily Amirpour, Director of A Girl Walks Home Alone at Night," *YouTube*, 6 November. Available online: https://www.youtube.com/watch?v=CtDim5P__Uo (accessed February 20, 2019).

Tiffany, K. (2017), "Ana Lily Amirpour on Romance in the Desert and the Racial Controversy over her New Film, The Bad Batch," *The Verge*, 23 July. Available online: https://theverge.com/2017/6/23/15855842/the-bad-batch-interview-ana-lily-amirpour-dystopia (accessed February 20, 2019).

Vice Films. (2014), "A Girl Walks Home Alone at Night," *Vice*, n.d. Available online: https://films.vice.com/a-girl-walks-home/ (accessed February 25, 2019).

11

"It Is in Our House Now"

Twin Peaks, Nostalgia, and David Lynch's Weird Spaces

Oliver Moisich and Markus Wierschem

Ever since *Eraserhead* (1977), the work of David Lynch has sounded an influential note in American Weird Fiction, combining Americana, comedy, and surrealist horror. The dark highways of the artist's imagination often lead to unlikely spaces of "otherness" where reality warps, time stutters and loops, and space becomes bendable. More often than not, Lynch's weird spaces constitute interpretive enigmas, offering profound challenges to characters and viewers alike. At the same time, these spaces shape and reflect the way in which we experience film and television.

The original ABC show *Twin Peaks* (1990–91), created by Lynch and Mark Frost, combined diverse genres such as mystery, crime procedural, and soap opera, and helped spawn well-known TV shows of the 1990s and 2000s with a similar formula. Detailing the FBI investigation into the murder of a high school girl in an idyllic small town in Washington, the show became a veritable pop phenomenon centered around the question "Who killed Laura Palmer?" A dedicated audience and fourteen Emmy nominations notwithstanding, ABC allotted the show's second season a Saturday-night graveyard time slot, resulting in subsequent cancellation, according to at least one executive because it was deemed "too weird for the US" (Woods 2000: 110). Yet in 2017—in a decade which saw a large number of 1980s and 1990s TV shows return to the screen as revivals, reboots, or continuations of earlier seasons—*Twin Peaks* returned with a third season. Fundamentally different in tone and structure in comparison to its preceding two seasons, *Twin Peaks: The Return* (hereafter *TP:R*) presents its audience with a narrative that seems deliberately designed to frustrate the serial-viewing experience germane to ordinary TV shows.

In this chapter, we argue that Lynch's and Frost's efforts to obstruct serial narrative gratification results in a metacommentary on popular contemporary revival TV shows. Consciously drawing on Lynch's earlier work, the weird spaces in *Twin Peaks: The Return* unravel storyworld logic. Through heterotopias (Foucault) and spatiotemporally disordered *chronotopes* (Bakhtin), Lynch and Frost create fictitious places and spaces that narratively uncreate themselves. These spaces achieve an inherently weird and eerie foundation through dialogue, visual language, and anachronistic temporality. Focusing on the original *Twin Peaks*, the first part of this chapter explores Lynch's "weird spaces" in the context of chronotopic and heterotopic conceptualization. On this basis, the second part will then investigate the TV show *Twin Peaks: The Return* and its reception by viewers and fans as a weird space of nostalgia television.

"Weirdsville, USA": A General Look at Lynchian Spaces

"It's a strange world, isn't it?" Characterizing David Lynch's cinematic cosmos, one could adopt worse a motto than the quizzical musing that frames his crime mystery *Blue Velvet* (1986) like its blooming red roses, white picket fences, and blue skies, or the figurative rabbit hole of the human ear into which the camera descends. Strange and disjointed through their reputation, the general sights and locales of Lynch's worlds, by today, are rather well established. Suggesting a unified auteurial topography or road map to a cinematic cosmos that may be called "Lynchtown" (Chion 2006) or "Weirdsville, USA" (Woods 2000), the ontology that underlies the "strange worlds" of David Lynch encompasses complex relations of time and space, setting and place, agents and objects, that challenge the order of both real-world experience and cinematic storytelling conventions. Approaching them on an analytic level thus calls for a heuristic that, firstly, can harmonize considerations of narrative and setting—in Mikhail Bakthin's terms, its particular *chronotope(s)* or "time-spaces"—with the dream logic of Lynch's more localized nonplaces and other spaces, in Michel Foucault's terms, its *heterotopias*. Secondly, dealing with a cult auteur such as Lynch, these complex relations extend beyond the diegetic worlds of his films to cultural and sociohistorical contexts that inspire them, as well as to the audiences that watch and in turn relate to these strange worlds.

On a macro-level, Lynch's films bear out looking at what Bakhtin calls the narrative's predominant *chronotope*. Premising time as the fourth dimension of space, chronotopes designate "organizing centers for the fundamental narrative events . . . where the knots of narrative are tied and untied," and Bakhtin characterizes them as a particular "density and concreteness of time markers—the time of human life, of historical time—that occurs within well-delineated spatial areas" (1981: 250). As R. Barton Palmer suggests (2004: 56–7), the chronotope applies to the order of setting rather than place—to Victorian London rather than the Royal Hospital, or early 1990s Twin Peaks rather than the Great Northern Hotel or the Packard Sawmill. As a tool, it is "designed to account for the particular movement of narrative in both of its senses—that is, in terms of story and storytelling time—within a given fictional genre, showing how a characteristic form of setting becomes its reflex" (Palmer 2004: 58). Going beyond "the text itself," the chronotope can function as "an optic for reading texts as x-rays of the forces at work in the culture system from which they spring" (Bakhtin 1981: 425), allowing for insight into and representation of human relations unfolding within a given narrative space, the ideology, cultural and personal values, or auteurial visions that inform it. Accordingly, Bakhtin dubs the chronotope of Greek and chivalric romance "adventure time," while Vivian Sobchack, characterizing the time-space of film noir as one of postwar insecurity and crisis, designates it as "Lounge Time" (1998: 129).

What would be an appropriate name for the Lynchian chronotope? Exceptions like *The Elephant Man*'s (1980) Victorian London or the science fiction and desert vistas of *Dune* (1984) notwithstanding, Lynch's vision draws primarily on the historical and cultural capital of Americana: *Blue Velvet*'s suburban Lumberton with its flowerbeds and picket fences, the amber cornfields lining the country roads of *The Straight Story* (1999), or the desert highways beneath blue skies of *Wild at Heart* (1990). On the other hand, there is the American metropolis—from the industrial nightmare of *Eraserhead* that reflected Lynch's negative experience as an art student in Philadelphia, and the metaleptic and meta-cinematic dream narratives of present-day Los Angeles and Hollywood as presented in *Lost Highway* (1997), *Mulholland Drive* (2001), and *Inland Empire* (2006).

Whether rural or urban, surreal or hyperreal, Lynch's settings provide the backdrop to places that appear out of this world. In his lecture "Des Espace Autres," Michel Foucault speaks of two types of places that stand in reflective, inverse, or even contradictory relation to the ordinary places in which our lives unfold. First, there are the unreal spaces of *Utopia*, which stand in a relation of analogy to the societies that dream them up. Secondly, Foucault envisions

> something like counter-sites, a kind of effectively enacted utopia in which the real sites, all the other real sites that can be found within the culture, are

simultaneously represented, contested, and inverted. Places of this kind are outside of all places, even though it may be possible to indicate their location in reality. Because these places are absolutely different from all the sites that they reflect and speak about, I shall call them, by way of contrast to utopias, heterotopias. (1967: 24)

Presented in the same year as then art student David Lynch's first short film *Six Figures Getting Sick* (1967), Foucault formulated the principles of his provisional heterotopology with real places in mind, yet in many ways they elucidate the nature of Lynch's weirder locales. Foucault characterizes heterotopias as places of either crisis or deviation (e.g., prisons and mental asylums), which "have a function in relation to all the space that remains" (27; for example, illusion, compensation), yet may assume different functions at different points in history. Thus, the nightmarish industrial ruins and unhomely homes in *Eraserhead* are primarily connected through protagonist Henry Spencer's battered psyche to that strange planet house in which the disfigured "Man in the Planet" works his levers and broken machines, yet the stage within the radiator in Henry's flat provides a utopian space of comfort in the arms of the "Lady in the Radiator." Conversely, *Mulholland Drive*'s Club Silencio is the place from which Betty's oneiric wish-fulfillment fantasy and dream version of Hollywood dissolves to give way to her nightmarish reality. These examples indicate that heterotopoi may juxtapose otherwise incompatible real places, as do the theater and cinema (cf. 25). Linking to Bakhtin, these spaces usually "open onto . . . heterochronies" which reflect a break with "normal" time, while relying on "a system of opening and closing" (26) that isolates them while also rendering them permeable to human entry. This calls to mind the *Lost Highway* motel which exists at a warped, time-looping turning point of the Moebius-wound narrative of Fred Madison's personal purgatory. More pertinently, it applies to an infamous, otherworldly Lynchian space, which opens once every twenty-five years: *Twin Peaks*' Black Lodge. Focusing on the original iteration of the show, the next section investigates the Black Lodge as heterotopia; yet, before doing so, we shall situate it within the chronotope of Twin Peaks.

"Welcome to Twin Peaks," or Lodge Time Reconsidered

Though set in ostensibly "real" places across America—Lynchian weird space tends to resist representation of its internal cohesion as a set of coordinates, vectors, and relations. More fluid than stable, space appears to "move *around* the heroes" (Seeßlen 1994: 36); its order is not simply geographical and hence largely impossible to reconstruct on a map.[1] The "cinematic mediation" of this space "involves non-places [*Un-Orte*] between the seams which obfuscate the relationship of its singular elements" (Pabst 1999: 13).[2] In this regard, the town of Twin Peaks presents one notable exception. "We had drawn a map of the city. We knew where everything was located and that helped us determine the prevailing atmosphere and what might happen there" (Lynch cit. in Chion 2006: 98–9). Lynch and Frost drafted a web of streets and locales—from the Sheriff's Department, the Great Northern Hotel, and the Packard Sawmill, to Big Ed's Gas Farm, the Double-R Diner, and the Roadhouse, to cemetery and general store, to the homes of the Johnsons, Packards, Hornes, Haywards, and Palmers, and thus the blueprint for a "believable" microcosm in Washington's mountainous regions. More than its layout and geography, the show treated its viewers to a sense of a living, breathing *place*, drawn from the rich cultural soil of Americana: Twin Peaks was a predominantly white, yet "all-American," small town with a population of 51,209, where life followed its own, leisurely pace set by a slow-moving opening montage and Angelo Badalamenti's music. Here, the local diner sported Norman Rockwell aesthetics along with delicious cherry pie and "damn good coffee." As Cooper declares in a moment to his cynical FBI colleague Albert: "Life has meaning here. Every life. And that's a way of living I thought had vanished from this earth. It hasn't, Albert. It's right here in Twin Peaks" (S1E03).

Yet like *Blue Velvet*'s Lumberton, from the show's opening moments, the *locus amoenus* is haunted by the presence of evil, which washes up on the lakeshore in the shape of Laura Palmer's "beautiful," plastic-wrapped corpse. Through the investigation of FBI agent Dale Cooper, a "combination private-eye and (cult)ural ethnographer" (Lavery 1995: 13), Twin Peaks thus revealed itself as suggestive of America and a place in its history and mythology:

> a promised land where the American Dream is ever possible, and hopelessly infected by disease. The smalltown cleanliness, the freshness of youth, the wide open spaces of the northwestern frontier belie the corruption and crime that seem possible everywhere and at every moment. (Kaleta 1993: 136–7)

Though spreading infectiously to human hosts, the evil gradually revealed by the show is less "human" than "other." This other, Pabst argues, is mostly associated with a space beyond human control, or its prime marker: *architecture*. The architectural border marks "the place, where what has been separated is in contact . . . relates to its parts . . . which only unfold their respective meanings in the context of this relation" (Pabst 1999: 11). Hence, the central dichotomy at play is that between the existence of an "outside" and "beyond" that inevitably exerts its controlling influence upon the "inside" and stands in opposition to it. In Lynch's films as well as *Twin Peaks: The Return*, this "beyond" comes as a formless, undifferentiated black (or white) void associated with the "*Über-Raum*" (24) of outer space. In seasons one and two, it is predominantly the forest which serves as the frontier where "darkness and architecture . . . flow into one another" and architecture loses "its ordering potential, and every opening in its fixed structures is like the portal to another world" (25–6). As Sheriff Truman reveals to Agent Cooper: "There's a sort of evil out there. Something very, very strange in these old woods. And we've always been here to fight it" (S1E03).

Located in the portentously named Glastonbury Grove within Twin Peaks' Ghostwoods, a circle of sycamore trees marks the entrance into the Lynchian space and heterotopia par excellence—the "Black Lodge" of Deputy Hawk's ancestral Nez Perce mythology. Ironically, this "most distant and strangest of all places is not located beyond some sequence of elaborate barriers at some remote corner of the world, but simply behind a red curtain that opens with the ease of a simple hand movement" (Pabst 1999: 19). The lodge itself is a surreal, wholly other place of power. It is home to a number of the "spirits" living off of "garmonbozia" (pain and sorrow), such as the dancing "Man from Another Place," Mike, and the murderous BOB—and potentially a number of doppelgängers.[3] Inside its spare rooms and labyrinthine corridors of black-and-white zigzag patterned floors, the objects are arranged in ways that seem "less guided by any idea of use [*Idee des Gebrauchs*] than the inherent law of the objects [*Gesetze der Objekte*] themselves" (14). Time yields to heterochrony, is slowed down, halted, or reversed. Hence, the motion picture *Fire Walk With Me* constitutes "not so much a prequel as a 'time warped sequel,'" in which "events from the story's end intrude on its beginning; for example, Annie Blackburne appears to Laura from the future to inform her that 'The good Dale is in the lodge, and he can't leave. Write it in your diary'" (Lavery 1995: 11).

A more immediate example of these warping effects is the way speech "functions" in the Lodge—an uncanny effect achieved by all utterances being spoken and recorded phonetically backward and then played in reverse, with the same technique applying to movement and video recording (cf. Rodley 2005: 166–7). The entire phenomenology of the Black Lodge thus shows, more literally than expected, Foucault's notion that heterotopias fundamentally undermine language, because they make it impossible to name this and that, . . . because they destroy "syntax" in advance, and not only the syntax with which we construct sentences but also that less apparent syntax which causes words and things (next to and also opposite one another) to "hold together." [H]eterotopias . . . desiccate speech, stop words in their tracks, contest the very possibility of grammar at its source. (1994: xix)

At the same time, the curtains of the lodge evoke Lynch's other stages—themselves heterotopoi that mediate between reality and illusion, disclose the wondrous, and present the astonishing, but also spaces within which narrative inscribes action. Going with the uncanny iconicity and narrative centrality of the Black Lodge, it is thus tempting to call the Lynchian chronotope "Lodge Time."[4] As with the "outside" of architecture, the surreal horror of the show would have no place were it not for Lynch's and Frost's skillful manipulation of TV tropes and conventions, "sometimes humorous, other times nostalgic" (Kaleta 1993: 147). At the level of reception, the weirdness is of a distinct quality otherwise associated with the weird fiction of Franz Kafka:

[W]hat is characteristic of Twin Peaks is not that everyone is mad, but that those who are not mad do not find the eccentric characters eccentric; the Log lady is at home among these ordinary Eds and Donnas. Twin Peaks presents a non-psychological world. . . . It is the structure of Twin Peaks which is mad. (Chion 2006: 105)

Similarly, it is before the more grounded chronotope which defines its "artistic unity" of Twin Peaks "in relationship to an actual reality" (Bakhtin 1981: 243) that the weird can fully emerge, the interplay making for a show unlike any other. Following Umberto Eco's discussion of "Cult Movies and Intertextual Collage," David Lavery posits:

The success of any series . . . has always been dependent on whether or not the viewer will "invite" its characters or personalities . . . back into their living rooms. . . . In the cult TV experience something more happens . . . altering the personal culture of those individual viewers, already members of a "culture of instinctive semioticians" ready to seek, indeed anxious to seek, membership in a new *systeme*. . . . If one of the functions of a traditional genre is to build cultural consensus, The Cult serves to build cult consensus in a singular interpretive community, a community committed to difference. (1995: 4)

Lavery rightly identifies *Twin Peaks* as a fully realized and fleshed-out world, fit for fans to immerse themselves in. The internet still in its infancy, fandom nevertheless found fertile soil in the show's wealth of quotable lines ("Damn good coffee!") and quirky gestures like Cooper's "thumbs up," engaging in "Peakspeak," trading plot synopses, family trees, and theories about Laura's murderer, or the importing of Cooper's dreams, hosting conventions, and publishing a number of fanzines (cf. Lavery 1995: 7). The marketing of book tie-ins such as tourist guides, *The Secret Diary of Laura Palmer* (1990), and *The Autobiography of FBI Special Agent Dale Cooper* (1991) further fleshed out the secondary world and provided more fodder for those hungering for more *Twin Peaks*—a trend that continues to this day.

What is more pertinent to our purposes, however, is how all this reflects upon the show's chronotope. In this respect, the recent publications of *The Secret History of Twin Peaks* (2016) and *The Final Dossier* (2017), both penned by Mark Frost, are particularly suggestive. The *Secret History* situates Twin Peaks within the core of American national mythology—interweaving its legendary origins with those of historical figures like Merriweather Lewis or Chief Joseph of the Nez Perce, as well as a number of US presidents. Thus, the dossier retroactively prefigures some of the show's temporal anomalies, as those episodes that have Ben Horne, in a bout of temporary psychosis, mistake himself for Robert E. Lee and reenact the battles of the Civil War, or those that temporally misplace Major Briggs, who reemerges in a historical aviator's uniform that may be straight out of the First World War (cf. Chion 2006: 106).

By contrast, *The Final Dossier* provides some answers to questions lingering after the show's long hiatus and its new iteration ("Did Audrey survive the bank explosion?" or "How's Annie?"), yet also tackles the nation's more recent history in conjunction with the fates of its characters: 9/11 and the Iraq War, the blight of privately-run for-profit prisons, and "the rising forces of corporatism, the corruption of wealth inequality, and the corrosive effects of . . . 'cannibal capitalism' on the human mind, body, and spirit" (Frost 2017: 84) are featured in files dedicated to Benjamin Horne and Dr. Jacoby, who, to many viewers' delights, the new season presents a progressive version of internet pundit and conspiracy theorist Alex Jones. If, as Woods asserts, viewers of the original show could "recognise a little of their own lives and values in the show, whatever kind of absurdist mirror they had been reflected through" (2000: 111),[5] the same remains true in 2017's *Twin Peaks: The Return*. The narrative voice of Agent Preston may shy from applying the concept of the Black Lodge's "Dweller on the Threshold"—"the sum total of all the dark, negative, unresolved qualities that reside in every human being"—to "the fate of nations" (Frost 2017: 111). Yet Frost himself is certainly apprehensive about the possibility of America's shadow-self having emerged like Cooper's doppelgänger from the Black Lodge.[6]

Ultimately, it matters little whether we are engaging in the apocrypha of fan fiction or the canonical texts from the show's authors. In either case, to paraphrase Bakhtin, the show and the world it represents have become part of the real world, with the real world vice versa entering the world of Twin Peaks in an ongoing process of creative change and renewal, more than twenty-five years after its inception. "Of course, this process of exchange is itself chronotopic.... We might even speak of a special *creative* chronotope inside which this exchange between work and life occurs, and which constitutes the distinctive life of the work" (Bakhtin 1981: 254). As Chion rightly observes, "Lynch's worlds tend to fuse, oscillating dangerously from one to the other, each preying parasitically on the other.... The worlds overlap, interpenetrate and merge... they grind against and crush each other on two parallel planes" (2006: 148). Such possibilities are par for the course within the chronotope. However, the degree to which the world and the secondary world created by Lynch and Frost entangle, merge, and overlap along a temporal resonance yet heard and resounding two decades after the fact, however, surely constitutes a unique artistic characteristic of "Lodge Time."

Fan Reception and the Weird Space of Nostalgia

The chronotopes and heterotopias of Lynch's films find their creative culmination in *Twin Peaks: The Return*, the third season of a TV show that had been on hiatus for more than twenty-five years. The original *Twin Peaks* received critical and public acclaim in the early 1990s and prompted viewers to take part in a discussion about each week's episode and its secrets, both around the watercooler at work and in online forums. If *Twin Peaks: The Return* aimed at similar reactions in 2016, then the first two seasons' resounding success would have posed a great problem. After *Twin Peaks*, a variety of mystery shows aired on US television, all complete with their season-wide story arches (a narrative practice that was previously virtually absent in television) and long-running mystery puzzles. As influential as *Twin Peaks* had been to other mystery shows such as *The X-Files* or *Lost*, TV audiences and their viewing behaviors have changed since the 1990s. Fans binge-watch entire shows at home or on the go instead of having to wait for a prime time slot at some cable broadcaster. At the same time, fans treat their favorite show's season-wide mysteries like detective work, divulge every little detail to sizable, organized communities on the internet, and more often than not reveal pivotal twists in the narrative before shows have a chance to reveal these twists themselves. At the same time, revival TV shows have seen a resurgence of old shows from the 1980s and 1990s. Shows such as *Roseanne* (1988–97; 2018), *The X-Files* (1993–2002; 2016–18), and *Full House* (1987–95; revival *Fuller House* 2016–2020) seem to find an audience that looks back on the original shows with some degree of nostalgia.

Twin Peaks: The Return takes a different approach. Lynch and Frost created a revival show that is implicitly critical of the idea of a revival. While the *Twin Peaks* fandom revels in series staples, *The Return* actively undermines any nostalgic gratification and thus obfuscates its own cult following. The result is a critical examination of nostalgia as heterotopia in an age where chronotopes of Western pop and TV culture are invested in that same sensibility; a space removed from reality, an (to speak with Foucault) inverted utopia of a once real place. Nostalgia becomes a weird space of discourse for fans that find the continuation of beloved narratives, settings, and characters, either lacking or having lost the qualities that made them so appreciated within the viewer community in the first place. In this particular instance, Lynch removes any positive qualities that nostalgic indulgence might have had and exposes it as a place that does not exist, and might have never existed. *Twin Peaks: The Return* realizes this weird space through a wide-ranging number of stylistic and narrative choices, which recall two discussions—first, Svetlana Boym's study of Nostalgia in *The Future of Nostalgia* (2001), and second, Mark Fisher's collection of essays in *The Weird and the Eerie* (2016). The following analysis will present these two concepts and how they apply to narrative and themes in *Twin Peaks: The Return*.

"Is It Future, or Is It Past?" Nostalgia in *Twin Peaks: The Return*

Boym describes *nostalgia* as "a longing for a home that no longer exists or has never existed" (2001: xiii). She derives her definition in part by the word's etymology—*nostos*, to return home, and *-algia*, a longing, or pain and suffering. As such, Boym says, nostalgia can only ever exist if such a home is displaced or removed from the patient that suffers from nostalgia. It is also a feeling that is fundamentally paradoxical; if one were to reconcile the thing that we long for (e.g., the past) with the thing that we are currently in possession of (e.g., the present), the two would cancel each other out. It is quite easy to see how this particular notion of nostalgia transfers to fandom: The fondness for certain books, films, and TV shows that we consumed at earlier stages of our life might survive longer than clear memories of the books, films, and TV shows themselves. Instead of the piece of fiction itself, we cherish the memories associated with it. Boym goes on to differentiate between two kinds of nostalgia. *Restorative nostalgia* focuses on *nostos*, that is to say, the drive to rebuild and return to a state of the world as it once was. Fittingly, Boym identifies this category as the nostalgia of nationalists—myths and symbols as well as the rejection of the now in favor of the yesterday. By contrast, *reflective nostalgia* focuses on *-algia*, a creative encounter with feeling nostalgic that "lingers on ruins, the patina of time and history, in the dreams of another place and another time" (41).

While many revival shows indulge in restorative nostalgia, *Twin Peaks: The Return* (hereafter *TP:R*) transforms nostalgia for the show's previous two seasons into something more reflective. As for examples of restorative nostalgia, one needs look no further than successful movies and TV shows of recent memory; shows such as *Stranger Things* (ongoing since 2016) or the recent remakes of Stephen King's *It* (2017; 2019) revel in 1980s and early 1990s aesthetics, memorabilia, and music. In *TP:R*, none of these elements have any lasting presence. Characters that were beloved staples of the first two seasons, such as protagonist Dale Cooper, or his almost-love interest Audrey Horne, have either radically changed personalities or reduced screen time. Audrey, who was among the major character roster in earlier seasons, does not appear in *TP:R* until episode 12 (out of 18). The few scenes with her mostly revolve around arguments that she is having at home with her husband, a new character to the show. Episode 16 finally sees Audrey in a different setting, the Roadhouse bar in Twin Peaks, in which she performs her signature dance from season one, episode two. Only here the dance is violently interrupted when a bar fight breaks out and Audrey rushes to her husband to "get me out of here," upon which she finds herself in another place, wearing a hospital gown and staring into a mirror. *TP:R* leaves viewers with that image; it never explicitly reveals Audrey's fate.

Even more puzzling and frustrating to viewers' expectations for nostalgic gratification is Dale Cooper's narrative arc. In S03E03, we see Cooper return from the Black Lodge after a twenty-five-year imprisonment. His evil doppelgänger (who has much more screen time than the actual Cooper) created a trap for him that locks Cooper's mind in another doppelgänger named Dougie Jones. The real Cooper, protagonist of the *Twin Peaks* S01 and S02, appears for only brief scenes in S03's first three episodes and in S03E16 and 17. In Cooper's stead, actor Kyle MacLachlan plays two doppelgängers throughout much of

TP:R, a stark reminder of the season's ungratifying treatment of nostalgia, which defers its most beloved character's full return to the proverbial last minute. As Marcin Cichocki points out in one of the earliest, serious discussions of the show's treatment of nostalgia, "the irrevocability of the past" (Boym 2001: 49) is precisely what *TP:R* is about. In other words, the show

> is ironic about the idea of restoring. . . . Agent Cooper cannot fully return because the moment he is back in Twin Peaks, he is compelled to save Laura only to realise he cannot do so. *Twin Peaks The Return* cannot restore the original *Twin Peaks* and instead reflects on the idea of wanting to go back but it being impossible to go back. (Cichocki 2017)

What is more, after Cooper's return, the show does not take long to transform him into yet another character named Richard, who looks and dresses like Cooper, but is in fact the opposite of Coop's jolly and amicable demeanor. Like its first iteration, *TP:R* contains numerous other changes of personality and *doppelgängers*. One of the main plot points even involves the creation of so-called tulpas, the manifestation of paranormal beings (a concept that theosophists imported from Tibetan Buddhism), that is, of hollow copies; in this sense, a vacuous "revival" of past personae. Other aesthetic and narrative choices in *TP:R* drive home the point that nostalgia for earlier seasons all but focuses on the *-algia*, the pain and longing for the past. Music from previous seasons is often absent—if not, it is recontextualized in scenes such as Audrey's dance, or a faint reminder that this show is indeed still *Twin Peaks* (the original opening theme, for example). Toward the end of the season, Cooper travels back in time to prevent Laura's murder. This deed prompts a radical change in narrative in the last episode, in which both Kyle MacLachlan and Sheryl Lee portray entirely different characters, in a strangely empty and, to them, confusing world. Cooper drives Laura to her old home in Twin Peaks, only to find that Laura's family apparently never lived there. Baffled, Cooper wonders "What year is this?"—a lingering question that closes off the season. In this final scene, Frost and Lynch epitomize their approach toward nostalgia. As Boym suggested, the longing for things past are irreconcilable with the reality of the present. Restorative nostalgia's focus on "returning home" results in a place that should not be, a crooked version of what once was a home, a weird space of nostalgia. Mike, one of the Black Lodge inhabitants, asks Cooper, "Is it future or is it past?" in two almost identical scenes in S03E02 and S03E17. In the end, Cooper, who is driven to save young Laura from murder, is unable to answer this question. He is trapped in the weird space of nostalgia.

"It Is in Our House Now": The Weird and the Eerie in *Twin Peaks: The Return*

These observations bring us to what actually makes nostalgia a *weird* space in *TP:R*. Mark Fisher reiterated that *the weird* is "the thing that should not be" or, in his own words, "that which does not belong" (2016: 10). In addition, he identifies *the eerie* as either a failure of presence or a failure of absence, something that should be there when it is not or something that should not be there when it is (12). *Twin Peak*'s first two seasons were mainly occupied with *the weird*: Occurrences and characters do not belong, in the sense that they are not what we expect from a small US town, from the Black Lodge and all of its inhabitants to something as innocuous as the town's borderline doctrinal devotion to coffee and pie. These weird phenomena crept into the fabric of what *Twin Peaks* means to its fans; over the years, fandom adopted even the show's weirdest quirks and they are now canon to the discourse. *TP:R*, however, introduces new weird elements into this canon—for instance, a league of supernatural homeless people or a British man with superhuman powers that come from a rubber glove which he cannot remove from his hand—but the season also operates in a fundamentally eerie mode.

Cooper, while inside Dougie's tulpa body, spends the majority of *TP:R*'s runtime in a zombie-like state. Dougie reduces famous Cooper one-liners from previous seasons ("Damn good" pie and coffee) to mere acts of parroting other characters' remarks, the only means of conversation that Cooper is capable of while trapped inside Dougie. The two most prominent instances are in S03E05 and S03E11, when other characters remark upon the quality of both ("Damn good joe, huh, Dougie?"—"Damn good joe." and "This pie is so damn good."—"Damn good."). Not only does the show strip the former FBI agent of any agency, it also fails to present anything that viewers might find satisfactorily nostalgic. The Dale Cooper of the past is still here, but he fails to restore his own former personality and quirks. And when he finally does, the majority of the season is already over—again, the show rejects nostalgic gratification.

Another scene pertains to Fisher's other type of the eerie, a failure of absence. In S3E14, FBI agent Gordon Cole, Cooper's former superior (played by David Lynch himself), tells of a dream that he had in which he met with Monica Bellucci (incidentally played by herself) at a café in Paris. Cole says that she told him the "ancient phrase"—Bellucci: "We're like the dreamer, who dreams and then lives inside the dream. . . . But who is the dreamer?" While Cooper-as-Dougie lacks any real agency, the Monica Bellucci dream implies a breaking of the fourth wall. The dreamer, who dreams the world of *Twin Peaks* and lives inside this world, is an agent upon their reality, the manifestation of some omnipotent figure: a failure of absence. Fisher observes that "the eerie is fundamentally tied up with questions of agency. What kind of agent is acting here? Is there an agent at all?" (2016: 11) *TP:R* draws from questions of agency in both directions. Beyond the weird, the show also elicits a sense of a ruinous landscape. The Twin Peaks that once was is no more; it is as a waning dream, and its population slowly realizes that they are merely fictions.

Fisher derives the weird and the eerie from Freud's concept *unheimlich*, "unhomely" or outside of home, "which operates by always processing the outside through the gaps and impasses of the inside. The weird and the eerie make the opposite move: they allow us to see the inside from the perspective of the outside" (10). It is from the *unheimlich* (also known as "uncanny") perspective that Carel Struycken's character "The Fireman" says one of *TP:R*'s very first lines: "It is in our house now" (S03E01). Whatever "it" is on a narrative level, it also represents the new forcing itself upon the old, the intrusion of "unheimlich" into the home that nostalgia inhabits. *TP:R* makes an effort to destroy this home with the eerie, the outside that forces itself in, much like Laura's home is "destroyed" in the final scene of the show.[7] By extension, the show rejects current revival shows' trends to return to a home that (Boym's words) once existed—or might not have existed in the first place. The latter reading of nostalgia makes it an eerie occurrence—a failure of absence—and creates in turn a weird space of fan reception. The heterotopia that is fandom does not belong here; a suppression of nostalgic gratification should not elicit a nostalgic response, yet it does exist.

"A Wonderful Masochism": Heterotopia and Nostalgia in *Twin Peaks* Fandom

Having established that *TP:R* elicits a sense of reflective nostalgia throughout its narrative and that it achieves this sense by using the weird and the eerie as narrative modes, it remains to be seen how exactly viewers react to that narrative in order to come to any conclusion as to how *Twin Peaks* fan discourse is a weird space. Luckily, online discussions survive for both the old and the new seasons, and they offer some striking similarities. While 2010s online communities provide a rich variety of forums, the 1990s were more restricted when it came to the number of online services and number of users. Henry Jenkins provided an overview of the Usenet group alt.tv.twinpeaks only a few years after the show's second season ended (1995). Joel Bocko lists a few more standout comments on his blog *Lost in the Movies* (2014). Recent discussions about *TP:R* are archived and are available via the links provided in the following.

The favorite topic of *Twin Peaks* fans seems to be trying to unravel its many mysteries. Viewers gather to discuss and attempt to make sense of it together. Based on the latest episode, they form theories as to what might happen next and what the key is to understand the entire story. On October 10, 1990, a user named Jan D. Wolter posts on alt.twinpeaks.tv:

> Well, you folks had me half convinced with the Laura is Maddie theory and the Leland is the killer theory. But to my thinking, this episode scotches both. Maddie tells us "Everybody thinks I'm Laura. But I'm not. I'm a different person altogether." Within the story there seems no more reason to believe her than there was before, but from the outside it sounds like the writers are eliminating that option. And with Leland guilty of Jacques' murder, I don't buy him as Laura's killer as well. I just can't believe that with so many fine potential villains running around, all the murders are going to be foisted off on Leland. (cit. in: Bocko 2014)

Compare this post to one made twenty-seven years later, on the r/twinpeaks subreddit on September 4, 2017:

> My take: Cooper went back in time to save Laura. Judy sensed this and sucked Laura into an alternate/fake universe. Coop entered the other world with Diane's help. Coop met up with Laura and was able to wake her from the dream world. Notice the owners of the house were named Tremond and Chalfont, both names of the spirit woman Laura served meals on wheels to. Also, the diner where Laura works is named "Judy." When Laura realizes who she is she screams, the dream world shuts off, and all the lights go out. (drwrzd 2017)

Both users posted their opinions less than a day after the latest episode aired, S02E03 and S03E18. Both users theorize about minute details in the episode, such as character's lines, or minor characters' names, and their possible hidden meaning. Ironically enough, user Jan D. Wolter rejects the possibility of a twist that turns out be true after all a few episodes later. It is striking that both users treat the show as a code that needs decoding; there is no explicit appreciation for themes, narrative, acting, lighting, editing, and so on. While those kinds of posts surely exist, the majority of users indulged an overwhelming number of theories and conspiracies—a tendency that *TP:R* gladly encouraged by creating an unsuspecting website (thesearchforthezone.com) that turned out to be a secret *Twin Peaks*–related website. Chronotopic by nature of the dialog between the show and each user's embeddedness in a shared, real-world context, these forums are likewise heterotopias as Foucault laid them out:

1. Heterotopia of crisis: the search (longing) for meaning and truth;
2. Different functions throughout history, linked to slices in time: forums are at their most active while the show was still on the air and right after the end of the latest episode;
3. At once permeable and isolated: free for all to post, but impenetrable to casual viewers;
4. A function in relation to the space that remains: preservation and conservation of discourse.

Committed to the shared experience of "Lodge Time," *TP:R*'s fan reception in particular is also fundamentally weird as per Fisher's definition. The willful lack of nostalgic gratification and, in turn, the intrusion of the outside into the home of nostalgia should disappoint fans of the show's characters and narrative. Instead, fans come together and puzzle over what it all means. This final observation points toward viewers' appreciation of the new, of the *unheimlich*. Restorative instances of nostalgia may be a short-term remedy for the past, but it is reflective nostalgia that furthers understanding of both the past and the present. One alt.twinpeaks.tv user writes:

> I love what Lynch is doing to me as a viewer. It's a kind of a wonderful masochism. Part of me wishes the answer could never be revealed. . . . I am so hoping that when what is really going on in Twin Peaks is fully and completely revealed, perhaps at the end of one more season after this, that it will be so shocking and unexpected that it will turn our faces white as a sheet and then the series will end. (Quoted from Jenkins 1995: 63)

This particular fan had his wish fulfilled over two decades later. The shocking ending to *TP:R* does the opposite of revealing a mystery; it reestablishes mystery and recreates a sense of wonder and strangeness. And yet, with the woman who opens the door to what *should* be the Palmer residence being played by the actual owner of the Washington house, there is the troubling suggestion that the chronotopes of show and reality have collapsed into one another and that Cooper/Richard and Laura/Carrie Page have somehow wound up in "the real world" of America, ca. 2018: the void of reality, where hatred, violence, and rapacity are still all-too real, yet the stranger in the car that follows along has nothing to do with oneself, and all magic and meaning must yield to the crushing weight of cosmic indifference. The mystery may be that there is no mystery. Seen so, the show may paradoxically have offered up something infinitely more terrifying than its narrative proper could: a scream and the lights go out. It is not the end of the story, but the end of storytelling as such.

The weird space—appreciating intrusions of the strange transformation of nostalgia into something new—empowers fans to be reflective of their own engagement with *Twin Peaks*: "The sense of wrongness associated with the weird—the conviction that this does not belong—is often a sign that we are in the presence of the new. The weird here is a signal that the concepts and frameworks which we have previously employed are now obsolete" (Fisher 2016: 13). Ultimately, fans of *Twin Peaks* establish their enjoyment upon this weird space. Anything else would retread the familiar territory that we expect from nostalgic revival TV shows. In the end, *Twin Peak*'s protagonist FBI agent Dale Cooper embodies this transformative experience: "I have no idea where this will lead us. But I have a definite feeling it will be a place both wonderful and strange" (S02E18).

Notes

1. This and all following translations of texts originally published in German are the authors'.
2. Examples include the nightmarish joy rides and road trips of Lynch's characters, as in *Blue Velvet, Wild at Heart*, or *Lost Highway*, with their lingering shots of barely illuminated darkened roads and highways, of nonplaces in between more concrete locales. Insofar as one general distinction between "place" and "space" comes down to the former having been ascribed a definitive meaning through human practice, and the latter as devoid of, or as Foucault might say not yet desanctified *by* such meaning, Lynch's films arguably challenge that distinction by accessing locales that simultaneously suggest a wealth of meaning and frustrate attempts at definitive interpretation.
3. There is of course Cooper's doppelgänger—who may or may not be himself a partial host of BOB's—but also the "Man from another Place," a.k.a. "The Arm," who in *TP:R* has turned into a strange, organ-headed tree. This sculpture finds its precursor in one of the central room installations of Lynch's exhibition *Dark Splendor* (2007), standing in the barely lit entrance to a dark living room with red-and-black floors, yellow-spotted blue walls and zebra-patterned black-and-white armchairs that give off the impression of looking at 2-D surfaces that are actually three dimensional.
4. The alternative "Crazy Clown Time," suggested by Lynch's musical forays, comparatively seems less on point.

5 The mirror, as noted by Foucault, is likewise "a placeless place" that is at once "absolutely real and absolutely unreal" (1967: 24), opening to an "unreal, virtual space that opens up behind the surface; I am over there, there where I am not, a sort of shadow that gives my own visibility to myself, that enables me to see myself there where I am absent: such is the utopia of the mirror. But it is also a heterotopia in so far as the mirror does exist in reality, where it exerts a sort of counteraction on the position that I occupy" (24). Lynch's literal mirrors function much the same, such as when Leland Palmer and Cooper's doppelgänger behold themselves in the mirror, revealing the absence of self and the presence of the evil spirit BOB.

6 So, when minor female character Lana Budding Milford is mentioned as briefly dating "a notorious resident of a certain eponymous tower on Fifth Avenue," New York, and that same man is then spotted "wearing an unusual green ring" (Frost 2017: 77)—a marker of the corruption of the Black Lodge—the portentous weight of contemporary American political realities is palpable. No wonder, then, that *The Return* largely constitutes a darker chapter in the annals of the show.

7 As Schuster establishes in a related discussion, the "uncertain house" has long since functioned as a leitmotif for Lynch. Thus, in *Lost Highway*, the Mystery Man invades the Madison home and simultaneously one of Lynch's own actual houses—whereas paintings like *Here I am—Me as a House!* establish a connection of the home to personal identity. Evoking Freud's famous diagnosis of the Ego not being master in its own home, Schuster concludes: "For Lynch, the house is *the* metaphor for existential and social insecurity. Nowhere can you feel at home, not even at your own place. This is Lynch's most bitter truth" (2010: 128).

References

Bakhtin, M. (1981), *The Dialogic Imagination: Four Essays*, Austin: University of Texas Press.

Bocko, J. (2014), "Twin Peaks on the Internet . . . in 1990 (an alt.tv.twin-peaks archive)," *Lost in the Movies*, November 17. Available online: http://www.lostinthemovies.com/2014/11/twin-peaks-on-internetin-1990-alttvtwin.html (accessed February 12, 2019).

Boym, S. (2001), *The Future of Nostalgia*, New York: Basic Books.

Chion, M. (2006), *David Lynch*, London: British Film Institute.

Cichocki, M. (2017), "'That Gum You Like Is Going to Come Back in Style' Twin Peaks: The Return and Nostalgia," Lecture presented at UdS American Studies Graduate Forum, *Reading American TV Series: An Interdisciplinary Conference*, October 5–6.

drwrzd (2017), "[S3E17] & [S3E18] Post-Episodes Discussion - Parts 17 and 18," *Reddit .com/r/twinpeaks*, September 3. Available online: www.reddit.com/r/twinpeaks/

comments/6xxf7g/s3e17_s3e18_postepisodes_discussion_parts_17_and/dmj5sqk (accessed February 16, 2019).

Fisher, M. (2016), *The Weird and the Eerie*, London: Repeater Books.

Foucault, M. (1986 [1967]), "Of Other Spaces," trans. Jay Miskowiec, *Diacritics*, 16 (1) (Spring): 22–7.

Foucault, M. (1994), *The Order of Things: An Archeology of the Human Sciences*, London: Routledge.

Frost, M. (2016), *The Secret History of Twin Peaks*, New York: Flatiron Books.

Frost, M. (2017), *Twin Peaks: The Final Dossier*, London: Macmillan.

Frost, S. (1991), *The Autobiography of FBI Special Agent Dale Cooper: My Life, My Tapes*, London: Penguin.

Jenkins, H. (1995), "alt.tv.twinpeaks, the Trickster Author, and Viewer Mastery," in David Lavery (ed.), *Full of Secrets: Critical Approaches to Twin Peaks*, 51–69, Detroit: Wayne State UP.

Kaleta, K. (1993), *David Lynch*, New York: Twayne Publishers.

Lavery, D. (1995), "The Semiotics of Cobbler: *Twin Peaks*' Interpretive Community," in David Lavery (ed.), *Full of Secrets. Critical Approaches to Twin Peaks*, 1–21, Detroit: Wayne State University Press.

Lynch, J. (1990), *The Secret Diary of Laura Palmer*, New York: Simon & Schuster.

Pabst, E. (1999), "'He Will Look Where We Cannot.' Raum und Architektur in den Filmen David Lynchs," in Eckhard Pabst (ed.), *"A Strange World." Das Universum des David Lynch*, 11–30, Kiel: Verlag Ludwig.

Palmer, R. B. (2004), "Lounge Time Reconsidered: Spatial Discontinuity and Temporal Contingency in *Out of the Past*," in Alain Silver (ed.), *The Film Noir Reader*, vol. 4, 52–65, New Jersey: Limelight.

Rodley, C., ed. (2005), *Lynch on Lynch*, London: Faber and Faber.

Schuster, P.-K. (2010), "The Uncertain Houses: David Lynch in Hollywood," in W. Spies (ed.), *David Lynch – Dark Splendor: Raum Bilder Klang*, 109–32, Brühl: Max Ernst Museum Brühl.

Seeßlen, G. (1994), *David Lynch und seine Filme*, Marburg: Schüren.

Sobchack, V. (1998), "'Lounge Time': Post-War Crises and the Chronotope of Film Noir," in N. Browne (ed.), *Refiguring American Film Genres: History and Theory*, 129–70, Berkeley: U of California P.

Twin Peaks: The Entire Mystery (2016), [Blu-ray], Dir. David Lynch, USA: Universal.

Twin Peaks: A Limited Event Series, (2017), [Blu-ray], Dir. David Lynch, USA: Paramount.

Woods, P. (2000), *Weirdsville USA: The Obsessive Universe of David Lynch*, London: Plexus.

12

Demolishing the Blues

Captain Beefheart as Modernist Outsider

Paul Sheehan

In the annals of American popular culture, there are few artists as demanding, and as divisive, as Don Van Vliet—otherwise known as the doyen of dada-rock, Captain Beefheart. Although his time as a recording and performing artist was relatively brief—he effectively retired from the music business in 1982, at the age of just forty-one—the music that he made throughout his career casts a long shadow over the history of rock, and it persists today. I say "shadow" rather than "influence" because Beefheart's music is too refractory and unruly, too sui generis to allow any but the most dedicated of his followers to absorb it fully, in terms of sound or style. Although Beefheart's legacy is formidable, it is also, in a sense, forbidding, and forbiddingly off-putting, for musicians and fans alike. As the music critic Ian McDonald put it, in the late 1990s:

> The Moebius strip mind of Don Van Vliet, forever careering to and fro between far-horizon liberation and prickly paranoia, blew a peyote clarity through the blues substructure of rock from 1966 to 1972. Sadly, the *nagual* seeds he and his trickster sidemen scattered in the lumpy earth of the mainstream failed to sprout. (1999: 80)

Ironically, McDonald is making this claim at the very moment—indeed, the *only* moment—when it seemed as if Beefheart's "crooked cactus landscape" (*ibid*), as McDonald called it, might successfully be transposed to radically different climates. At this point, Tom Waits had already been mining a rich Beefheartian vein, with career-making returns, for about fifteen years, and his example had been followed by Beck, by P. J. Harvey, and by Tricky.[1] What all four sought to do, in their very different ways, was establish a mutant blues vernacular, taking their cues from the furrow that Beefheart had ploughed in his sixteen years as a recording artist. However, mutant blues was not the only marker of

Beefheart's legacy. In the late 1970s, the American band Pere Ubu refracted the spirit of Beefheart through the European avant-garde (as their name suggests), developing a kind of experimental primitivism that they dubbed "avant-garage"; and in the UK, the late Mark E. Smith, leader of The Fall, composed songs that wedded angular, post-Beefheartian rhythms to similarly dense and elusive wordplay.

To talk or write about Beefheart is, inevitably, to court contradiction. On the one hand, his body of work is notoriously alienating and rebarbative, seeming willfully to ignore the most basic rules of musical form. On the other hand, his songs continue deeply to affect, if that is the right word, generations of musicians. Just how "rebarbative" and "alienating" is his music? To ascertain this, we need look no further than the 100-second opening salvo of Beefheart's *Trout Mask Replica*, the 1969 (double) album that will be my case study for this chapter. Entitled "Frownland," the song features multiple, superimposed tonalities and polyrhythmic drum patterns, with musicians playing in different keys and at different tempi.[2] These unprecedented sonorities are fastened to a lyric that conjures up a homeland of the mind, freed from rapacious exploiters and predators ("Where black jagged shadows remind me of the coming of your doom"). Yet the song is also an environmentalist plea, filtered through a psychedelic lens—an appeal to see the world with new eyes, and to find within it a utopia of caring, creative individuals.

Not every song on *Trout Mask* is as jolting and discordant as "Frownland," but each of them does exhort us to suspend our disbelief and open our minds (and ears) to new horizons, to stretch ourselves as listeners. A key aspect of Beefheart's appeal, I suggest, is recognizing that beneath the abrasive surfaces, the off-kilter rhythms and jarring melody lines, there is in fact a kind of beauty, an aesthetic cogency, which is consequent upon Beefheart inviting us into his world (whether or not we accept that invitation is, of course, a matter of choice). "The Dust Blows Forward 'n' the Dust Blows Back," for example—an a-capella improvisation that follows the polytonal storm of "Frownland"—is sung by Beefheart as if he were "stitching a song from oral formulas and pausing at the breaks" (Ford 2008: 120). Greil Marcus may have located the "old, weird America" in the context of Bob Dylan and the Band, to give a kind of geo-imaginary backdrop to the songs and impromptus that became *The Basement Tapes*, but a significant part of Beefheart's oeuvre actually fits the term better. In this kind of song, like "The Dust Blows Forward," a pretechnological America is reinhabited, conveyed through keen observations that posit a simpler, more direct relationship with the natural world. In true dialectical fashion, however, an equally significant part of the Beefheart corpus sets its sights on the present, or near future, when the environment has been ravaged, and the Third World War is just around the corner. "Dachau Blues," in the most notorious instance, draws an oblique and wayward line from the atrocities committed in the Second World War to the barbarisms of Vietnam, thence to the horrors that await in the next global war ("They're counting out the devil with two fingers on their hands / Begging the Lord don't let the third one land").

What I am arguing, then, is that it is *the weird* in Beefheart music—be it the dreamy, old America or the nightmarish, new America—that underpins its aesthetic force. To further define this Beefheartian weird, let us take a brief detour through Russian formalist poetics. The spokesman for this credo, Viktor Shklovsky, made the famous claim that it is the mission of art to *make it strange*, to expand and complexify our perceptual faculties through linguistic figuration. As Shklovsky notes, in his *Theory of Prose*: "A crooked road, a road in which the foot feels acutely the stones beneath it, a road that turns back on itself—this is the road of art" (1990: 15). I contend that Beefheart's penchant for *making it weird* has some common ground with Shklovsky's dictum. The "crooked road" becomes Beefheart's "crooked cactus landscape"; the "stones beneath [the foot]" convoke the kind of earthy, elemental connection to the world of matter that Beefheart often solicits; and "a road that turns in on itself" implies a reflexive turn, a specular quality that is the very essence of the Beefheartian sound (a point to which I will return later).

Beefheart's *making weird* is therefore not so far removed from Shklovsky's *making strange*. And if there is a ground zero or first principle for his creative vision, then it is *weirding the blues*, turning the music of his youth, that most primal, but also plaintive and soulful, form of folk expression, inside out. In *The Weird and the Eerie* (2016: 10), Mark Fisher defines the weird as *things that don't belong together*—like, say, African American blues and European dada translated into primitivism-meets-jaded sophistication. Incongruity is thus central to the Beefheartian method: violent rhythmic changes, strange time signatures, and abstract sound textures. And then, cutting through the finely calibrated mayhem, there is Beefheart's voice. Once described as "cosmic vaudeville" (Edmonds 1970), it oscillates between a raspy, lower-register growl and a higher and hoarser bellow—the "dirty timbres," as Allan Moore puts it (2002: 1), of vocalic blues expression. These "weirding" tendencies mean *demolishing* the blues, but not in the sense of eradicating or even just traducing it as a musical form. It means, rather, bending it out of shape, harnessing its primal, tightly bound energies along more free-form and heterogeneous lines (hence the old adage that Beefheart "plays the blues as if it were jazz"). It is germane to ask, then, how is it that the blues form can lend itself to this kind of radical makeover?

The blues evolved from African chants and spirituals, which became secularized in America as work songs and field hollers. It both gave voice to, and made more bearable, the hardship and destitution that became the lot of black farmworkers and sharecroppers in the post-bellum American South (see Palmer 1982: 34–6). Listen to early recordings by Son House, by Lead Belly, by Charley Patton, and there is a spooky, otherworldly quality to them—a *haunted* quality, that inflects their tales of loss and regret, of misfortune and woe. "You can't play no blues," the Chicago bluesman Howlin' Wolf once declared, "unless you have some hard times" (Guralnick 2003: 164). This tenebrous mood or aura is toned down and eventually lost when the blues form develops further, first into the urban, electric blues dynamic of R & B (rhythm and blues) in the 1940s, and then into rock & roll in the 1950s. Beefheart is, therefore, restoring to the blues this quality of estrangement, but doing it in the most confrontational way possible, through jagged song structures and instrumental discord.

Furthermore, in the Delta blues tradition, which comes into its own in the 1920s and 1930s, there is an implosive energy, as if the performer were holding something back, keeping it in reserve.[3] A similar kind of tension is almost palpable in Beefheart music. The players possess considerable musical power, but they almost never get to unleash it fully; which is to say, nothing on *Trout Mask Replica* sounds like 1960s blues-rock. Even a song such as "Moonlight on Vermont," which leads with the drums and features some manic bottleneck-guitar lines (a Delta blues trope), is polyphonic, rather than monolithic; it seems almost to be finding its own form, sweeping each instrument along as it unfolds.

Just Another Freak: *Trout Mask Replica* and Outsider Art

For the nonexpert, one of the great mysteries is how this music could have come into being. What were the conditions that enabled Beefheart and his so-called Magic Band to break the formulaic imperatives of blues-driven rock so comprehensively—from the actual notes that they played, to the kind of baroque arrangements that gave each song its singular identity? This is more than just an idle or scholastic enquiry. To address this question is to get to the heart of *the weird*, and the limits of popular culture in accommodating—or at least tolerating—work that strays so far from mainstream acceptability. Over the years, a number of critics and music historians have grappled with the implications of this question, and more or less agreed on three key elements.

In the first place, Beefheart, although he was nominally a "musician," could not actually play any instrument. Despite this limitation, he bought an upright piano, and set about composing songs on it. What emerged from these attempts were, unsurprisingly, not "songs," as such, but fragments of what could, with the right musical know-how, be bound into coherent musical pieces. The fact that most of the tracks on *Trout Mask* are under three minutes long points to the second key element: Beefheart's frustratingly short attention span. Many of his musicians have observed that getting him to rehearse, or even just to elaborate on his compositional fragments, was nigh on impossible. So he needed dedicated sidemen to give life to his vivid, impressionistic, yet essentially one-off sonic textures; to shape them into something that could be performed more than once. And this brings us to the third and most crucial element, at least on a practical level: the kind of band that Beefheart assembled.

It has become a truism, in accounts of the Vietnam War, to say that you can make nineteen-year-olds—nineteen-year-old men, in particular—do anything. Teach them how to kill, send them into the jungle, subject them to various degrees of privation and terror, and they won't utter a word of protest. Beefheart somehow acquired a similar insight into the late-teenage mindset and turned it to his advantage. Just twenty-seven years old himself, when he began writing songs for the *Trout Mask* album, he traded on his aura of "seniority" and his imposing, charismatic personality and, one by one, replaced his original band members with nineteen-year-old players. These young men were not only highly skilled musicians, prepared to give everything for their (or rather, his) art, but also compliant, naive, and easily manipulable. And so for nine months, starting in the autumn of 1968, Beefheart staged his own "Vietnam War" in a house in Woodland Hills, about twenty miles outside the city of Los Angeles. Keeping his players under what was effectively house arrest, Beefheart gave them zany stage names, spiked their tea with acid, starved them, berated them (sometimes for days at a time), and paid them almost nothing, until they were sufficiently "broken down" to follow his demanding and unorthodox musical directives (see Barnes, 2000: 119–20). The drummer in the band during this period, John French, describes Beefheart's ruthless ability to "pull [sound] out of the players" (2010: 385), like a midwife or surgeon. Given, then, Beefheart's lack of musical training, his reluctance to rehearse, and his unorthodox behavior, a further question becomes paramount: Does his work qualify as Outsider Art? Further, what is gained or lost by thinking about *Trout Mask Replica* in this way?

Outsider Art, also known as *art brut*, refers to cultural artifacts that exist alongside of or in opposition to the conventional art world (see Maclagan 2009: 8). The "outsider arts," in the broader sense of the term, go by various names—naïve art, visionary art, spiritual or mediumistic art—but are brought together under the umbrella term of folk art. As for folk *music*, Marybeth Hamilton notes that it "was composed anonymously, transmitted orally, and suffused with the spirit of the peasantry" (Hamilton 2008: 94). The blues is, therefore, a genuine folk form; but in the absence of a traditional peasant class, the music emerges instead from a disenfranchised slave culture. And like other modes of folk expression the blues was, for much of the last century, seen as a "low" cultural form, a primitive outpouring of the African American underclass. This impression was reinforced by the fact that, as David Evans notes, the blues "thrived among hobos and hustlers in the underworld of gambling, moonshining, and prostitution, and among the people floating in and out of prisons" (2002: 20). With this kind of reputation, it is no surprise that the blues was treated as a form of Outsider Art, only able to flourish at a distance from the civilized precincts of modern-day America.

The music of Captain Beefheart has often been seen in the same light—despite Van Vliet's tireless insistence that it *not* be taken that way. As he said to a journalist, in 1970, he "didn't like the idea of being labeled and put aside as just another freak" (Edmonds 1970). Underlying this objection is an uneasy awareness that Outsider Art is not simply a form of aesthetic (or "anti-aesthetic") practice; it is also a psychiatric category. This may be self-evident, when a term such as "psychotic art" or "art of the mentally challenged" is applied to an artist's work; or it can be implicit, as two items from 2000 show.

Songs in the Key of Z is a compilation album and book, and it aims to be a kind of field guide to Outsider Music. Beefheart is in both, of course, where he keeps company with the Pink Floyd founder Syd Barrett, who became an early acid casualty in the late 1960s, before making a couple of whimsical, quietly deranged solo albums; and the recently deceased Daniel Johnston, a diagnosed schizophrenic and manic depressive who recorded thirteen albums over a ten-year period. Now, Beefheart's working technique, as we have seen, was to lean heavily on his musicians and their "translation" abilities, whether by singing, whistling, or playing short piano compositions to them. Yet despite this, even the more enlightened music journalists insist on regarding him as they would a Barrett or a Johnston. Sean O'Hagan, for example, in his 2010 obituary, describes Beefheart as a "sonic and linguistic visionary, an outsider artist," and laments the fact that "[t]here is no place now in pop for the madcap and the beautifully demented" (O'Hagan 2010).

Beefheart himself has to shoulder some of the blame for this prejudice. Almost from the moment that *Trout Mask* first appeared, he was spinning a vainglorious myth of its genesis—how he composed the entire twenty-eight-track opus in a single, eight-and-a-half hour burst of creativity; and then spent the next few months teaching his musicians how to play it, note by note. The founding document here is a piece that Langdon Winner wrote in *Rolling Stone* in 1970, which took Beefheart's claims at face value and gave them an enduring validity (see Winner 1970). (It is disheartening to see a piece written ten years later, by the fabled rock critic Lester Bangs, reiterating the same fallacies [1980]). These claims circulated far and wide for decades, until the late 1990s, when the counter-texts began to arrive. Two of Beefheart's musicians, Bill Harkleroad (*Lunar Notes: Zoot Horn Rollo's Beefheart Experience*) and John French (*Beefheart: Throught the Eyes of Magic*), who had also acted as his musical directors, recount in painstaking detail the erratic, haphazard, and painfully unsystematic process that gave birth to Beefheart's most outré compositions.[4] Their stories are supported by Mike Barnes, whose 2000 biography presents a less flattering, though still respectful, portrait of Don Van Vliet and his compositional practices, based on research rather than music-press hearsay.

The effect of these alternative accounts, once they became known, is that the myth of the solitary musical genius was well and truly exploded. "We could have played the songs backward and he wouldn't have known it," Harkleroad has said. "[Beefheart] had the big picture, he just didn't have the musical skills or knowledge to understand how to stick things together" (Paytress 2005: 54). By the same token, the dedication that Harkleroad and Co. showed in piecing together the fragments that Beefheart gave them, and making these shards work as musical passages that could be rehearsed and refined, is partly a function of their youthful determination and pliability. Their leader may have abused his position of seniority and caused a great deal of anguish and unhappiness, but he also knew what he had: a quartet of indefatigable musical adventurers, primed for the task of giving life to his spontaneous outpourings.[5]

The Road to Modernism

Yet although Beefheart refused to be seen as a "freak-show" performer, he was nonetheless an outsider in other ways—outside the mainstream, outside the business side of things, even outside the normal processes by which a songwriter or bandleader conveys ideas and instructions to his sidemen. In addition, and as we have seen, one of Beefheart's most persistent mannerisms was to present himself as an utterly singular and intuitive creative genius. In keeping with this self-styled outsider stance, the most useful comparison might be not with another musical artist, but with a filmmaker—one who also, as Van Vliet did, has a parallel career as a painter. David Lynch epitomizes, for many, the weird-making possibilities of the screen, in his exploration of the disorienting dynamics of switched identities (*Lost Highway, Mulholland Drive, Inland Empire*) and menacing psychosexual nightmares (*Eraserhead, Blue Velvet*). The comparison is sustained further by the fact that Lynch is closely involved with the soundtracks of his films, most often via collaborations with Angelo Badalamenti, and has even made three solo albums himself.

Both Beefheart and Lynch explore the underside of a mundane, prosaic American reality, probing the inherent strangeness that simply being in the world entails. This everyday surrealism points, however, in different directions—for Lynch, it suggests a primordial encounter with the fearsome and formless *Real*, envisaged as a staging ground for malevolent desire,[6] while for Beefheart it connotes an unqualified immersion in the natural world, alongside a menagerie of nonhuman creatures both real (blue jay, squid, bear, rooster, swan, and numerous insects) and imaginary (chrome bird and octafish). Yet despite these contrapuntal destinations, the two artists share a predilection for marginal, unsociable figures of all kinds. Thus, where Lynch's cinema often features deviants (thieves, mobsters, hit-men, prostitutes and cowboys), Beefheart populates his songs with outcasts: hobos, pirates, hermits, pachucos (Mexican-American youths) and old farts. Outsiderness, for each, has therefore as much to do with subject matter as it does with working method.

But the Lynch-Beefheart connection does not stop there. Lynch has often expressed his admiration for Beefheart's music, demonstrated in 2008 when he read the lyrics to the *Trout Mask* song "Pena," for a Beefheart tribute; and in 1994 when Lynch told Van Vliet "directly" (through the medium of Anton Corbijn's short film, *Some Yo Yo Stuff*) how much he liked "The Dust Blows forward."[7] The appeal for Lynch lies, I suggest, in Beefheart's unerring ability to *make modernism weird*. The profusion of dreamlike imagery, the startling leaps of logic, the absurdist approach to language and form, and the use of conventional instrumentation to produce unearthly sounds are, however, only part of the picture; what completes it is that this preposterous mix of elements is made to yield something incontrovertibly American. Lynch may not have any kind of passion for blues music (at least in his professional life),[8] but he does nonetheless understand its mythical underpinnings—its conjuration of dark forces, for instance, or its piercing emotional intensity—and how this is necessarily repressed for postindustrial America to thrive.⁹ Beefheart brings it back to the surface, in his weird-modernist ways, using it to distil his own oddball observations and deliberations.

I want to argue now that Beefheart's "outsiderness" is not just clarified through the lens of David Lynch; it also brings him into proximity with a different kind of artistic dissidence. One of Shklovsky's claims, as I mentioned earlier, is that the "road that turns back on itself" is the one that *makes strange* the operations of art. This is also the road of aesthetic modernism. It's a road that is acutely aware of its own quality of being *made*, affirming that the materials of art, its self-constitutive particularities, should not be hidden from the observer (or reader, or viewer, or listener). Such a quality is evident enough in Beefheart music: in breaking the rules of form, tempo, tonality, and so on, its sonic materiality becomes evident. I am suggesting, then, that there is an emphatic *reflexivity* present throughout *Trout Mask Replica*, and I suggest that this quality is maintained through the notion of the field recording.

Even for those who have never had direct contact with *Trout Mask*, one credit on the sleeve inevitably prompts recognition: "Produced by Frank Zappa." Beefheart, or rather, Don Van Vliet, and Zappa were school friends, in the 1950s, and musical rivals in the 1960s and 1970s. The rivalry was, however, somewhat one-sided. The hopelessly impractical Beefheart envied Zappa his business acumen, while Zappa, for his part, generously put that acumen at the disposal of his old friend. So it was that in 1968 he gave Beefheart a free hand to write and rehearse what would become *Trout Mask Replica*. Zappa then recorded and produced it and oversaw its release on his Straight record label. After the album had arrived in the world, Beefheart was typically dismissive of Zappa's input, saying that he "fell asleep" at the console (see French, 2010: 463). Once again, the myth of the solitary genius overrides the reality. Put the myth aside, however, and Zappa's contributions can be heard all over the record.

In fact, Zappa had a clear-cut vision for how he wanted *Trout Mask Replica* to sound. He originally thought of it as an "anthropological field recording" (French 2010: 456), and to that end, arranged to capture the band's performances in the Woodland Hills house (the "Trout House," as it has become known), to showcase the Magic Band in their natural habitat, as it were. Beefheart initially went along with this idea, until his paranoia was stirred, and he accused Zappa of trying to "do it on the cheap." So studio time was booked, and the instrumental tracks cut in a matter of hours. Despite this, Zappa's original plan is still evident. It is Zappa, I suggest, who makes the album a performance piece par excellence, bringing out Beefheart's absurdist humor, and turning the artifact into a document of *itself*.

"Dachau Blues," for example, has appended to it a "monologue" by an Amway salesman, secretly recorded after he had dropped some of his products off at the Trout House; he can be heard talking about a rat infestation on a movie set (see French 2010: 799). This part of the song is a genuine field recording—and so, too, is "China Pig," a voice-and-guitar duet performed by Beefheart and a former Magic Band guitarist, Doug Moon. Recorded in the living room of the Trout House, it is the roughest-sounding of the twenty-eight songs and concludes with a tape hiccup—a sudden reminder of the mediated, lo-fi nature of the performance. "She's Too Much for My Mirror" is slicker, introduced by the studio engineer, Dick Kunc: "Here you would have, famous version of 'She's Too Much for My Mirror.' Note the clever slate," while a barely audible Beefheart exclaims, as the song ends, "Shit, I don't know how I'm going to get that in there." Possibly the strangest track on the album, "The Blimp," does not feature Beefheart at all. Instead, the alarmed voice of guitarist Jeff Cotton shrieks insistently through the telephone line ("Frank, it's the big hit, It's the blimp, Frank . . . It's the mothership," etc.), backed by a studio-recorded rhythm-track played by Zappa's musicians. Zappa himself both introduces the piece ("You ready?") and later, when Cotton asks, "Did you get it?," signs it off ("Sure did. It's beautiful!"). The instrumental, "Hair Pie: Bake One," is even more unbounded. After the instruments taper off at the end, a conversation between Zappa and some neighborhood youths about politics takes over.

What we get throughout the *Trout Mask* set is, then, a whole series of sonic "accidents": mishaps, false starts, snatches of incidental dialogue, tape glitches, all left there deliberately by Zappa, in his capacity as producer. It is as if he were allowing the environment itself to "speak," conveying its ambient temperature through peripheral, apparently incidental sounds. Now, for those Delta bluesmen that I mentioned earlier, the environment—the ultra lo-fi recording context—was part of the song. Studio technology was fairly rudimentary, up until the 1940s; performances were basically captured live, "warts and all," and cut direct-to-disc. It is possible to see Zappa's production design as a further way of keeping Beefheart close to his roots. By revealing something of the conditions under which the recordings were made, by giving the listener intermittent reminders about the production process, that this is a *recorded artifact, Trout Mask* is renewing the spirit of the blues—or at least, Beefheart's somewhat antic and polymorphic take on that spirit.

So, to recap: Beefheart's weird, "crooked cactus" blues is often jarring and discordant—even for a carefully crafted sound—but it does hark back to tradition. The Delta blues songs from the 1920s and 1930s that have survived also contain their own unearthly, trance-like qualities. But Beefheart music is not just about further weirding this strange, haunting musical form. It is also about taking the blues in a modernist direction—and this, I want to suggest now, *is* unprecedented.

The folkloric dimension of the blues means that it holds fast to its primitivist origins. Jazz, by contrast, which is born around the same time as the blues, evolves through regional particularism and takes the modernist turn in the early 1940s, with the advent of bebop. Although scorned by certain jazz purists,[10] bop allowed for much greater rhythmic and harmonic complexity, thereby making it, in some ways, more blues oriented. The overall fate of the blues was, of course, much less auspicious. Some of it becomes the lingua franca of rock & roll—the twelve-bar blues scale, the accentuated backbeat—and much of it was fetishized by the revivalists of the early 1960s, who fueled the blues-rock boom. The avant-blues idiom that Beefheart fashions on *Trout Mask Replica* is, then, carving out a different future for this primal yet protean musical form.

It is a well-documented fact of musical history that Bob Dylan modernized folk music in the mid-1960s, remaking its simple, anthemic structures and heartfelt yet impersonal declamations. Dylan infuses this somewhat earnest genre with irony, surrealist wordplay and a heightened subjectivity—as he put it, in late 1964: "From now on, I want to write from inside me" (Hentoff 1964)—and gives it a ferocious rock edge. Four years later, Beefheart modernizes the blues—or rather, he provides a multiform sonic template for such a project, making exorbitant demands on his musicians as well as his audience. Yet in the same stroke the template is demolished, so that anyone reckless enough to follow in Beefheart's footsteps does so at his or her peril. What results from this weird-blues stew of the archaic (the old, weird America) and the avant-garde, as I have argued, is the tradition turned inside out, as much *of it* as *against it*. This could be seen as Beefheart's ultimate "outsider" statement: singular, heterodox, and unrepeatable.

Notes

1 Waits was given a songwriting contract in the early 1970s by Beefheart's manager, Herb Cohen, at the start of Waits's career. Beefheart's influence did not really take hold, however—reportedly at the behest of Waits's wife, Kathleen Brennan (see

Hoskyns, 2009: 277)—until the early 1980s, and the trio of albums that followed in quick succession (*Swordfishtrombones* [1983], *Rain Dogs* [1985], and *Frank's Wild Years* [1987]). As for the three other artists, Beefheartian approaches to the blues can be heard on Beck's *Mellow Gold* (1994), P. J. Harvey's *To Bring You My Love* (1995) and Tricky's *Pre-Millennium Tension* (1996). Four years later, in a more literal vein, the White Stripes released a single consisting of three Beefheart covers, including "Party of Special Things to Do."

2 Samuel Andreyev, the classical composer and performer, undertook an extraordinary musicological study of "Frownland" in 2017. Posted on his YouTube channel, the thirty-two-minute analysis breaks the song down into seven "blocks" or movements of sound, and transcribes the twenty instrumental "cells" that make up each movement.

3 Peter Guralnick writes of the "packed structures and nervous energy" (2003: 92) that characterize Delta blues music—energy that is more effective for being partly withheld.

4 Although French's exhaustive memoir was not published until 2010, he had already "rehearsed" some of the same material ten years earlier, in an essay written for Beefheart's *Grow Fins* boxed set (1999).

5 For an account of the *Trout Mask* rehearsal process that focuses on the damage that Beefheart caused, rather than the astonishing music that it spawned, see Sanjek 2012.

6 Lacanian readings of Lynch's films are, not surprisingly, plentiful. Slavoj Žižek is best known for promoting this kind of approach, but see also McGowan 2007.

7 These are both publicly available. The Lynch reading—which was a recording—can be found here: https://soundcloud.com/garylucas/pena-composition-by-don-van-vliet-read-by-david-lynch (accessed August 10, 2019). And the Corbijn short is on YouTube: https://www.youtube.com/watch?v=iwytKykXbpM&t=264s (accessed August 10, 2019).

8 Like Lynch, the Coen brothers have been studiously developing their own (more sardonic) forms of American Weird Cinema for almost four decades. Unlike Lynch, though, they have incorporated roots music into some of these forms—as can be seen, most evidently, in their blues-and-bluegrass opus, *O Brother, Where Art Thou?* (2000). In addition, cult favorite *The Big Lebowski* (1998) contains a scene in which the Dude is seen listening to a Beefheart song, "Her Eyes Are a Blue Million Miles."

9 In a 2013 interview, Alan Greenberg, the author of *Love in Vain: A Vision of Robert Johnson*, claimed that the screenplay adapted from his book would be filmed by David Lynch (see Morgenstern 2013). Six years later, Lynch still expresses enthusiasm for the project, but has yet to commit fully to it.

10 Perhaps most (in)famously, the poet and occasional jazz critic Philip Larkin decried the young Turks of bebop (Davis, Parker, Coleman) because they "attacked and overthrew the melodic principles of [his] childhood heroes Armstrong, Bechet, Waller and the Condon groups" (Motion 1993: 397).

References

Andreyev, S. (2017), "Anatomy of a Song." Available online: https://www.youtube.com/watch?vFhhB9teHqU&list=PLPyqt9rE6s4s11WzsBLQCK35GHEPdoprB (accessed August 12, 2019).

Bangs, L. (1980), "He's Alive, But So Is Paint: Are You?," *Village Voice*, 1 October. Available online: https://www.laweekly.com/captain-beefheart-the-legendary-1980-profile-by-lester-bangs/ (accessed August 22, 2019).

Barnes, M. (2000), *Captain Beefheart*, London: Quartet.

Chusid, I. (2000), *Songs in the Key of Z: The Curious Universe of Outsider Music*, Chicago, IL: A Cappella.

Edmonds, B. (1970), "I Wouldn't Call It Dada Rock Exactly: What It Is, Is . . . ," *Creem*, 2 (13) (Spring). Available online: http://beefheart.xyz/argue/argue6571/dada2.html (accessed August 12, 2019).

Evans, D. (2002), "The Development of the Blues," in A. Moore (ed.), *The Cambridge Companion to Blues and Gospel Music*, 20–43, Cambridge: Cambridge University Press.

Fisher, M. (2016), *The Weird and the Eerie*, London: Repeater.

Ford, P. (2008), "Taboo: Time and Belief in Exotica," *Representations*, 103 (Summer): 107–35.

French, J. (2010), *Beefheart: Through the Eyes of Magic*, London: Proper.

Guralnick, G. (2003), *Feel Like Going Home: Portraits in Blues and Rock'n'Roll*, Edinburgh: Canongate.

Hamilton, M. (2008), *In Search of the Blues*, New York: Basic.

Harkleroad, B. (with B. James) (1998), *Lunar Notes: Zoot Horn Rollo's Captain Beefheart Experience*, Wembley: SAF Publishing Ltd.

Hentoff, N. (1964), "The Crackin', Shakin', Breakin' Sounds," *New Yorker*, 24 October. Available online: https://www.newyorker.com/magazine/1964/10/24/the-crackin-shakin-breakin-sounds (accessed August 22, 2019).

Hoskyns, B. (2009), *Lowside of the Road: A Life of Tom Waits*, London: Faber and Faber.

McDonald, I. (1999), "Abracadabra!," rev. of *Grow Fins: Rarities (1965-1982)* and *The Dust Blows Forward (An Anthology)*, *Uncut*, 28 (September): 80.

McGowan, T. (2007), *The Impossible David Lynch*, New York: Columbia University Press.

Mclagan, D. (2009), *Outsider Art: From the Margins to the Marketplace*, London: Reaktion.

Moore, A. (2002), "Surveying the Field: Our Knowledge of Blues and Gospel Music," in A. Moore (ed.), *The Cambridge Companion to the Blues and Gospel*, 1–12, Cambridge: Cambridge University Press.

Morgenstern, H. (2013), "My Interview with Writer / Filmmaker Alan Greenberg Covers Work with Werner Herzog and David Lynch," *Independent Ethos*, 6 June. Available online: https://indieethos.com/2013/06/06/my-interview-with-writerfi

lmmaker-alan-greenberg-covers-work-with-werner-herzog-and-david-lynch/ (accessed August 12, 2019).

Motion, M. (1993), *Philip Larkin: A Writer's Life*, New York: Farrar Straus Giroux.

O'Hagan, S. (2010), "Captain Beefheart Obituary: Rock's Father of Invention," *The Observer*, 19 December. Available online: https://www.theguardian.com/music/2010/dec/19/captain-beefheart-tribute-legacy (accessed August 22, 2019).

Palmer, R. (1982), *Deep Blues*, London: Macmillan.

Paytress, M. (2005), "The Ultimate 'Out There!' Album," *Mojo*, 136 (March): 54.

Sanjek, D. (2012), "Life in the Fast and Bulbous Lane: Captain Beefheart (1941–2010)," *Popular Music and Society*, 35 (2): 301–13.

Shklovsky, V. (1990), *Theory of Prose*, trans. Benjamin Sher, Elmwood Park, IL: Dalkey Archive Press.

Winner, L. (1970), "I'm Not Even Here I Just Stick Around for My Friends," *Rolling Stone*, 58 (14 May). Available online: https://www.rollingstone.com/music/music-news/the-odyssey-of-captain-beefheart-rolling-stones-1970-cover-story-237400/ (accessed August 22, 2019).

13

Weird Visual Mythopoeia

On Matthew Barney's *Cremaster Cycle*

Florian Zappe

Around the turn of the twenty-first century, the idiosyncratic performance artist, sculptor, and filmmaker Matthew Barney has risen to become one of the biggest celebrities of the international art world and one can certainly claim that this stardom is, at least to a certain extent, based on the aura of weirdness that surrounds his persona and his work. If one browses through journalistic reviews of Barney's projects or through the commentary sections of YouTube and other online outlets that feature snippets of his work—particularly from his opus magnum the *Cremaster Cycle* (1994–2002) a "*Gesamtkunstwerk* that uses performance art, music, film, dance, installation, sculpture and photography" (Danto 2003) with a body of five experimental films with a total running time of almost seven hours at its center—one is likely to find numerous comments that range from blunt assertions that refer to the content as simply "weird" (e.g., Jones 2002) to other expressions of utter confusion. To cite just a few examples: a user calling himself Supple Chap rates a clip from *Cremaster 3* as "[a]nother video to add to my weird playlist" (Supple Chap 2019). Another online commentator professed to be "disturbed for the rest of [her] life" since what she has seen is so "fricken weird" (MichellAnna88 2008). A well-respected newspaper like the *The Telegraph* praises the artist's cinematic endeavors as "Very weird—and totally wonderful" (Sandhu 2002), and when Barney split up with his long-time partner, the pop singer Björk, the gossip blog *Defamer* (a subsite of the now defunct *Gawker* network) ran the headline "Salty Weirdo Matthew Barney Sues Björk For Custody of Their Daughter" (Evans 2015).

Naturally, these associations of Barney and "the weird" may seem trivial but they are also substantially indicative of a certain form of aesthetic experience that triggers a strong emotional reaction in many recipients of the artist's work, especially in those who encounter it for the first time. If we follow Paul J. Locher, the initial aesthetic response to any work of visual art "includes a sense of a work's pictorial content, its global structural organization, its semantic meaning, and an initial affective response to it," a first impression that he calls the "gist" of the work (Locher 2015: 76). Reading the above-quoted comments on Barney's *Cremaster Cycle* films through that lens, one has to assert that the "gist" of the visual vocabulary employed there is hard to grasp: The pictorial content of the cinematic images escapes established modes of readability, the structural organization of the films defies the Aristotelian unity of time, place, and action that still holds a firm grip on cinema, and their semantic content is impossible to trace for a first-time viewer. As a result, the initial affective response seems to be one of utter disorientation. The comments can thus be understood as expressions of what I like to call "gut weirdness"—an affective reaction to the work of an artist that defies easy categorization, expressed in vernacular terms.

On Modes: The Weird and the Mythical

But to what extent can this Barneyesque weirdness be theorized, especially in the discursive context of the present volume? Obviously, the *Cremaster Cycle*, titled after a muscle in the system of male genitalia[1] that serves as a "conceptual departure point" (Spector 2004b: 30) for the entire project, strikes audiences as "weird" but this goes, as I want to argue in this chapter, beyond a simplistic equation of weirdness with oddity.

Once more one may turn to Mark Fisher who has rightfully remarked that "the weird," similar to related notions of "the eerie" and the "the uncanny," is one of those concepts that not only describe affects but also *modes*: "modes of film and fiction, modes of perception, ultimately, you might even say, modes of being. Even so, they are not quite genres" (Fisher 2016: 9). Fisher's observation that the weird goes beyond the question of generic categorization and touches upon questions of representation, epistemology, and, "you might even say," existence provides a fruitful starting point for an investigation of Barney's *Cremaster Cycle* beyond the affective "gut weirdness" it evokes. Going beyond the long-established tradition of defining the weird through popular culture—be it in literature, film or music—I want to argue that the cycle, this "apparent paradox of [a] neo-avant-garde blockbuster franchise" (Keller and Ward 2006: 4), belongs to an expanded canon of weird arthouse cinema—a canon that is defined by *mode* rather than by genre. In this, Barney bears not only a close kinship with congenial filmmakers such as David Lynch, David Cronenberg, Nobuo Nakagawa, and Alejandro Jodorowsky but also carries on the legacy of weird mythopoeia.[2]

"Mythopoeia" is a somewhat peculiar term in literary and cultural studies as it is, according to Kirstin Johnson "virtually unknown in most circles and used to the point of meaninglessness in others" (Johnson 2007: 26). Originally coined in 1931 by J. R. R. Tolkien in a poem of the same title, mythopoeia is most commonly defined by its verbatim translation from Greek as "myth-making," a "definition that, particularly in consideration of the multiple definitions of myth, is not very helpful" (27). Consequently, any discussion of mythopoeia has to be preceded by a definition of "myth." For the purposes of this chapter, I will draw on a modern classic of myth theory: Roland Barthes's *Mythologies*. Barthes rejects the notion that myth is a generic category; he rather sees it as a "a type of speech . . . that . . . cannot possibly be an object, a concept, or an idea; it is a mode of signification, a form" (Barthes 1991: 107). As a consequence, everything can become a myth when it is expressed in mythical communication, which means when it is "adapted to a certain type of consumption, laden with literary self-indulgence, revolt, images, in short with a type of social usage which is added to pure matter" (107–8). This mode of communication is by no means limited to language: "It can consist of modes of writing or of representations; not only written discourse, but also photography, cinema, reporting, sport, shows, publicity, all these can serve as a support to mythical speech" (108). From this Barthesian perspective on myth, certain criticisms of mythopoeia must necessarily fall short. David E. Cooper, for example, claims that "reference as a story as myth . . . implies that it is false. This raises a problem concerning the devising of myths—mythopoeia. How can anyone openly promulgate a myth, for to do so, it seems, is to offer for acceptance something which, by calling it a myth, one admits is false?" (Cooper 1998: 99). If we follow Barthes's understanding, such a definition based by the truth value of its content is completely futile, as "[m]yth can be defined neither by its object nor by its material, for any material can arbitrarily be endowed with meaning" (Barthes 1991: 108).

The relationship between mythopoeia and myth, self-evidently, is a close one but there is one important difference between the two concepts: the former usually can be attributed to an originator, whereas the latter is the result of nonauthorial emergence, "a type of speech chosen by history" (108). Mythopoeia is therefore a form of masquerade. It poses as myth by imitating its manifestations in many ways, albeit not its modes of communication. Its relationship to the mythical can—on the level of structure and content—be characterized by reference, mimicry, homage, appropriation, plagiarism, opposition, or even blatantly shown indifference.

And yet, all this marks no strict demarcation between the two in the event of the appropriation of an object originating from mythopoeic authorship by a mythical mode of depersonalized discourse. Fisher reminds us that the strange case of H. P. Lovecraft, undoubtedly the master of weird mythopoesis, provides a notorious example here by pointing to the fact that "more than a few readers have contacted the British Library asking for a copy of the *Necronomicon*, the book of ancient lore which is frequently referred to in many of Lovecraft's stories" (Fisher 2016: 24). The fictitious grimoire has become fully detached from its mythopoeic provenance and entered the realm of the mythical.

In order to understand the specific characteristics of weird mythopoeia, a short excursion on how the weird and myth as modes (rather than merely genres) operate in the sociocultural realm seems useful. The traditional function of myths is to offer narratives that render the unknown familiar, provide order and meaning to a world of (apparent) contingency and, as Barthes has famously put it, transform "history into nature" (Barthes 1991: 128). The mythologies created by artists of the weird on the other hand, operate in the opposite direction. They subvert (pseudo)natural ontologies, disrupt the familiarity of the material world and our established epistemological mechanisms to make sense of it, and bring the unknown lurking behind the familiar to the surface. In that respect, weirding in the broadest sense can be seen as a form of *ostranenie* (in the Shklovskian fashion) and weird mythopoeia as that particular mode of making the myth(ologie)s we experience as stabilizing factor in our existence "strange."

Matthew Barney: Mythmaker and Sorcerer

Barney has repeatedly been described as a mythmaker (see Jones 2002; Hoby 2013) but also as "something of a sorcerer" (Hoby 2013), a conjuror of an aesthetic cosmos of uncategorizable otherness that paradoxically seems to be radically dispersed and at the same time fundamentally organic. And indeed, to some extent, one can see the entire project as an artistic exercise in (black?) magic. Any trained art historian will be able to retrace an array of influences on the *Cremaster Cycle* and its mythology. Given the fact that Barney has had a long career as a performance artist, the *Cremaster Cycle* is also strongly rooted in this tradition and especially that of the radical transgressive body artists of the 1960s and 1970s such as Marina Abramović, Chris Burden, or Gina Pane, who are frequently cited as a major inspiration (see Keller and Ward 2006: 3 and Wruck 2014: 33–46).

But there are also less avant-gardistic paragons. Keller and Ward have noted that "*Cremaster*'s lush aesthetic is shot through not just with references to but nostalgia for the film styles of a number of Hollywood moments" while "its epic running times, monumental sets and huge budgets place *Cremaster* in line with ... blockbuster cinema" (Keller and Ward 2006: 3). There is, however, yet another quite conspicuous genealogy that critics largely and counterintuitively have overlooked: that of mythopoeia in experimental film. P. Adams Sitney traces the origins of mythopoeic cinema back to the second American film avant-garde of the last century: "The triumph of the mythopoeic film in the early sixties sprang from the film-makers' liberation from the repetition of traditional mythology and from the enthusiasm with which they forged a cinematic form for the creation or revelation of new myths" (Sitney 2002: 109). Indeed, there is a certain kinship between Barney and Kenneth Anger, Sitney's exemplary representative of the mythopoeic film, not only because both are interested in occult symbolism and queer(ed) readings of pop culture. Similar to Anger, Barney blends a plethora of appropriated ancient myths and popular mythologies, scientific as well as autobiographical references, and somewhat outlandish symbolic systems into an eclectic assemblage.

Such a genealogy of influences is, however, soon exhausted if one wants to approach an interpretative mythography of the cycle—an enterprise that seems to be a sheer impossibility without paratextual support. This is provided by the catalog of the *Cremaster* project, which has been published by the Guggenheim Museum. Nancy Spector, Barney's long-time curator, collaborator, and editor defines this huge, over 500-page-strong volume as "encyclopedia" and "user's guide or source book for the entire *Cremaster* cycle" (Spector 2004a: xiv). The layout of the book recalls that of a grimoire. The cover is adorned with five pseudo-occult symbols, all based on Barney's "field emblem," a central icon in the *Cremaster* cosmos.[3] In her introductory essay "Only the Perverse Fantasy Can Still Save Us," a hybrid of exegesis and manifesto that not only makes a claim of undisputable philosophical validity in its title but also constitutes the most helpful tool to decrypt the cycle, Spector describes the emblem's significance as follows:

> His "field emblem"—an ellipsis bisected horizontally by a single bar—signifies the orifice and its closure, the hermetic body, an arena of possibility. The motif is ubiquitous in Barney's oeuvre. Like a traditional heraldic emblem it encapsulates and translates the artist's complex symbology into visual shorthand. But the field emblem also functions like a corporate logo, ensuring a certain brand identity by virtue of its constant presence in the work. Mixing the archaic and the pop,

this graphic image epitomizes Barney's unique aesthetic language, which is continuously evolving in its construction of a new-millennium mythology. (Spector 2004b: 7)

This new mythology is developed over the course of the five films of the cycle, which were produced in anti-numerical order: *Cremaster 4* (42 minutes), chronologically the first film, was made in 1994, *Cremaster 1* (40 minutes) in 1995, *Cremaster 5* (45 minutes) in 1997, *Cremaster 2* (79 minutes) in 1999, and *Cremaster 3*, with a running time of 182 minutes by far the longest part, in 2002.

Given the scope, intricacy, and exceptional idiosyncrasy of the *Cremaster Cycle*, any attempted synopsis within the limits of this chapter will inevitably have to remain an exercise in futility. I therefore refer the reader to the comprehensive and potentially more prolific attempts by Spector (2004b: 30–73) and Wruck (2014: 62–124). Nevertheless, I consider it a propaedeutic necessity for the ensuing exegesis of the weirdness of the work to give at least a selective and inevitably cursory inventory of some central elements and motifs: *Cremaster 1* with its pop art aesthetics is set on the mythical battlefield of American popular culture—the football ground. Two small airships branded with Goodyear ads float over the field, which both are inhabited by two identical extravagantly dressed women who—an information we have to derive from the catalog—are both named Goodyear. We watch them sitting under two tables and playing around with grapes, dropping them from the airships. A chorus line reminiscent of those in a classic Hollywood musical appears whose dancing follows a choreography directed by grapes falling from the vessels.

The second part of the cycle is probably the most narrative as it oscillates between several complexly intertwined, yet identifiable plotlines. The first adapts motifs and story fragments from *The Executioner's Song* (1979), Norman Mailer's Pulitzer Prize–winning novel about the real-life case of Gary Gilmore, who was the first criminal to be executed after the reintroduction of the death penalty in the United States in 1976. The second plotline follows the legendary escape artist Harry Houdini at the Chicago world fair of 1893. Houdini is played by Norman Mailer himself. With this unusual and surprising casting choice, the film playfully reflects on Mailer's (disputed) claim that Gilmore and Houdini were related. In addition to a variety of other narrative fragments and innumerable cameos (among them a Mormon choir and the heavy metal drummer Dave Lombardo), the film climaxes in a somewhat bizarre Rodeo in the Bonneville Salt Flats in Utah during which the Gilmore character (played by Barney himself) is executed.

Cremaster 3 is the longest and most complex of the five films of the cycle. Most of its action is set in New York. After a short opening sequence retelling a Celtic story about a giant, Barney introduces a zombie version of Gary Gilmore, returning from the dead after he had been executed in part two. Beyond that, the film depicts a crash car race ruining a faithful reproduction of the lobby of the Chrysler Building. The central piece of part three (and the entire cycle) is a segment called "The Order" which uses the Guggenheim Museum in New York as setting for a complex performance art piece based on a Masonic initiation ritual. Barney himself plays a character called Entered Apprentice (a Masonic rank), who has to undergo a five-stage-long initiation rite. "The Order" stars not only Barney as the protagonist but also Aimee Mullins, a former paralympic athlete who lost both her legs due to disease while she was still an infant and later became famous as fashion model. In total, Mullins plays six different characters in the cycle where she shares the cast list with such unlikely collaborators such as the hardcore punk band Agnostic Front and the sculptor Richard Serra.

Part four shows a montage of different quasi-plotless currents of action. Its temporal structure defined by two racing motorcycles which follow the track of the Tourist Trophy (albeit in opposite direction), a traditional and notoriously dangerous racing event held annually at the British Isle for over a century. The film also features a protagonist called the Loughton Candidate, a satyr (again played by Barney) who, hoping for the initiation into an obscure social order, tap-dances himself through the floor of a Victorian pier house and falls into the sea. Back at land, he follows a bizarre trail that leads him through a grease-filled corridor in order to reach a couple of fairies he interacts with before returning to the pier house again.

Cremaster 5 is the most turgid and Dionysian part of the cycle. Its action is primarily set in Budapest's opera house as well as the city's famous Gellért Baths and features the former James Bond actress Ursula Andress in the role of the flamboyant "Queen of Chain" as a central character.

As this (admittedly sketchy) outline of the cycle demonstrates, the inventory of characters consists of an array of historic and fictitious personalities, mythological figures ranging from centaurs to tap-dancing androgynous satyrs or grotesque creatures reminiscent of the broken and subversive corporeality we know from fantastic genres like body horror. And yet, the content of the cycle is anything but random; it is a carefully orchestrated abundance of visual tropes—we must not forget that Barney's preferred medium is the image, not the (spoken) word—that negotiates topics like the fluidity of gender identity (and the validity of the concept of identity in general), the status of metaphysics in the context of consumer culture, the iconography of "America" (as an idea and an ideology), and of the institution of art as a quasi-religious system in contemporary society.

Spector has described Barney's visual style as "protean" and "the iconography [as] multivalent and allusive. Objects and images, always striking, bizarre and seductive, function simultaneously on various levels of meaning" (Spector 2004b: 4). Viewers lacking the epistemological crutch of the paratextual information supplied by Spector's essay or Neville Wakefield's "The Cremaster Glossary," which lists a multitude of quotes from fiction, theory, and philosophy addressing key objects (in alphabetical order from "anus-island" to "zombie") that played a part in conceptualizing the cycle (see Wakefield 2004: 93–114), will undoubtedly encounter problems accessing these levels of meaning.

Being confronted with Barney's mythological universe somewhat "unarmed" has undoubtedly a be*weird*ing effect. At the beginning of *The Weird and the Eerie*, Fisher initially defines "the weird as that *which does not belong*" and therefore claims that "[t]he form that is perhaps most appropriate to the weird is montage—the conjoining of *two or more things which do not belong together*" (Fisher 2016: 10–11, emphases in the original).

In their usual contexts, audiences experience these objects, characters, and motifs presented in the *Cremaster Cycle* as familiar—entertainment, art, and sports are contemporary mythological systems that people know well and engage in actively and the references to ancient myths draw on the canon of Western culture. Accordingly, the cycle's weirdness is not evoked by the content itself but by the mode Barney appropriates and reworks to create entities in which the constituent components are defamiliarized by the wayward ways in which they "do not belong" together. In doing so, he stands, of course, on the shoulders of a tradition. Montage is a long-established avant-garde technique that artists have used it for more than a century to evoke weirdness. A merely formalist analysis of the "weird" structure of the *Cremaster* films, of their ritual-based narratives and their solipsistic repetitions would, however, only offer limited insights if one wants to get to the "gist" of his visual poetics. I agree with Graham Harman's claim that "[f]ormalism obviously belittles content, since it treats content as mere fodder for larger structural relation— for gestures of irony and paradox in which the exact content in these structures is either reversible, or else is simply whatever random content happens to be on hand" (Harman 2012: 253).

Its overabundant and seemingly impenetrable mythological content opens the cycle up for a variety of interpretations. For some critics, the hermetic aestheticism of the cycle is nothing but an extravagant yet largely apolitical "art for art's sake" enterprise that offers, as Keller and Ward claim "no ... institutional commentary or critique" (Keller and Ward 2006: 6). Micheal Jay McClure reads the cycle through the lens of queer theory and argues that identity in the films "does not occupy a 'space' within a semantic taxonomy, but one that seems riven with contingency" (McClure 2010: 157)—a quality that, according to his reading, scrutinizes the dominant heteronormative and abelist matrices of Western culture. Annette Jael Lehmann's reading goes in the opposite direction and sees Barney as a tacit conservative. She argues—aptly pointing to the fact that the eponymous cremaster muscle is an "exclusively male organ" (Lehman 2007: 69)—that Barney's points of reference "implicitly deploy a re-empowerment of masculinity at a time when the crisis of white middle-class masculinity has been diagnosed at large" (79). While all these interpretations certainly make important and valid points, they also express a little tinge of dissatisfaction as they focus on selective content, a fact that demonstrates that even professionals in the field of interpreting complex forms of art struggle in the light of the difficulty—if not impossibility—to satisfactorily decipher and disentangle the complex web of symbols, objects, images, and cultural references Barney has created.

Collapsing Epistemologies

According to Fisher, we have to understand

> the weird as a particular perturbation. It involves a sensation of wrongness: a weird entity or object is so strange that it makes us feel that it should not exist, or at least it should not exist here. Yet if the entity or object is here, then the categories which we have up until now used to make sense of the world cannot be valid. (2016: 15)

In other words, the experience of "weirdness," be it affective, aesthetic, or intellectual is the product of the gap that opens between objects and our habitual modes of perception and representation. It is the result of a moment of epistemology collapsing.

Barney's prime mode of evoking those moments is the production of "gaps"—which seems at first surprising given his aesthetics of overabundance. But maybe this becomes clearer if we have a closer look at the role of gaps in

Harman's theory of "weird realism." For him, gaps have, first of all, a philosophical function, as "[o]ne of the most important decisions made by philosophers concerns the production or destruction of gaps in the cosmos" (Harman 2012: 2). Generally, he distinguishes between two kinds of philosophers: "[T]hose who destroy gaps by imploding them into a single principle are generally called reductionists, let's coin the word productionists to describe philosophers who find new gaps in the world where there were formerly none" (3). These two fundamentally divergent philosophical approaches are also applicable to artistic production, a fact he sees paradigmatically embodied in a writer like Lovecraft who

> is clearly a productionist author. No other writer is so perplexed by the gap between objects and the power of language to describe them, or between the objects and the qualities they possess. . . . Indeed, there are times when Lovecraft echoes cubist painting in a manner amounting almost to a parody of Hume. While Hume thinks that objects are a simple amassing of familiar qualities, Lovecraft resembles Braque, Picasso, and the philosopher Edmund Husserl by slicing an object into vast cross-sections of qualities, planes, or adumbrations, which even when added up do not exhaust the reality of the object they compose. (3)

Lovecraft's productionist weird has its roots, according to Harman, in his ability to accept and to cope with the limits of paraphrase, the fact that the weird is not representable by language. Based on this notion, Harman would be reluctant to ascribe similar qualities to Barney as he attributes the gap-producing qualities to "the indirect character of literature as opposed to painting or cinema" (Harman 2012: 24), a claim that echoes narratological film theory, especially Seymour Chatman's classic distinction between literature as an "assertive" and film as a "presentational" art form. While such distinctions may have some validity with regard to traditional narrative cinema, they do not apply to those forms of experimental film scrutinizing the (re)presentational qualities of the image. Barney follows essentially a protactionist strategy similiar to Lovecraft's, albeit in a visual medium. He presents objects, familiar objects even, but his weird defamiliarization does not allow us to say much about their qualities. His weird visual mythopoeia is not affirmative of the myths we use to cope with the object world. It rather opens up epistemological chasms—gaps—between them and the qualities that we, in our usual patterns of meaning-making, associate with them. Some critics have placed his work in the tradition of surrealism (see Jones 2002), and there may be arguments for that kinship but the major difference here is that Barney did not rely on a foundational doctrine (like, for example, the surrealists had in psychoanalysis). He is the creator of his own mythological system built on appropriated elements of other cultural myths, both highbrow and lowbrow. But that system is not just a case of simple montage of symbols and images but a composition of reworked fragments. It is less a cut-up that could theoretically be disassembled and rearranged into its original material, but rather a pick-up in a Deleuzean sense that "does not happen between persons, it happens between ideas, each one being deterritorialized in the other, following a line or lines which are neither in one nor the other, and which carry off a 'bloc'" (Deleuze and Parnet 1987: 18).

Conclusion: The Weirdest Series of Films Ever Made?

In 2017, the Flatpack Film Festival in Birmingham hosted a rare screening of the complete *Cremaster Cycle* which prompted the film critic Matt Turner to revisit the films and to write a short review with the title "Is this the weirdest series of films ever made?," praising the cycle's "recalcitrant, rebellious weirdness, its corporeal, queasy physicality, and a psychedelic, symbolic density" (Turner 2017). When he describes the be*weird*ed audience's response to the film, he observes that "little to no consensus was made over what had been seen, or even its value. Those that stayed to the end seemed worn down, weakened, and not necessarily convinced, but still fascinated by Barney's strange, deeply self-indulgent act of creation" (Turner 2017).

The discussion of the significance of Barney's idiosyncratic work beyond the art world is a recurring one; it also surrounds the post-*Cremaster* projects *River of Fundament* (2014) and *Redoubt* (2019). The accusations are usually the same: beautiful but unimpenetrable, megalomaniac and solipsistic, an apolitical exercise in *l'art pour l'art*. Understanding Barney as a weird mythopoet, however, may offer a new perspective on this artist's work. It has always been the avant-garde's project to disturb but it has been repeatedly pointed out that this seems to be an impossibility after postmodernism (allegedly) fulfilled the aesthetico-political axioms formulated by the modernist avant-gardes a century ago. It is certainly no coincidence that the weird—as popular genre—blossomed for the first time simultaneously to the various manifestations of modernist avant-gardes, which brought about their own weirdness. Both phenomena were reactions to the human condition in the modern age and both challenge, on very different battlefields, the dominant mythologies of their time. It may therefore also not be a coincidence that a neo-avant-garde project such as the *Cremaster Cycle* emerged contemporaneously with the phenomenon of New Weird fiction.

"With a particular type of horror," Barney once said, "you can really fit your head up your ass—turn yourself inside out to form a kind of visceral landscape— where you can chase the demons around" (Barney qtd. in Spector 2004b: 11). The demons of the early twentieth century were certainly different than the demons of the new millennium, but the weird mode of mythopoeia seems to be an enduring tool to scrutinize them.

Notes

1. By hoisting and lowering the scrotum, the cremaster muscle helps regulating the ideal temperature active sperm cells need to survive in the male body. The prenatal formation of this muscle occurs in the same embryonic stage in which the biological differentiation of the sexes is completed. It is therefore not surprising that Barney takes it as a departure point for his scrutiny of binary gender categories, although Danto speculates that the "the poetics of ascent and descent" (Danto 2003) may have contributed to the decision.
2. The specter of genre is, however, a haunting presence in the *Cremaster* Cycle. Annette Jael Lehman, for example, refers to *Cremaster 2* as "a gothic Western" and to *Cremaster 3* as "part zombie-thriller, part gangster film" (Lehmann 2007: 74 and 77). In addition to that it is worth mentioning that popular genre fiction has always been an important influence for Barney. The visual aesthetics of his video installation *OTTOshaft* (1992) strongly recalls David Cronenberg's body horror. Nancy Spector also notes that Barney's "metamorphic vocabulary . . . invokes the defining characteristics of literary fantasy" (Spector 2004b: 23), and in an interview Barney himself cites "a real classic, cabin-in-the-woods horror film"—Sam Raimi's *Evil Dead II* (1987)—as a major cinematic influence on the *Cremaster Cycle*, as one particular scene "when the lightbulbs start bleeding" gave him a notion that "evil lives in the architecture rather than in the person" (Porter and Barney 2000: 31).
3. Each of these five symbols combines the field emblem with a symbolic reference to one of the parts of the cycle: the first (representing *Cremaster 1*), on top of the book's cover, features talaria, equally referring to Hermes, the messenger god of Greek mythology and to the Goodyear corporate logo, that features prominently in this part (not least because the central female character is named Goodyear). The second (representing *Cremaster 2*) shows a beehive, referencing the flag of the state of Utah where parts of this segments of the cycle were shot (in the Bonneville Salt Flats), as well as an American flag and the Canadian Red Ensign (the former national flag of Canada) in the version of 1873, as well as the Canadian Rockies were also a location for the film (Spector 2004b: 32). The third symbol, arranged adequately at the center of the cover to represent the centerpiece of the cycle (*Cremaster 3*),

features the silhouette of the Chrysler building, which is one of the film's iconic New York locations, combined with "the Masonic symbol of the compass and square, along with the double-headed eagle, the symbol used for the Scottish Rite, a form of Freemasonry the developed on the Continent in the eighteenth century and spread rapidly throughout the world" (Brunet 2009: 99). The variation representing *Cremaster 4* shows the so-called Manx triskelion, central to the flag of the Isle of Man which is the setting of this film. The final symbol features a stylized calla lily, a flower that plays a significant role in the visual vocabulary of *Cremaster 5*.

References

Barthes, R. (1991), *Mythologies*, New York: The Noonday Press.
Brunet, L. (2009), "Homage to Freemasonry or Indictment?: The Cremaster Cycle," *PAJ: A Journal of Performance and Art, PAJ 91*, 31 (1): 98–112.
Cooper, D. E. (1998), "'Reactionary Modernism' and Self-Conscious Myth," in M. Bell and P. Poellner (eds.), *Myth and the Making of Modernity: The Problem of Grounding in Early Twentieth-Century Literature*, 99–114. Amsterdam: Rodopi.
Danto, A. C. (2003), "The Anatomy Lesson: Matthew Barney's Cremaster Cycle," *The Nation*, 17 April. Available online: https://www.thenation.com/article/anatomy-les son/ (accessed October 23, 2019).
Deleuze, G., and C. Parnet (1987), *Dialogues*, New York: Columbia University Press.
Evans, D. (2015), "Salty Weirdo Matthew Barney Sues Björk For Custody of Their Daughter," *Defamer*, 2 April. Available online: http://defamer.gawker.com/salty-weirdo-matthew -barney-sues-bjork-for-custody-of-t-1695226159 (accessed October 25, 2019).
Fisher, M. (2016), *The Weird and the Eerie*, London: Repeater Books.
Harman, G. (2012), *Weird Realism: Lovecraft and Philosophy*, Winchester: Zero Books.
Hoby, H. (2013), "Matthew Barney Interview: It's What's Outside the Frame That's Scary," *The Telegraph*, 13 July. Available online: https://www.telegraph.co.uk/culture/ art/art-features/10153609/Matthew-Barney-interview-Its-whats-outside-the-frame- thats-scary.html (accessed March 23, 2018).
Jones, J. (2002), "The Myth-Maker," *The Guardian*, 16 October. Available online: https:// www.theguardian.com/film/2002/oct/16/artsfeatures (accessed November 2, 2019).
Johnson, K. (2007), "Tolkien's Mythopoesis," in T. Hart and I. Khovacs (eds.), *Tree of Tales: Tolkien, Literature and Theology*, 25–38, Waco: Baylor University Press.
Keller, A., and F. Ward (2006), "Matthew Barney and the Paradox of the Neo-Avant-Garde Blockbuster," *Cinema Journal*, 45 (2): 3–16.
Lehmann, A. J. (2007), "Myth of Reproduction in Matthew Barney's Cremaster Cycle," in S. Sielke and N. Schäfer-Wünsche (eds.), *The Body as Interface: Dialogues Between the Disciplines*, 69–81, Heidelberg: Winter.
Locher, P. J. (2015), "The Aesthetic Experience with Visual Art 'At First Glance,'" in P. F. Bundgaard and F. Stjernfelt (eds.), *Investigations Into the Phenomenology and the*

Ontology of the Work of Art: What Are Artworks and How Do We Experience Them?, 75–88, Cham, Heidelberg et al.: Springer.

McClure, M. J. (2010), "Queerd Cinema: Film, Matter, and Matthew Barney," *Discourse* 32 (2): 150–69.

MichelleAnna88. (2008), Comment on the youtube clip "Matthew Barney—The Order From Cremaster." Available online: https://www.youtube.com/watch?v=IdxRPavq uIQ&lc=Ugy8HrpBdt1s22_P3J54AaABAg (accessed November 4, 2019).

Porter, A. J., and M. Barney (2000) "Fluid Talk," *Circa*, 92: 30–1.

Sandhu, S. (2002), "Very Weird—and Totally Wonderful," *The Telegraph*, 31 October. Available online: https://www.telegraph.co.uk/culture/film/3585007/Very-weird-and-totally-wonderful.html (accessed March 27, 2018).

Sitney, P. A. (2002), *Visionary Film. The American Avant-Garde 1943–2000*, Oxford and New York: Oxford University Press.

Spector, N. (2004a), "Acknowledgements," in M. Barney and N. Spector (eds.), *Matthew Barney: The Cremaster Cycle*, xiv–xvi, New York, Guggenheim Museum.

Spector, N. (2004b), "Only The Perverse Fantasy Can Still Save Us," in M. Barney and N. Spector (eds.), *Matthew Barney: The Cremaster Cycle*, 3–91, New York, Guggenheim Museum.

Supple Chup (2019), Comment on the youtube clip "The Order—Matthew Barney." Avilable online: https://www.youtube.com/watch?v=y_S3fX4F9nU (accessed October 27, 2019).

Turner, M. (2017), "Is this the Weirdest Series of Films Ever Made?," *Little White Lies*, 30 April. Available online: https://lwlies.com/festivals/the-cremaster-cycle-matthew-barney-flatpack-festival/ (accessed November 9, 2019).

Wakefield, N. (2004), "The Cremaster Glossary," in M. Barney and N. Spector (eds.), *Matthew Barney: The Cremaster Cycle*, 93–114, New York, Guggenheim Museum.

Wruck, E. (2014), *Matthew Barneys Cremaster Cycle. Narration—Landschaft—Skulptur*, Berlin: Reimer.

14

Hidden Cultures and the Representation and Creation of Weird Reality in Alan Moore's *Providence*

Alexander Greiffenstern

"The aim of all commentary on art now should be to make works of art—and, by analogy, our own experience—more, rather than less, real to us."
—Susan Sontag, "Against Interpretation"

Reality has always been a weird concept and a concept of the weird. In the 1980s, during the heyday of television, Jean Baudrillard wrote about the "Evil Demon of Images." He showed that the relation between signifier and signified between representation and reality became increasingly blurred—the actual accident at the nuclear power plant in Harrisburg in 1979 seemed to imitate the plot of the previously shown TV movie *The China-Syndrome*. In his text Baudrillard writes: "It is precisely when it appears most truthful, most faithful and most in conformity to reality that the image is most diabolical" (Baudrillard 1987: 13). A concept like truth had already been abandoned by philosophers, so Gilles Deleuze was concerned about the usage of the concept of truth by his friend Michel Foucault, who resuscitated this old philosophical concept for his analysis of power and sexuality (see Dosse 2010: 318). Since the 1970s, both concepts—truth and reality—have been the subject of further fierce debates and the advent of the internet, social media, and cable news have potentiated the problem. British comic book writer Alan Moore puts the question of reality in the foreground when he engages with the work of H. P. Lovecraft in his recent series *Providence* (2015–17).

Alan Moore is one of the key figures of the British invasion of American comics in the 1980s and 1990s. Besides Moore's comics, one could name Neil Gaiman's *Sandman* or the long-running series *Hellblazer* and *Preacher,* written and drawn by British artists such as Garth Ennis, Warren Ellis, Steve Dillon, and Peter Milligan for American publishers. Although these artists are British and some of their work is clearly focused on British politics and history, many are set in the United States with American characters. *Watchmen*, created by Moore and Dave Gibbons and published by DC Comics from 1986 to 1987, revolutionized the superhero genre and changed the US comic industry. One can detect the influences of many authors and artists in the work of Alan Moore, and H. P. Lovecraft is certainly one of them. But it is only in his more recent books that Moore began very consciously to deal with Lovecraft's writing and biography.

The Genealogy of *Providence*

The history of Moore's *Providence* begins in 1994 as a short story that Moore contributed to *The Starry Wisdom*, a collection of tribute stories to H. P. Lovecraft that, among others, included texts by William S. Burroughs and J. G. Ballard. Moore's story "The Courtyard" was turned into a comic miniseries in 2003 under the supervision of Moore, and in 2010 Moore published a four-issue sequel called *Neonomicon*. *Providence* is prequel and sequel to *Neonomicon* published from 2015 to 2017.

All these Lovecraft-related comics are published by the small American publisher Avatar Press that gave Moore full artistic control. Moore tested and exploited this artistic freedom in *Neonomicon*, about which he remarked afterward:

> Funnily enough, that is one of the most unpleasant things I have ever written.... So *Neonomicon* is very black, and I'm only using "black" to describe it because there isn't a darker color.... It's got all of the things that tend to be glossed over in Lovecraft: the racism, the suppressed sex. Lovecraft will refer to nameless rites that are obviously sexual, but he will never give them name. I put all that stuff back in. There is sexuality in this, quite violent sexuality which is very unpleasant. (Thill 2010)

Neonomicon continues the FBI investigation of a series of gruesome murders that started in "The Courtyard." Merril Brears, the female protagonist of *Neonomicon*, quickly understands the connection of these cases to the writing of Lovecraft, and the story develops into a new take on Lovecraft's story "The Shadow over Innsmouth." Lovecraft never explicitly deals with sexuality, and a female protagonist would have never occurred to him, but in "The Shadow over

Innsmouth" interspecies breeding between humans and "deep-ones" is part of the story and the narrator understands at the end of the story that he is the child of such a relation. In contrast to Lovecraft, Moore brings the sexual subtext of the story to the surface when he shows the prolonged sexual abuse of Merril by a group of cultists and then by a "deep-one."[1]

Although *Providence* has some disturbing scenes as well, the overall tone is different and Moore sets out to explore a wider range of topics. Every issue, or chapter, takes on other stories of Lovecraft, which makes the series a form of fictional commentary to Lovecraft's work and its reception. It was published in twelve issues or chapters and tells the story of young journalist Robert Black, who embarks on a journey through New England in 1919 to find evidence of the hidden occult America, to speak to its protagonists and write a book about this. Another goal of his is to find inspiration for some kind of mystery novel in the vein of Edgar Allan Poe. Similar to *Neonomicon*, Moore changes the typical Lovecraft protagonist by making Black a homosexual and Jewish, which enables Moore to approach Lovecraft's texts from a different perspective. The story of Black is told in issues 1–10 as a comic as well as a first-person narrative in a commonplace book, in which Black chronicles his journey and notes his ideas at the end of each chapter. Moore uses this technique often: the "main narrative" of the comic is accompanied by newspaper clippings, diaries, excerpts from books mentioned in the comic, medical records, letters, and so on. In many ways, this assemblage of texts creates a broader narrative structure. *Providence* adds only the commonplace book of Black, which becomes the source for Lovecraft's stories after Black lends it to him, and two texts Black picks up during his research. Issue 11 is about Black's return to New York City and then follows the subsequent reception of Lovecraft's stories through the following decades up to the events of *Neonomicon* in 2006. Issue 12 is set after the events of *Neonomicon*, providing an end for both stories.

Providence and *Gay New York*

Robert Black's homosexuality is already suggested on the first pages. At first, one sees the back of a male person tearing up what appears to be a love letter. On the next page, the reader sees Black, clearly positioned in the front of the picture and furthermore distinguished from the other figures in the picture by his blueish suit and green tie, which contrasts the black, brown, and white clothes of the other three. This difference in fashion colors is continued on the following pages, and what seems to be a simple signifier for the reader to recognize the hero or lead character is actually based on Moore's reading of George Chauncey's *Gay New York: Gender, Urban Culture, and the Making of the Gay Male World, 1890-1940*, first published in 1994.[2] This historical study describes and analyzes the surprising visibility of gay life in the first part of the twentieth century in New York City. Besides the very visible nightlife in bars and clubs, a parallel gay world existed, visible only to the people familiar with its code. Part of this code was a certain colorful fashion, such as red or green ties and, of course, a coded language that helped homosexual men to recognize each other but stay invisible to outsiders.

> [G]ay men devised a variety of tactics that allowed them to move freely about the city, to appropriate for themselves spaces that were not marked as gay, and to construct a gay city in the midst of, yet invisible to, the dominant city. They were aided in this effort, as always, by the disinclination of most people to believe that any "normal"-looking man could be anything other than "normal," and by their access, as men, to public space. (Chauncey 1994: 180)

Moore uses Chauncey's examples when Robert Black meets an acquaintance, and they talk about their relationships with other men by using female names for their male partners and coded language (see Moore and Burrows 2016-2017: "Chapter 1: The Yellow Sign," 7).[3] Furthermore, Moore sets this dialogue in an Automat, a popular form of self-service cafeteria in the 1920s and 1930s.

> The growth of such facilities is exemplified by the history of two of New York's most famous cafeteria chains, Childs and Horn & Hardart, both of which came to play major roles in the gay world. . . . The cafeterias and Automats were not just cheap places to take meals. Many people also used them as meeting places, where they gathered on an almost nightly basis. . . . Some of these cafeterias, Automats, and lunchrooms catered to a gay clientele, while others were simply taken over by gay men, who were allowed to remain so long as they increased business without drawing the attention of the police. (Chauncey 1994: 164-5)

Providence is set in Moore's altered version of history—cities are covered by domes and there is a suicide chamber in Central Park that is used by Black's former lover in "Chapter 1."[4] But most readers are probably not aware of the historic reality of the depiction of New York's gay life. Chauncey's book shows not only the existence of a hidden gay world in New York during the first half of the twentieth century, but that it was thriving. Moore was obviously intrigued by Chauncey's study and used this historical background as analogy to Robert Black's search for the hidden America of occult believes and practices. Robert Black is already part of a hidden culture, or only partly visible culture, which makes him the ideal person to explore another hidden culture—the occult. But it is not just any hidden occult culture, it is Lovecraft's occult New England that Black starts to explore.

In Lovecraft's texts, the protagonists are often oblivious to the danger and the depth of the ancient culture they immerse themselves in, and Black is no exception here. He only realizes what position he has got himself into when it is too late. Interestingly, shortly before he also realizes that Lovecraft, whom he meets and befriends in the course of the story, is a homophobic anti-Semite and therefore nobody he can really be friends with. It is also interesting to note that, although Robert Black, a Jew and a homosexual, is a fictional character, Lovecraft befriended several other writers that can be compared to Black; Samuel Loveman and Robert Bloch were Jewish and Robert Barlow a homosexual. Robert Black shares the same initials with the latter two and Loveman is discussed by (Moore's) Lovecraft and Black in "Chapter 10: The Haunted Palace," which starts with a quote from "The Haunter of the Dark," a story dedicated to Robert Bloch. In *Providence*, Black does not know how to react to the homophobic and anti-Semitic remarks of Lovecraft in regard to Samuel Loveman, but it is important for Moore to add this perspective on the complicated inner workings of Lovecraft. The contradictions in Lovecraft's writing and biography have led to a great deal of speculation, but in recent years it became clear that these contradictions are an important key to the understanding of Lovecraft's writing. With a nod to Michel Houellebecq's characterization of Lovecraft's racism as self-loathing, Stephen Shapiro and Philip Barnard examine Lovecraft as a regional writer who is interested in the architecture of New England, and they show the complex relation of Lovecraft to the history of slavery:

> Lovecraft's prose not only seeks to indicate that New England's material architecture of cultural prestige is founded on the profits from slavery, but also to signal how the ensuing historical amnesia about the origins of its institutional endowments creates epistemological limits to what can be rationally seen, recognized, or said within its walls. (Shapiro and Barnard 2017: 136)

The difficult relation of US society with its own history is represented in Lovecraft's weird tales, and Moore makes the contradictions in Lovecraft's personal relations visible as well.

Art and Politics

The question of representation and art gets another twist when Moore takes on Lovecraft's story "Pickman's Model" (1927) in "Chapter Seven: The Picture."

After a harrowing journey through remote parts of Lovecraft's New England, Robert Black arrives in Boston on September 10, 1919.[5] The Boston police force had gone on strike, and there were incidents of looting and violence in the streets. Governor Calvin Coolidge used the strike as an opportunity to gain political points in Washington with a hard course against unions and by calling the striking policemen "traitors" and "communists." He succeeded and became vice president the following year.

Moore establishes the historical context on the first page when a drinking policeman in a looted bar tells Black: "I doubt that you've more of a screw loose than Governor Coolidge." (Moore and Burrows 2016-2017: "Chapter Seven: The Picture," 1) He continues four panels later: "Us flatties wanted decent pay; But with the Red Scare they refused. Said we were *Bolsheviks*. Now we're on *strike*" (3, emphasis in the original). The historical context here seems to have a different function to that of the beginning in chapter one. While it helps the reader to get an impression of what was happening in Boston in 1919, it clouds Robert Black's perception when he meets Ronald Pitman.

Obviously, Pitman is Moore's version of Lovecraft's Pickman. In Lovecraft's story, Richard Upton Pickman has been thrown out of the Boston Art Club, because of his disturbing images. The narrator, Thurber, is fascinated by Pickman's pictures and takes his side until he discovers that his monsters don't stem from imagination, but from reality. Moore's Pitman is essentially the same character; both have knowledge of monsters living under Boston and both create paintings from photographs of said monsters. Although, or rather because, Black has already had some disturbing experiences at this point in the story, he is unable to realize what is happening around him. When he sees Pitman's paintings, he interprets them as social criticism. The monsters "represent the anger of the downtrodden lower *classes*, am I right? Erupting into *violence*, like with the *police* strike." (Moore and Burrows 2016–2017: "Chapter 7: The Picture" 12, emphasis in the original). Although Pitman regards his pictures as realism, Black views them as symbolism. Because Black has obviously some knowledge about the occult, Pitman tries to explain to Black that these creatures are real by introducing him to one. For safety reasons, Black is not supposed to look at the creature, and although he seems genuinely frightened, he refuses to accept the reality of speaking to a monster and rather tells himself that Pitman is a good ventriloquist. Analogous to the way Calvin Coolidge used the Red Scare to change the perception of unions and reasonable demands for higher wages, Black regards Pitman's pictures as the artistic expression of the violence he saw in Boston. Furthermore, the traumatic experiences that Black lives through and his naivety lead him to rely on art theory rather than trusting his own perception.

The image of artist Jacen Burrows is very close to Lovecraft's text as it is described by the narrator Thurber:

> Gad, how that man could paint! There was a study called "Subway Accident," in which a flock of vile things were clambering up from some unknown catacomb through a crack in the floor of the Boylston Street subway and attacking a crowd of people on the platform. (Lovecraft 1963: 20)

Although Pickman's pictures are compared to Goya, Thurber describes Pickman as realist artist. "Pickman was in every sense—in conception and in execution—a thorough, painstaking, and almost scientific *realist*" (Lovecraft 1963: 21, emphasis in the original). The punchline, of course, is that neither Lovecraft's Pickman nor Moore's Pitman are really artists who create original art; they copy photos they have taken of the monsters. Their pictures seem like visionary art, sprung from imagination, because they present a reality that is fundamentally different to common experience. So, Moore is basically following Lovecraft's story and his intention here, with two important differences: On the one hand, the narrator of "Pickman's Model" realizes at the end what Pickman is doing, while Robert Black refuses to see the truth behind Pitman's art. The second difference, related to the first, is the police strike, which does not come up in Lovecraft's story. In "Pickman's Model," Lovecraft describes the hidden places beneath Boston and their relation to American history. For Pickman, place and history are important for his art: "The Place for the artist to live is the North End. . . . Don't you realise that places like that weren't merely *made*, but actually *grew*?" (Lovecraft 1963: 15, emphasis in the original). Of course, Pickman and his weird art represent also Lovecraft, who was fascinated by the history of New England.

Moore starts this chapter with a quote from an actual letter by Lovecraft that shows the importance of Boston's historical architecture for "Pickman's Model," and similar to Lovecraft's approach, Moore uses historical context for his adaptation of Lovecraft's stories. In this case, he uses some of Lovecraft's other writing to add to the story of Robert Black, as Lovecraft himself warned against Bolshevism in his publication *Conservative* in July 1919. He writes:

> Even in this traditionally orderly nation the number of Bolsheviki, both open and veiled, is considerable enough to require remedial measures. The repeated and unreasonable strikes of important workers, seemingly with the object to indiscriminate extortion rather than rational wage increase, constitute a menace which should be checked. (Lovecraft 2006: 37)

During the Red Scare of 1919, Lovecraft sided with people like Calvin Coolidge and believed that unions could lead to communism and the downfall of the United States. Lovecraft was not an author with a social conscious as Black sees Pitman, but in *Providence* conflicts of his time become visible.

Lovecraft sometimes used artists as protagonists in his stories, though "Pickman's Model" certainly stands out as a reflection of his own approach. Moore uses the story to reflect on his new interpretation of Lovecraft: he wants to show Lovecraft's darker sides. Black searches for them in the "real New England"[6] and Pitman/Pickman shows them in his pictures. Additionally, Moore has learned from Lovecraft to value history, and the incorporation of the Boston police strike is also a commentary on today's political discourse.[7] "Pickman's Model" is about the difficulties of interpretation and the relation of the artist and his art and Moore's *Providence* tries to cope with these difficulties in an artistic way.

After Black's storyline ends in chapter eleven, Moore follows the history of Lovecraft's texts through the twentieth century, until he catches up with the events of *Neonomicon*. For this part about Lovecraft's reception, he uses four pages or fourteen panels—not counting two images of a record that is repeated throughout the issue—and, interestingly, William S. Burroughs appears in three of these panels.

Providence and William S. Burroughs

Alan Moore has made references to Burroughs before; most notably in his best-known work *Watchmen* where a newspaper is called after Burroughs's cut-up novel *Nova Express* and one of the main characters, Adrian Veidt, talks about the power of cut-ups for an entire page at the start of chapter eleven. Furthermore, Burroughs had some connections to Lovecraft as well,[8] and Moore makes them clear in the three panels. The first panel shows Burroughs standing in the background, while in the foreground two paramedics bend over a dead man whose vomit suggest an overdose. The text in the panel is from an actual letter that Burroughs wrote on January 11, 1951, from Mexico City to Allen Ginsberg:

> A queer Professor from K.C., Mo., head of the Anthropology dept. here at M.C.C. where I collect my $75 per month, knocked himself off a few days ago with overdose of goof balls. Vomit all over the bed. I can't see this suicide kick. (Burroughs 1993: 78; Moore and Burrows 2016–2017: "Chapter Eleven: The Unnamable" 23)

The queer professor who killed himself after "a disgruntled student threatened to expose him as a homosexual" (La Farge 2017) was Robert Barlow, one of Lovecraft's correspondents in the 1930s. Lovecraft visited Barlow in Florida in 1934 and only then discovered the young age of his pen friend. When forty-three-year-old Lovecraft met his young fan for the first time, Barlow was just sixteen years old. After Lovecraft's death in 1937, Barlow became his literary executor, but he was quickly ousted by other Lovecraft disciples, and Barlow followed his passion for Mayan culture that led him to the position at Mexico City College. Burroughs obviously knew Barlow through his studies of Mayan culture, but it is unclear whether there were any meetings between the two outside of a lecture, or whether Burroughs was aware that Barlow was a friend of Lovecraft. But it is interesting to note that Burroughs's study of Mayan culture became very influential for his writing, best seen in *Ah Pook is Here*. In later works, like *Cities of the Red Night*, Mayan mythology merges with other influences, and Lovecraft's Cthulhu mythos is one of them.

The third panel shows Burroughs on his death bed, a cat on his chest and *The Starry Wisdom*, to which he had also contributed, in his lap. In the background, one can recognize James Grauerholz, Burroughs's companion, editor, and manager since the 1970s. The picture seems to be intended as statement by Moore about the importance of Burroughs for the continuation of Lovecraft's legacy because the picture appears as mirror image—or fold-in—to Lovecraft's death exactly four pages earlier. In this context, Burroughs can be seen as stand-in for many authors and artists who were influenced by Lovecraft, but there are more aspects that can be compared to Lovecraft. Burroughs was also an outsider of the literary establishment of his time—Ted Morgan's biography of Burroughs is even called *Literary Outlaw*. His early biography also resembles that of Robert Black: as a young homosexual, he often came to New York City and explored the possibilities that it offered (see Miles 2013: 56).

But for Moore, Burroughs is more than an example of an author influenced by Lovecraft, and the second panel shows more clearly why Moore brings up Burroughs. One can see Burroughs "dropping in" to the printing of the *Simon Necronomicon* in 1977 and the speech balloon of Burroughs, "'Kutulu,' Huh? Maybe I'll use that in this new thing I'm doing" (Moore and Burrows 2016–2017: "Chapter Eleven: The Unnamable" 25) suggests that Burroughs discovered or rediscovered Lovecraft before writing *Cities of the Red Night*, which was published in 1981 and begins with an "Invocation" that contains references to Lovecraft:

> This book is dedicated to the Ancient Ones, . . . to Kutulu, the Sleeping Serpent who cannot be summoned, . . . to the *Great Old One* and the *Star Beast*, to *Pan*,

God of Panic, to the nameless gods of dispersal and emptiness, to *Hassan I Sabbah*, Master of the Assassins.

To all the scribes and artists and practitioners of magic through whom these spirits have been manifested. (Burroughs 1981: xvii–xviii)

Similar to Alan Moore, Burroughs believed in the existence of certain forms of magic, which is probably why both have been drawn to Lovecraft's *Necronomicon*. The *Necronomicon* might be Lovecraft's most famous invention. It is a fictional grimoire that appears in several stories and has been taken up as a reference point by other authors who were collaborating with Lovecraft or later wanted to pay homage to him. Since Lovecraft also invented a history for the book, which was supposedly written by the mad Arab poet Abdul Alhzared around 730 A.D. in Damascus, people began to believe that it was a real book. As Timothy Evans points out, the combination of real history and invented myths is one of the strengths of Lovecraft's texts:

> Lovecraft drew on real and invented traditions to create a new aesthetic, which in turn defined a new reality. This *bricolage*, this creating meaning out of seemingly unconnected bits and pieces, is seen by de Certeau and others as characteristic of postmodernity; it is this quality more than anything else that makes the stories of the conservative Lovecraft, who liked to imagine himself an eighteenth-century gentleman, resonate with audiences in the twenty-first century. (2005: 127)

Mark Fisher has a similar view and adds that "Lovecraft generates a 'reality-effect' by only ever showing us tiny fragments of the *Necronomicon*" (24). Therefore, it seems inevitable that several versions of the book were published over the years. The so-called *Simon Necronomicon*, published in 1977 in New York City, is the most successful version, nonetheless because Burroughs wrote a blurb for it.[9] Moore's intention is not to make fun of this development, but rather show how an idea can become reality. In *Providence*, Lovecraft's stories are based in reality, and, in the end, Cthulhu is brought into the world quite literally.

Weird Reality and Magic

In *Providence*, reality, dream, and literature are often hard to distinguish. This is, first of all, true for its protagonist Robert Black, but also for the reader, which is part of Moore's approach. This becomes especially apparent with regard to the *Necronomicon* and the Cthulhu mythos. In "Chapter Six: Out of Time," Black finds and reads *Hali's Booke of the Wisdom of The Stars* and makes excerpts in his commonplace book. In the world of Moore's *Providence*, this book is a real magic book, and it becomes the model for the *Necronomicon* after the fictional Lovecraft uses Black's commonplace book as inspiration for his stories. After Lovecraft's death, his stories grow in popularity, in *Providence* as well as in reality. The *Simon Necronomicon* is a fake book, in *Providence* as well as in reality, but in *Providence* this is all part of a sinister plot by a secret society of cultist. The monster Cthulhu can only appear in the world when enough people "believe" in its existence. Although Moore surely does not think that it will come this far, the story of the *Necronomicon* shows how a fictional book can become real and people believe it contains forbidden knowledge of magic. *Providence* becomes allegorical and truly weird at the end when Cthulhu is born by the FBI agent Merril Brears, who is raped in *Neonomicon*, and Lovecraft's biographer S. T. Joshi is part of the group that is present at his "birth." The mixture of historical facts and fictional characters create in *Providence* a truly weird reality.

The power of art to change our perception of reality is what fascinates Moore and what also drew Burroughs to Lovecraft. Alan Moore said in an interview:

> It's pretty much a fact that our entire universe is a mental construct. We don't actually deal with reality directly. We simply compose a picture of reality from what's going on in our retinas, in the timpani of our ears, and in our nerve endings. We perceive our own perception, and that perception is to us the entirety of the universe. I believe magic is, on one level, the willful attempt to alter those perceptions. (Bebergal 2013)

This is a definition of magic with which Burroughs could go along, and something that Lovecraft achieved in a way when people perceive the *Necronomicon* as real book, even some who never read Lovecraft in the first place. It is a definition of magic that Moore locates deeply embedded in Western culture, as he uses Shakespeare's Prospero in his comic series *The League of Extraordinary Gentlemen*, and, incidentally, this Prospero looks very similar to Moore himself.

William Burroughs used a similar definition for the function of art:

> I would say that the function of art or, in fact, of any creative thought is to make people aware of what they know and don't know. For example, in the Middle Ages, the people living on the seacoast knew that the earth was round, but they believed the earth was flat. It took Galileo to come and tell them what they knew already—that the earth was round. When Cézanne first exhibited his canvasses, people were so incensed they attacked the canvasses physically in some cases because it was something they weren't used to seeing. They didn't realize that this

> was a pear—just from a different angle, in different light. Ok, then after the furor died down, then everybody accepts it. There's been an advance in awareness. People now know that the earth is round because they couldn't navigate without knowing it. Any child will now recognize the objects in a Cézanne painting—no one is even bothered by that. James Joyce made them aware of their own stream of consciousness, and was accused of being unintelligible, but I don't think very many people would find it very unintelligible now, certainly not *Ulysses*. So that is my working definition of the function of art. (Burroughs 1999: 124)

Burroughs used these examples of art changing our perception often when he was asked about the function of art and, of course, he considered cut-ups in the same vein. Collage and montage techniques have been around in painting for about a century, and they have been applied to other art forms like video and film as well. But it will probably take some time until we regard cut-ups in a similar way we now look at an impressionist painting. Nevertheless, everyone who engages with Burroughs's cut-ups over a longer period of time will experience an alteration of his or her perception of texts.

In *Watchmen*, one can see that Moore was thinking about Burroughs's cut-ups when he inserted Burroughs so prominently into *Providence*. Character Adrian Veidt states before the final showdown of *Watchmen*:

> Multi-Screen viewing is seemingly anticipated by Burroughs' *cut-up* technique. He suggested re-arranging words and images to evade rational analysis, allowing the *future* to leak through. . . . As an afterthought, the method has an *earlier* precursor than Burroughs in the *shamanistic* tradition of divining randomly scattered *goat innards*. (Moore and Gibbons 2013: 349–50, emphasis in the original)

Burroughs ascribed forms of supernatural power to the cut-up technique, and Moore sees Burroughs's cut-ups as exactly this: a way to avoid "rational analysis" and enter the realm of magic and shamanistic rituals. The cut-ups are not primarily for destruction but intended for creation. Burroughs is part of the hidden world that Robert Black is searching for in *Providence* because he uses similar methods as some of the magic practitioners Black encounters and he had the same goal: changing our perception of the world.

In 1964, Susan Sontag called for a different approach to art in general and literature in particular when she published "Against Interpretation." At the very end of her essay, she suggests a new form of interpretation that she calls "an erotics of art" (Sontag, 14). What she means is a conjunction of art and art critique, of creation and interpretation. Furthermore, she embraces the concept of mimicry when she writes "The aim of all commentary on art now should be to make works of art—and, by analogy, our own experience—more, rather than less, real to us" (14). This is what Moore does when he recreates some of Lovecraft's stories. Additionally, his new take on Lovecraft is situated in the best tradition of comparative literature when he holds up William Burroughs and New York's gay culture to shed new light on the work of Lovecraft.

In *Providence* Alan Moore creates a weird reality that assembles historical figures, a new reading of Lovecraft's creations, and Lovecraft himself in a setting that is deeply rooted in political and literary history. As Timothy Evans and Mark Fisher point out, Lovecraft did something similar when he combined history and myths in his own unique way. Moore is aware of Lovecraft's strength and its influence and reception in the arts of the twentieth century. He also knows that all engagement with and interpretation of texts is a form of destruction; *Providence* ends with the tearing apart of Robert Black's commonplace book.

> To all the scribes and artists and practitioners of magic through whom these spirits have been manifested. . . .
>
> NOTHING IS TRUE. EVERYTHING IS PERMITTED. (Burroughs 1981: xviii, capitalization in the original)

Notes

1. With the growing popularity of comics or graphic novels in recent years, the interest in Moore's work has increased as well and sexuality has been one of the topics of discussion (cf. Comer and Sommers 2012).
2. Moore talks about Chauncey's book in at least two videos that can be found on "YouTube." One is *Alan Moore—Providence, a follow-up to Neonomicon* (Baker 2012) that can be found here: https://www.youtube.com/watch?v=DFuqI4j-9h4&t; the other is *The Alan Moore Lecture 2013* (NorthamptonCollege01 2013), https://www.youtube.com/watch?v=rAxDDqi2tBg. Especially in the second video, Moore gives a good summary of some of Chauncey's thesis, and one can find these points later appearing in *Providence*.
3. The three volumes' hardcover edition does not have page numbers. Commentary sites on the internet start counting on the first page of the comic, which will also be done here.
4. Moore likes to play with altered historical timelines. In *Watchmen*, the existence of a being with supernatural powers, Dr. Manhattan, changes American history significantly: the United States wins the war in Vietnam, and, later, the "Watergate"

story isn't published thanks to another "Watchman." So, in *Watchmen*, which starts in October 1985, Richard Nixon is still president. Although one of Dr. Manhattan's most prominent powers is to travel through time, he seems unable to change the course of history according to his own wishes.

5   Through the information in the comic and the dating of the commonplace book, the reader is able to follow Black's journey through New England very accurately, which is very important for Moore's approach.

6   The full quote at the end of the chapter is: "I'm a writer who's trying to get a picture of the *real* New England. My name's *Black*" (Moore and Burrows 2016–2017: "Chapter Seven: The Picture" 26, emphasis in the original).

7   In *Providence*, Moore makes other political comments that fit the setting of 1919, but can also be seen as contemporary. The first chapter starts with the editor in chief, Ephraim Posey, complaining that William Hurst "dragged us all into the gutter" (Moore and Burrows 2016–2017: "Chapter One: The Yellow Sign" 2).

8   Burroughs probably read Lovecraft as a boy and Lovecraft's influence on Burroughs's writing can easily be detected in his later work, especially in the 1980s. But in *Naked Lunch* and the *Nova*-trilogy the case is more difficult. These texts borrow from pulp science fiction, but some ideas might be traced rather to Lovecraft disciples than to Lovecraft himself (cf. Murphy 2009).

9   The blurb reads: "Let the secrets of the ages be revealed. The publication of *The Necronomicon* may well be a landmark in the liberation of the human spirit" (Reality Studio 2019).

References

Baker, A. (2012), *Alan Moore – Providence, a Follow-up to Neonomicon.* Available at: https://www.youtube.com/watch?v=DFuqI4j-9h4&t (accessed September 10, 2019).

Baudrillard, J. (1987), *The Evil Demon of Images*, Sydney: Power Institute of Fine Arts, University of Sydney.

Bebergal, P. (2013), "An Interview with Alan Moore," *The Believer* 99, June 2013, https://believermag.com/an-interview-with-alan-moore/ (accessed September 10, 2019).

Burroughs, W. S. (1981), *Cities of the Red Night*, New York: Picador.

Burroughs, W. S. (1993), *The Letters of William S. Burroughs: 1945–1959*, ed. Oliver Harris, London and New York, Penguin.

Burroughs, W. S. (1999), *Conversations with William S. Burroughs*, ed. Allen Hibbard, Jackson: UP of Mississippi.

Chauncey, G. (1994), *Gay New York: Gender, Urban Culture, and the Making of the Gay Male World, 1890–1940*, New York: Basic Books.

Comer, T. A., and J. M. Sommers, eds. (2012), *Sexual Ideology in the Works of Alan Moore*, Jefferson, NC, and London: McFarland & Company.

Dosse, F. (2010), *Gilles Deleuze and Félix Guattari: Intersecting Lives*, trans. Deborah Glassman, NY: Columbia UP.

Evans, T. H. (2005), "A Last Defense against the Dark: Folklore, Horror, and the Uses of Tradition in the Works of H. P. Lovecraft," *Journal of Folklore Research*, 42 (1): 99–135, Indiana UP.

Fisher, M. (2016), *The Weird and the Eerie*, New York: Random House.

La Farge, P. (2017), "The Complicated Friendship of H. P. Lovecraft and Robert Barlow, One of his Biggest Fans," *The New Yorker*, March 9, 2017, https://www.newyorker.com/books/page-turner/the-complicated-friendship-of-h-p-lovecraft-and-robert-barlow-one-of-his-biggest-fans (accessed September 10, 2019).

Lovecraft, H. P. (1963), "Pickman's Model," *The Dunwich Horror and Others*, 12–25, Sauk City: Arkham House.

Lovecraft, H. P. (2006), "Bolshevism," in S. T. Joshi (ed.), *Collected Essays: Volume 5: Philosophy, Autobiography & Miscellany*, 37–8, New York: Hippocampus Press.

Miles, B. (2013), *Call Me Burroughs: A Life*, New York & Boston: Hachette.

Mitchell, D. M., ed. (2003), *The Starry Wisdom: A Tribute to H. P. Lovecraft*, London: Creation Books.

Moore, A., and J. Burrows (2016–2017), *Providence*, 3 vols, Rantoul, IL: Avatar Press.

Moore, A., and J. Burrows (2017), *Neonomicon*, Rantoul, IL: Avatar Press.

Moore, A., and D. Gibbons (2013), *Watchmen*, Burbank, CA: DC Comics.

Murphy, T. S. (2009), "Random Insect Doom: The Pulp Science Fiction of *Naked Lunch*," in O. Harris and I. MacFadyen (eds.), *Naked Lunch@50: Anniversary Essay*, 223–32, Carbondale: Southern Illinois UP.

NorthamptonCollege01 (2013), *The Alan Moore Lecture 2013*, Available online: https://www.youtube.com/watch?v=rAxDDqi2tBg (accessed September 10, 2019).

RealityStudio (2019), *Burroughs Blurps*, Available Online: https://realitystudio.org/texts/burroughs-blurbs/ (accessed September 10, 2019).

Shapiro, S., and P. Barnard (2017), *Pentecostal Modernism: Lovecraft, Los Angeles, and World-Systems Culture*, London and New York: Bloomsbury.

Sontag, S. (2009), "Against Interpretation," in Sontag, *Against Interpretation and Other Essays*, 3–14, London and New York: Penguin.

Thill, S. (2010), "Alan Moore Gets Psychogeographical With *Unearthing*," *Wired.com*, August 9, 2010, www.wired.com/2010/08/alan-moore/ (accessed September 10, 2019).

15

Alien Beauty

The Glamor of the Eerie

Fred Francis

In February 2018, online readers of *Vogue* could have been forgiven for thinking they were accidentally reading copy from a new collection of weird fiction. An article on the emerging North American design duo Fecal Matter—titled "Yes, 'Fecal Matter' Is the Name of an Instagram You Should Be Following"—described "heels of feet . . . warped into skin-covered scythes" and "a zombie, complete with totally greened-out eyes and a severed breathing tube stuck in her nostrils" (Satenstein 2018b). The author of the piece, seeking to acknowledge that the looks may fall outside the scope of *Vogue*'s usual coverage, suggests that Fecal Matter's designs "could also strike one as eerily beautiful" (Satenstein 2018b).

Fecal Matter draw on a wide range of aesthetic inspirations in their work. The article in *Vogue* notes their commitment to "Victorian-era" waistlines, and the combination of pink pastels and black leather in their designs evokes the looks developed in club, BDSM, and rave culture. However, as *Vogue*'s description of "a freakish fairy tale, or rather a nightmare" might suggest, the influence of the weird in fiction, art, and film is a significant and recurring touchstone in their work (Satenstein 2018b). The breathing tubes and biomechanical appendages favored by Steven Raj Bhaskaran remind the viewer of H. R. Giger and *Alien*, whereas the neon colors and decaying flora and fauna often worn by Hannah Rose Dalton evoke Jeff VanderMeer's *Southern Reach* trilogy and the color palette and variety of human-plant hybrid forms of its 2018 movie adaptation *Annihilation*.[1]

Given the visible relationship between Fecal Matter's designs and a number of high-profile weird works, the most interesting element of the article that brought the duo to the mainstream is the refusal of the fashion world to name the weird at all. "Freakish," "extreme," and—most interesting within the context of this current collection—"eerily beautiful" are all used to describe the weirdness evoked by Fecal Matter's designs, yet the word "weird" itself does not appear (Satenstein 2018b). A similar article about the duo in *i-D* asks: "[W]hy is everyone obsessed with alien beauty, and is it a new kind of subculture?" Focusing on "alien beauty" as a style promoted by several designers, models, and artists, including Fecal Matter, Salvia, MLMA, and Aryuna, the article variously describes the emerging trend as "post-humanist," "dark," and "gothic," but not as weird (Pressigny 2018).

The vocabulary choices made by writers at *Vogue* and *i-D* are reflected across the industry. Another piece about Fecal Matter, in *Indie*, writes that their "gothic, extraterrestrial beauty provoke(s) a conversation about the meaning of 'ugly'" (Phillips 2018). Again, the word "weird" is absent in favor of a claim to an "extraterrestrial beauty"—a phrase reminiscent of the "unearthly cosmic beauty" described by the narrator of H. P. Lovecraft's novella *At the Mountains of Madness* (Lovecraft 2013: 280). Despite the absence of the weird as a term to describe the duo's work, the suggestion that Fecal Matter challenge what we know about ugliness evokes one of the central tenets of scholarship on the weird: the uncanny, fearful, or disquieting properties of the weird have a critical function, and can even be a form of radical resistance. The critical potential of Fecal Matter's designs is fleshed out further in the *Vogue* article, which promotes the duo's critical position toward mainstream fashion as a key selling point. The article quotes Bhaskaran: "[I]t's things that we don't like in the industry, like the child labor, the waste that goes on in the fabric industry, the dyes that are harmful for the environment." To combat this, Fecal Matter is intended to be "a platform of how to discuss uncensored ideas and promote critical thinking" (Satenstein 2018b).

Scholars of the weird might well ask, at this point, whether "eerie" or "alien" beauty is not simply another word for "weird." Although the weird is notoriously hard to pin down, the brief sketch I have outlined of both the form and function of Fecal Matter's "alien beauty" seems to place it squarely within what we know about the weird. If this is the case, the absence of the word itself in writing about the duo, at least within the framework of fashion journalism, begins to make the weird itself look like an ineffable horror—a thing which cannot be named. In *i-D*, the only appearance of the word is in the acknowledgment that "beauty looks that elevate what society traditionally considered ugly or weird is hardly a new idea" (Pressigny 2018). *Indie* argues that, like punk before it, alien beauty is "subverting traditional standards of beauty" (Phillips 2018). In the fashion world, at least, it seems that the weird is not beautiful in the traditional sense, but the ugliness or weirdness can be "elevated" to the level of beauty.

Fashion magazines appear to bracket "weird" with "ugly" as words to be overcome—ideas that do not endear art to their audience. This is hardly surprising: weirdness is deliberately off-putting, challenging, and subversive. In the furthest-reaching of positive scholarly appraisals, weirdness presents a threat to the entire capitalist order. The reticence of fashion writers to use the term "weird" is perhaps understandable, in this light. However, as the appearance of Fecal Matter in *Vogue* proves, the weird—even by another name—has the potential to generate money in the mainstream. Indeed, throughout its history the concept of the weird as an outsider form, a space for critical thinking, has been directly at odds with its commercial success. While some "weird culture" remains underground and jealously guarded by aficionados, the origins of weird fiction are in the disposable magazine and comics culture of twentieth-century North America (Luckhurst 2017: 1042–4). Furthermore, the sizable and continuous revenue generated from writers like Lovecraft (even in the face of efforts to highlight his unsavory politics) is evidence enough that—like it or not—*weirdness sells*. In fact, I feel confident in suggesting that any reader of this volume is interested enough in the weird as a mode to have paid money to enjoy some of its cultural products—even if they are then able to argue that the product itself critiques or undermines a capitalist system. The same can be said of "alien beauty." Although both *Vogue* and *Indie* are keen to herald the subversive power of Fecal Matter, their work has now clearly breached the mainstream. By December of 2018, the duo had staged their first catwalk show, as well as appearing in the music video for A$AP Rocky's song "Fukk Sleep" (featuring FKA twigs), which has over seventeen million views on YouTube at the time of writing.

This chapter focuses on the disjunction between the critical and commercial potentials of the weird highlighted by the example of writing about Fecal Matter and their aesthetics of what has been termed "alien beauty." If the weird is so critical and challenging, what is it that provokes us to spend our hard-earned money on it? If the weird is often "ugly" or off-putting, what is it about these products that entrances us? When does the weird cease to be weird and instead become "dark," "gothic," "alien," or "eerie"? The answer to these questions, I will propose in this chapter, is hidden in the division enacted between the idea of "the weird" as an ugly form and its counterpart in "eerie beauty." Beginning from Mark Fisher's separation of the weird and the eerie in his book of the same name (see Fisher 2016), I will argue that the language deployed by fashion writers reflects a broader cultural approach to the weird and the eerie. Where the weird denotes that which is unsettling—a mode which should put off engagement—

the eerie denotes an attractive weirdness which compels us toward it. Once we understand the difference between these two modes, it then becomes clear that the process by which weirdness can be made eerie is also a process in which something off-putting can be made attractive, and the application of eeriness becomes a technology to make weirdness commercially viable. In other words, I want to argue that eeriness is the mechanism by which weirdness becomes marketable—it is the weird's glamorous counterpart.

An Eerie Presence

The distinction between weirdness and eeriness highlighted by the language used to write about alien beauty is also the focus of Mark Fisher's *The Weird and the Eerie*. In his book, Fisher aims to separate weirdness and eeriness as related but critically distinguishable modes. He begins with the sensation of the weird, which he suggests is provoked by "that which does not belong" (Fisher 2016: 61). The encounter with a weird object creates a "sensation of *wrongness*" in the subject because the presence of something weird challenges what the subject knows (or, previously knew) to be the truth and scope of their world (15). Fisher draws out this relationship between the weird and an apparent challenge to what is "natural" through the idea of the black hole: "the bizarre ways in which it bends time and space" challenge the very idea of what we know about the operation of the universe (15).

Fisher's approach to the weird adds weight to the assertion that "alien beauty" is at least significantly similar, if not functionally the same, as the weird. In fact, two of the key characteristics visible in writing about alien beauty are present in Fisher's definition: the idea that the mode has critical potential and its relationship to ugliness. Alien beauty is regularly described as "subversive" or "posthuman," and Clementine de Pressigny notes in *i-D* that "challenging binary ideas of gender is a clear part of the impetus behind alien glamour" (2018). Bhaskaran and Dalton's designs achieve this effect by either removing or reworking typically gender-marked clothing, as in their most well-known creation: the skin heels. Realized by American sculptor and artist Sarah Sitkin, the skin heels mimic the shape of a stiletto shoe but appear to have the texture of human flesh, creating the illusion that the wearer's legs end in sharp talons. By presenting one of fashion's most familiar objects, the high heel, as an outgrowth of the human form, Bhaskaran and Dalton highlight the cruelty of the object's shape while simultaneously challenging the idea that heels should be gendered at all. The rendering of the object as "natural" is a challenge to the normalization of such footwear, and to the restriction that this footwear is only for women.

Weirdness, in this paradigm, depends on visibility. In order to unsettle or be subversive, a weird object has to come into view within the world we currently perceive. As Fisher puts it, weirdness relies on "presence" (2016: 61). In this light, the idea of the weird as "ugly" reveals the ways in which the presence of "ugliness" is itself a challenge. When Bhaskaran comments that "in Paris, people spit at us and call us the devil," these reactions are only one more outcropping of the systematic violence targeted toward people who do not conform to gender norms (Satenstein 2018b). Fecal Matter's visibility, and the violence that attends their visibility, not only is an essential part of their weirdness but also forms the most significant part of their critical work. Bhaskaran suggests that their designs challenge ideas of gender, and of beauty, because "we want the masses to accept [difference] and see it as something not scary or intimidating" (Satenstein 2018b).

Eeriness, on the other hand, is a counterpart to weirdness distinguished by its inversion of the idea of "presence." For Fisher, the eerie "occurs either when there is something present where there should be nothing, or there is nothing present where there should be something." The eerie, then, is "constituted by a *failure of absence* or a *failure of presence*" (Fisher 2016: 61). However, I would like to suggest here that Fisher's account of the eerie is instructive but requires some further examination. Rather than divide the eerie into two parts, pursuing Fisher's logic reveals the eerie as a unified phenomenon, which is always about both absence and presence, where the object provoking the sensation of the eerie provokes speculation as to its original source.

Fisher's first definition of the eerie presents it as a *failure of absence*. In this case, the eerie is a sensation that occurs when an object is present which should not be. The idea of a "thing that should not be" has clear origins in Lovecraftian weirdness, to the degree that it seems difficult to draw out what is different about a weird object that disrupts our knowledge of what is natural (what *can* be) and an eerie object which breaks the particular rule of "something that should not be here." Fisher's example is of a bird's eerie cry. It is eerie if it suggests that there is something more than the biological animal in its source: an "intent" not normally associated with the bird that provokes questions of possession, of abnormality, of the supernatural. In the case of the bird's cry, the source of the cry must be obscured from view either by the absence of the physical bird or by the invisibility of the "form of intent we do not usually associate with a bird" (Fisher 2016: 62). This absence must be the case if the speculation necessary for the sensation of eeriness can occur. In other words, if something is eerie, there must be something the observer cannot know or verify. If the bird's cry was a marker of a verifiable supernatural possession, this would render the sensation not eerie but weird, horrific, or some other associated but definably separate affect. Since Fisher is clear that mystery or speculation is vital to the eerie, it follows that this mystery must always rely on a failure of presence: a lacuna or absence, which is not (and perhaps cannot be) filled. I would suggest, in this case, that it is not the presence (Fisher's "failure of absence") that is causing eeriness, but the absence of something else: the context or explanation for the presence.

Fisher's second type of eeriness—the failure of presence—already relies on this absence of context to achieve its effect. He writes that the eeriness caused by a failure of presence is most obviously provoked by "ruins, or . . . other abandoned structures" (Fisher 2016: 62). In this case, an object hints that something necessary to understand the object is not present: a building in ruins, in a desolate landscape. Making the comparison between the eeriness of Stonehenge and eerie architecture in postapocalyptic science fiction, Fisher argues that both environments share this particular lacuna. The presence of the structure highlights the absence of the framework or society which explains that structure. As Fisher puts it, "The symbolic structures which made sense of the monuments have rotted away" (63). For Fisher, the value of thinking about the eerie can be demonstrated by the critique this approach enables. The viewer of the eerie object is forced to question what brought the object into being, and reckon with absent and abstract forces that no longer exist: in his argument, the eerie can provoke engagement with the absent-presence of capital or other invisible structuring mechanisms at work and reveal that "a force like capital does not exist in any substantial sense" (64). Eeriness, therefore, maintains the same critical power as weirdness, although expressed in terms of absence—or invisibility—rather than visibility. The critical power of the weird is in its ability to reveal the limits of human knowledge in the face of nature's great scope: Fecal Matter's designs reveal that a binary view of gender is inadequate to capture the breadth of human experience, just like a black hole reveals the limitations of human understanding about the laws of nature. Conversely, and yet producing a similar result, the eerie has a critical function when it reveals the limits of human knowledge through absence—what we know to be true is missing, yet the traces of its presence remain.

In both of Fisher's examples, the eerie affect is reliant on the question or mystery that the object provokes. Once the reason behind the bird's cry or the abandoned structure is understood, the situation may resolve into either the weird—the bird was in fact possessed, and "that which does not belong" is definitely present—or the quotidian (i.e., there was nothing untoward). Developing Fisher's theory to focus on the mystery produces new ways to explore the attraction potential of eeriness. Firstly, focusing on the question the eerie provokes reveals that the *failure of presence* is at the heart of the eerie. For the mystery to exist, something must be missing which the observer hopes, and fails, to fill in. Fisher's description of the *failure of absence* is only a restatement of this same logic. In his argument, the *failure of absence* produces eeriness when it points to something supernatural or inexplicable. However, something that is truly visible as supernatural is no longer eerie. Rather, failure of absence only produces eeriness when it points beyond itself to a further *failure of presence* upon which speculation can take place—as Fisher puts it, "when knowledge is achieved, the eerie disappears" (62). It is then possible to make a firmer restatement of the conditions for the eerie: the eerie is revealed as a *presence which points to absence*—an object that points to something unknown beyond itself.

Eerie Capitalism

Fisher is careful to point out that "not all mysteries generate the eerie," and eeriness must also involve a sensation of alterity or "forms of knowledge, subjectivity, and sensation that lie beyond common experience" (Fisher 2016: 62). However, the mystery at the heart of the eerie, and in particular the sense of something missing, is the first clue to understanding the commercial appeal of weirdness and eeriness. If weirdness relies on the presence of things we did not know could exist, the appearance of these objects certainly expands the space for commerce: a weird object, in a commercial space, might be one we did not know was possible until confronted by it. This is no doubt the case with Fecal Matter's skin heels: the idea was first realized with the sole purpose of deceiving the eye through a combination of prosthetics and digital manipulation, and only ever intended to be seen in the context of a photo shoot. Despite their origins as a critique of high fashion, and their apparent ugliness, the skin heels quickly became a commercial reality—retailing for somewhere in the region of $10,000. The second life of the shoes as a purchasable object (albeit highly limited) only came about once they had been seen to exist: their visibility, central to their weirdness, created the market the duo could then exploit. However, the value of the shoes as weird objects is also their significant limitation: because the shoes are designed to challenge the mainstream, Bhaskaran acknowledges that "the bottom line is the masses aren't going to adapt to this. It isn't like tomorrow everyone is going to be wearing these heels" (Satenstein 2018b).

The weird, by this reckoning, has commercial value as a site for innovation, but the unsettling sensations it produces limit its appeal. How then, as *Vogue* suggests is the case for other designs by Fecal Matter, might an object contain or present eeriness instead of weirdness? If the eerie is a *presence which points to absence*, then the eerie is a sensation or affect that must be attached to a particular object: something must be present in order to reveal the absence beyond that presence. For Fisher, "there is no doubt that the sensation of the eerie clings to certain kinds of physical spaces and landscapes," but the statement can be pushed beyond the immediately physical (2016: 61). When Fisher gives the example of the bird's cry as an eerie object, both the cry itself and the absence to which it points—the unknown origin of the cry that goes beyond the bird—have no stable, tangible presence. In fact, it is perhaps in their absence of physicality that the eeriness originates. One notable similarity between Fisher's two examples he does not consider is the way they evoke the idea of the temporary, and of temporality (albeit over very different timescales). The bird's cry is fleeting, perhaps never to be repeated, and creates the sensation of eeriness once it is finished and the environment returns to silence. Similarly, a ruined building is eerie because it catches the moment of returning to silence, or to absence, over a longer time frame. In both cases, the observer must face the process of presence becoming absence—of something that was once present, but which is, or will be, no longer.

If the object requires no physical presence, it follows that the object to which the eerie clings can be constituted within, or by, other objects. In other words, there is no reason we cannot create eerie objects out of thin air. Fisher writes that "although [the eerie] is certainly triggered by particular cultural forms, it does not originate in them. You could say rather that certain tales, certain novels, certain films evoke the feeling of the eerie" (2016: 61). Again, this argument requires some investigation. If I were to describe a book as "evoking the feeling of the eerie," for example this would be an immediately appreciable review that might stimulate people to go and spend money. However, it is rarely the case that the book itself, as opposed to the objects constituted within the book (descriptions of ruins, etc.), evokes the eerie. An eerie book, *as object*, would be one that pointed beyond itself to some kind of missing knowledge—perhaps asking the question: Where did this book come from? This is rarely, if ever, what is meant when we call a book eerie. The description of an "eerie book" more obviously points to the way objects created within the book make the subject feel, and the way in which that eeriness seems to permeate the container object (such that a text can both contain eeriness and become eerie as a whole). This usage presents a further point of investigation: we need to understand how the sensation of eeriness can overflow the specific object within the text to which it is attached and permeate or saturate a text in its entirety, and we need to know why this saturation is appealing.

Fisher points toward these problems when he looks at Christopher Priest's novel *The Glamour*. The "glamor" of the novel recalls the original sense of the word as a spell or charm cast upon an object; in this case, the glamor is a spell of invisibility that makes people disappear. According to Fisher, this glamor within the novel that accounts for the eeriness of the novel as a whole (2016: 74). The invisibility glamor hides something which should be present—characters and their experiences. When this glamor is revealed, the book is made eerie since we can no longer trust the narrative provided by the main character. As an eerie object, and like any spell that affects the way we perceive the world, a glamor is eerie since the knowledge of its existence points to what it hides. At the same time, within the novel the spell functions similarly to eeriness as an affect. Both the glamor and eeriness "cling" to objects, overflow them and give them resonances beyond themselves.

Fisher's focus on the idea of glamor, albeit brief, has some obvious resonances with the usage of eerie when discussing high fashion. Other treatments of glamor offer further insight in this matter and point to the relationship between glamor and eeriness that Fisher highlights. In "The Material Practices of Glamour," Nigel Thrift suggests glamor as the answer to the question: "Why are people attracted to goods?" (2008: 9). Thrift draws on the same etymology for glamor as Fisher, taking its original meaning and describing glamor today as a kind of "secular magic" (9). Reversing the object-human relationship generally created by glamor spells—a situation where a human actor bewitches an object to accord it some affective power—Thrift proposes that the spell of glamor is not attached to objects. Rather, objects *cast* glamor as a spell: the signals that we receive in the act of sensing an object are "magical" in that they "provide associations and conjunctions, dissociations and echoes, that stimulate perception and imagination and, indeed, enjoyment" (11). The extra-sensory "echoes" that are part and parcel of the sensation of an object, and go beyond its purely physical nature, are the key to understanding how eeriness can overflow the object to which it clings. In Thrift's theory of glamor, the fact that objects point beyond themselves is the source of their magic. In the same way, Fisher's eerie object is *always* pointing beyond itself to the "dissociations and echoes" created by the realization of temporality, or the recognition of something ineffable.

Eeriness and glamor, then, rely on strikingly similar affective mechanisms. Where an eerie object points to an enigmatic or disconcerting absence, a glamorous object is one that points to an absence we desire. For Thrift, glamorous objects point beyond themselves to "a world without troubles," offering the promise of a paradise or utopia which achievable through purchase (2008: 14). These utopian worlds, according to Thrift, are often "spaces formed by capitalism": he notes the purpose-built store or shopping mall as examples (2008: 14). To maintain the illusion, glamor must be effortless—it is a manipulation that relies on not being noticed, and discordant details that could "break the spell" must be silently removed. The intentional removal of the structuring devices used to create the spell of glamor recalls Fisher's argument that eeriness occurs when "the symbolic structures which made sense of the monuments have rotted away" (Fisher 2016: 63). Thrift's argument is that spaces like malls are "spaces formed by capitalism whose aim is not to create subjects . . . so much as the world within which the subject exists" (Thrift 2008: 12), but this world is revealed as false when the abandoned mall outlives capitalism itself—a conclusion validated by the number of eerie abandoned shopping malls in weird fiction.

Following this line of thought, I want to argue that any object casting glamor is also eerie, at least by the definition I have proposed. The enigma at the heart of the eerie—the missing piece—is no different to the "mechanism of fascination" which drives glamor. In both cases, a perceptible object points to something absent—either a more perfect world or a deeper unknown—and encourages us toward it. This conclusion is supported by tracing both Thrift and Fisher's work back to a common source in Graham Harman's philosophy of "allure," which could be broadly presented as the appeal of the gap between the sensual and the real. Harman argues for a "dual polarization that occurs in the world" as we perceive, with the result being significant conceptual and perceptual gaps between "the real and the sensual" and between "objects and their qualities" (Harman 2012b: 4). One of the key outcomes of these gaps is that the surface impressions which objects produce can be manipulated and made to give hints of qualities separate from the "reality" of the object—this reality being inaccessible to sensory perception (Harman 2012a: 187). It is these impressions that make the object "alluring" to us—in this case, we want to have the object to get closer to the unreachable pleasure it offers.

The gap between real and sensory object takes on a variety of guises. In one case, it can be the magic of glamor, in another the horror of the ineffable, in another the chill of the eerie. Harman acknowledges as much when he postulates an alternate version of Lovecraft:

> One could imagine a very different writer who used Lovecraft's staple techniques for other purposes—perhaps a sensual fantasist who would place us in a world of strange and indescribable pleasures, in which candles, cloves, and coconut milk were of such unearthly perfection that language would declare itself nearly powerless to describe them. (Harman 2012b: 4)

Harman is able to imagine Lovecraft as a writer of what might be best described as an old-world glamor because, in his assessment, both unknowable horror and pleasure beyond the accessible proceed from the same alluring gap between sensation and reality. This argument means horror is not a necessary part of Lovecraft's style, and Harman separates the horror of Lovecraft's "literal content" from his ability to write into the spaces "between objects and their qualities"— Lovecraft's skill is not simply as writer of horror but as a "writer of gaps" (Harman 2012b: 4). Furthermore, Harman argues that Lovecraft's ability to conjure up and exploit the space between experience and reality preempts Harman's own philosophy (2012b: 4). Although we might balk at this self-centered interpretation of literary history, it is true that Harman's work (and, more broadly, the group of philosophies known as speculative realism) has had a significant impact on the theorization of affect. Harman is cited in both Fisher's and Thrift's arguments, and his proposal of a textual object that offers pleasure beyond the worldly is strikingly similar to Thrift's proposal of glamor as a "technology of allure." In both cases, an object created from thin air can entrance the viewer through a glimpse at a better and beautiful, but ultimately inaccessible, world. By tracing the origins of Thrift's and Fisher's ideas to Harman, it becomes apparent that the shimmering or deceptive quality of the object, presenting an always-tempting but unknowable reality, gives rise to Thrift's idea of the glamorous in the same way as it produces Fisher's sense of the eerie.

Conclusion: The Glamor of the Eerie

The eerie, then, occupies a strange middle ground between the weird and the glamorous. Understanding this position helps to make sense of both why fashion magazines would see an eerie beauty as a positive attribute and how weirdness can become a commercial prospect. In the first instance, I have argued that Fecal Matter's designs both draw on and have begun to influence weird culture. Furthermore, the duo's work is deliberately challenging and subversive, in line with common critical interpretations of the weird. However, "alien beauty" is also glamorous. Its critical work aims at creating a new, better world for marginalized groups, and promises this world in the objects it creates. Simon Huck, designer of the exhibition *A.Human*, has suggested that "when you think of the future, you think dark, dystopian—there are all these images that come to mind. I didn't want to create a utopian world, but I definitely wanted to create a world that was optimistic" (Yotka 2018). Huck's exhibition features "a conch-shell-like permanent heel"—these designs being a recurring theme in the "alien beauty" trend (Yotka 2018). Similarly, Bhaskaran's comments justifying the decision to sell the skin heels evokes an optimistic vision of the potential of the design: "through our platform, a lot of people are gaining confidence and living their lives without fear" (Satenstein 2018a). From this perspective, Fecal Matter's designs seem to combine Thrift's concept of glamor as promising a "world without troubles" and the visible challenge to the norm that defines the weird for Fisher. The result is an object that promises happiness by looking to an optimistic future where gender-based violence no longer occurs. This object, as *Vogue* describes it, might well be considered "eerily beautiful."

However, as a counterpart to this critical function, I want to note that Thrift closes his argument with the idea that "not everyone is taken in by the secular magic of glamour and other forms of allure but sometimes even the most hardened feel its tug—in an impulse purchase, in some small sign of obeisance to a persona they can't help but fantasize about, in an object placed just so in a room" (2008: 21). This, I think, is the danger to which scholarship on the weird often succumbs. The allure, and particularly the allure that an object will have critical value, is fundamental to understanding why we want to buy weird objects. If eeriness functions like glamor, containing its own "allure" when it promises the resolution to a mystery, then it also becomes an exploitable technology. In other words, we need to be aware of the fact that the eerie can be faked and used to sell us things. The same blend of meticulous attention and apparent nonchalance used to produce glamor can produce an eeriness or weirdness which relies on its own fascinating effect: rather than promise a perfect world, it promises an enigmatic world—a mystery that can be solved through purchase. This being the case, we would do well to watch out for the glamor of the eerie—both in order that we can appreciate when it haunts and makes weird the spaces used to sell us things, and so that we can ask ourselves what it is about haunting and weirdness that we find so appealing.

Note

1   In the time since this chapter was first written, the relationship of influence between Fecal Matter's designs and contemporaneous horror and weird cinema has already begun to swing in the opposite direction. Although a more recent article describes one of Dalton's outfits as "a twisted sequel to *Midsommar*" (Fraser 2019), I would argue that the duo's growth in popularity predates this film and that several design choices in *Midsommar* demonstrate the spread of their aesthetic influence (as two examples, the scene where one character has duct-taped a hose to their mouth and the outfit of flowers at the film's climax).

References

de Pressigny, C. (2018), "Why Is Everyone Obsessed with Alien Beauty," *i-D*. 10 October. https://i-d.vice.com/en_uk/article/7x3dy9/why-is-everyone-obsessed-with-alien-beauty-instagram-fecal-matter (accessed August 17, 2019).

Fisher, M. (2016), *The Weird and the Eerie*, London: Repeater.

Fraser, E. (2019), "From Flesh Boots to Skin Ruffles, How Fashion Embraces Fantasy and Horror," *SyFyWire*. 21 August. https://www.syfy.com/syfywire/from-flesh-boots-to-skin-ruffles-how-fashion-embraces-fantasy-and-horror (accessed August 24, 2019).

Harman, G. (2012a), "The Well-Wrought Broken Hammer: Object-Oriented Literary Criticism," *New Literary History*, (43): 183–203.

Harman, G. (2012b), *Weird Realism: Lovecraft and Philosophy*, Winchester, UK: Zero Books.

Lovecraft, H. P. (2013), "At the Mountains of Madness," In Roger Luckhurst (ed.), *The Classic Horror Stories*, 182–285, Oxford: Oxford University Press.

Luckhurst, R. (2017), "The Weird: A Dis/orientation," *Textual Practice*, 31 (6): 1041–61.

Phillips, E. L. (2018), "Instagram's Alien Entities Are the Manifestation of Millennial Punk," *Indie*. 4 December. https://indie-mag.com/2018/12/alien-beauty/ (accessed August 17, 2019).

Satenstein, L. (2018a), "Fecal Matter Has Made Its Photoshopped Skin Shoes into Actual Wearable Heels—and They're $10,000," *Vogue*. 24 October. https://www.vogue.com/article/fecal-matter-releases-photoshopped-skin-heels-for-real-life (accessed August 17, 2019).

Satenstein, L. (2018b), "Yes, 'Fecal Matter' Is the Name of an Instagram You Should Be Following," *Vogue*. 27 February. https://www.vogue.com/vogueworld/article/fecal-matter-instagram-duo-to-follow (accessed August 17, 2019).

Thrift, N. (2008), "The Material Practices of Glamour," *Journal of Cultural Economy*, 1 (1): 9–23.

Yotka, S. (2018), "Would You Get High Heels Implanted into Your Feet? This Exhibit Wants You to Consider It," *Vogue*. 27 August. https://www.vogue.com/article/a-human-body-modification-simon-huck-exhibit (accessed August 17, 2019).

16

Conspiracy Hermeneutics

The Secret World as Weird Tale[1]

Tanya Krzywinska

Through close consideration of the multiplayer online game *The Secret World* (2012), this chapter works toward a definition of "weird games" as a basis for advocating the aesthetic potential of the concept of the weird for digital games. While the weird tale shares some features with the gothic, it has a very distinctive form that is beautifully summed by H. P. Lovecraft in his essay *Supernatural Horror in Literature*:

> The true weird tale has something more than secret murder, bloody bones, or a sheeted form clanking chains according to rule. A certain atmosphere of breathless and unexplainable dread of outer, unknown forces must be present; and there must be a hint, expressed with a seriousness and portentousness becoming its subject, of that most terrible conception of the human brain—*a malign and particular suspension or defeat of those fixed laws of Nature which are our only safeguard against the assaults of chaos and the daemons of unplumbed space.* (Lovecraft 1973: 15; emphasis added)

The weird tale may be regarded broadly as a part of twentieth-century populist or even trash writing, but it also has a place in digital games and like the gothic it crosses genres and (plat)forms. Indicative of its presence in "Indie" games (those games that actively seek to go against mainstream formats and experience) are: *Alone* (Greenwood Games, 2013), developed for the immersive context provided by Oculus Rift providing many opportunities for breaking the fourth wall; *Dear Esther* (the Chinese Room, 2012), which pushed horror grammar toward atmosphere rather than action, and, in the surreal, visually innovative, and well-written *Truberbrook* (Headup/Whisper Games, 2019).

To these I add examples from prior, bigger budget games such as the Lovecraftian homage *Eternal Darkness: Sanity's Requiem* (Silicon Knights,

2002), the early entries in the Silent Hill series (particularly 1 and 2), and the Twin Peaks-like *Deadly Premonition* (Access Games, 2010/2012), where a real-time mechanic contributes to the creation of its version of the weird. More than simply adaptation, the weird is exerting an influence on the formation of innovative contemporary game grammar, largely in contention with established conventions. The analytic framework around this assertion is based on an investigation of the ways that the participatory and rule-based nature of digital game form shapes, at a fundamental level, the ways that the weird tale manifests itself in games, and I will truncate the term "weird tale" to the weird which further helps relocate its presence outside text-based literature and places emphasis on its affective coordinates. As such, this chapter works toward the proposition that there are certain properties of digital games that are capable of generating a new dimension to the affective experience of the weird.

The Secret World (Funcom, 2012; *TSW* hereafter) is a massively multiplayer role-playing game (MMORPG) that provides an excellent example of the ludic adaptation of the weird tale and offers a means of exploring the adaptive possibilities within games for weird fiction. As will be shown, in *TSW* these possibilities emerge through the specific use of intertextuality, which is pivotal in the production of what I will call the "Conspiracy Hermeneutic." As a disturbance in the symbolic order generated by the specific nature of computer-based media, the conspiracy hermeneutic is aimed to create for players a strong sensation of the weird. Central to the argument of this chapter is the idea that at the conjunction of participatory game media and the characteristic features of weird fiction there lurks a powerful means of fundamental disturbance that has transformational and critical potency. Such potential is ably illustrated by the derangement of schematic and conventionalized boundaries between the signification of fact and fiction. Such derangement produces a vast and dizzying network of looped refractions and recursive intertexts that are intended to induce vertigo and to scatter asunder the coherence and stability of the symbolic order. Working with, and undermining, our inbuilt will to mastery and knowledge, the weird of the game carves a frisson of doubt into any comforting sense of rational certainty and authority. It does this by casting precarious the base distinction between fiction and fact and thereby causing the frameworks by which we assign meaning to fall into disarray. We may have physical mastery over the game's interface, but unlike the affective trajectory of standard games, that mastery is frequently belittled and devalued in the face of monumental, obscured, and occulted powers—even if with a rather less melancholic affect than the case with games such as *Eternal Darkness: Sanity's Requiem* or *Limbo*

(Playdead, 2010). *TSW* is therefore trying to innovate on "action-based" game grammar in an open world setting rather than reframe it elsewhere or use a more linear, closed world, as is the case with *Limbo, Eternal Darkness,* or *Alan Wake* (Remedy Entertainment, 2010). In blending together H. P. Lovecraft's critical attempts to locate the sphere of the weird with a type of paranoiac, everything-is-true reading that underlies conspiracy theory and Graham Harman's *Weird Realism: Lovecraft and Philosophy* (2012), this chapter claims that the weird has an aptitude for ludic participation that is most apparent in its power to recast tired regimes of player sovereignty. Seeded from Harman's tree, this chapter thus shows that the weird becomes present where the medium of games *is used against itself*.

Lovecraftian Principles

The weird tale can appear hard to distinguish from other related genres such as fantasy, supernatural, horror, gothic, and science fiction; often based on taste, critics tend to overly tribalize such imagination-based fiction (much as occurs with rock music). The value of such labor is not so much that we can beat our friends in late-night arguments about what stories belong to which tribes (as fun as that might be), but instead lies in the help that such distinctions can provide in the identification of the more subtle threads, tangential intertexts, and elusive affective intentions of weird fiction. In their introduction to *Realms of Fantasy* (1983), Malcolm Edwards and Robert Holdstock outline five settings for stories that fall into the fantasy, supernatural, horror, gothic, and science fiction camp: stories set in the past; those set in present-day lost worlds; those on other planets; those in the distant future; and those in fantasy Earths quite separate from our own (but with affinities to it) (see Edwards & Holdstock 1983: 7). The weird does not however fit neatly with any of these, and the fact that it does not tells us a great about the weirdness of weird. Principally, weird fiction takes place in the here and now: there is no comforting distancing device of placing events in the past or the future, or indeed in a constructed "secondary creation" such as Middle Earth or Azeroth. Equally, the weird is devoid of the epic qualities so common in fantasy and has no principled, valiant, or intrepid heroes such as Aragorn and Conan, nor even an anti-hero like Moorcock's Elric. There is never too much action, bar perhaps some wild flailing about and, possibly, some running away. The weird might therefore be said to be in its best sense the antithesis of epic fantasy and technological optimism: tech-noir, for example, is marked off by its weird negativism and pessimism. While I have rather confidently asserted its differences, Joshi cautions that "the weird tale ... did not (and perhaps does not now) exist as a genre but as a consequence of a world view.... If the weird tale exists *now* as a genre, it may only be because critics and publishers have deemed it so by fiat" (Joshi 1990: 1).

This does not mean that newer, altered uses of the term "weird" are not legitimate or interesting, far from it. The adoption of the Anglo-Saxon word "wyrd," for example, has rich resonance with outsider art, mystical, and/or occult fiction and shamanistic practices. However, the definition of weird in play in this chapter and its address in the context of games is guided by Lovecraft, mainly to provide a starting point for understanding its presence in games and its existing and possible relationships with the games and game form. Joshi suggests that it is Lovecraft's insistence on psychological realism that leads it away from the gothic, although in an overly tidy maneuver he locates the gothic temporally within novels written in late eighteenth and early nineteenth century. While E. T. A. Hoffmann's short tales (see Hoffmann 1982) might be said to be characterized by psychological realism, tellingly their distinction is apparent. For example, the plot of "The Sandman" (1816) revolves around the fatal, conspiratorial misreading of events on the part of the mad central character, thereby framing the supernatural as subjective and not as a property of objective reality. This diegetically grounded "conspiracy hermeneutic" is therefore a feature of the gothic, rather fully occupying the domain of the weird. Specifically, the weird is a property of reality; it is not an effect of psychology, even though it might be taken as symptomatic of a character's imagination by that or other characters. The supernatural in the context of weird fiction is not metaphysical or mystical, even though it might appear to have such properties. As Joshi says, it is "not *ontological* but *epistemological*: it is only our ignorance of certain laws that creates the illusion of *supernaturalism*" (Joshi 1990: 7); as is evident in Lovecraft's post-Euclidean, post-Einsteinian, post-human tale, "Dreams in the Witch House" (1933). Adding a further dimension, appropriately, to this conception, Harman places emphasis on the otherness of the real when explaining the value of Lovecraft's weird, "reality itself is weird because reality itself is incommensurable with any attempt to represent or measure it ... when it comes to grasping reality, illusion and innuendo are the best we can do" (Harman 2012: 51). Harman insists that Lovecraft is a writer of great allusive subtlety rather than a literalist genre hack, while Joshi claims that the appearance of Lovecraft's work in the pulp magazine *Weird Tales* may have made the weird into a genre but caused "the contemptuous dismissal of all weird work on the part of academic critics"

(Joshi 1990: 3). The appearance, then, of the weird in games has much to live up to, mixing, as it does, horror with allusive intimations of the dark sublime. The weird clearly has the power to appeal across the pulp versus elite divide, and like the weird tale, digital games have been lauded as wasteful, populist adolescent pulp *and* a new, highly sophisticated art form. In his essay *Supernatural Horror in Literature* (1927), Lovecraft lists some characteristics that help identify the properties of the weird:

> Indeed we may say that this school [romantic, semi Gothic, quasi moral] still survives; for to it clearly belong such of our contemporary horror-tales as specialize in events rather than atmospheric details, address the intellect rather than the impressionistic imagination, cultivate a luminous glamour rather than a malign tensity or psychological verisimilitude, and take a definite stand in sympathy with mankind and its welfare. It has its undeniable strength, and because the "human element" commands a wider audience than does the sheer artistic nightmare. If not quite so potent as the latter, it is because a diluted product can never achieve the intensity of a concentrated essence. (Lovecraft 1973: 43)

We can summarize these Lovecraftian principles as the following: atmosphere over events, malign tensity, psychological verisimilitude, appeal to the impressionistic imagination, and a lack of any sympathy for humanity. These are helpful coordinates through which to assess any claims to the weird in games) and as a lens through which to evaluate *TSW* as weird fiction.

Atmosphere, Tensity, and Imagination in *The Secret World*

In setting the scene for the analysis of *TSW* as a ludic addition to the pantheon of weird tales, it is noteworthy that prototypical weird tales have made use of codes and ludic elements. As John Peterson (2012) has argued, Stevenson's *Treasure Island* (1883) contains various elements that have proved important to games. In addition to this, an important pre-Lovecraft weird tale to which we will return later is Poe's short story "The Gold-Bug" (1843). As with *Treasure Island*, maps are central to the search for the "phat lewt" that serves as engine for its plot. Crucially, this is a story based on a cryptographic puzzle which works to involve the reader as puzzle solver above and beyond narration. This extends therefore beyond that of the usual code of enigma that Barthes's *S/Z* claims is integral to storytelling:[2] the enigma is not solved simply by "reading on," forward through the text, but instead the reader has to put some work in, becoming more than a reader. The enigmatic dimension to storytelling, reading, and games proves important for the discussion of the conspiracy hermeneutic of *TSW*. Suffice to say for the present that connections with games are seeded into the weird tale from early, on and it is this capacity that contemporary games regularly mined. In its highly reflexive and baroque way, *TSW* invokes a complex web of literary and popular cultural sources as a means of producing the weird, and in so doing constructs its conspiracy hermeneutic by attempting to dissolve the boundaries between myth, fiction, and reality.

It is part of normative game grammar for players to act on the situation that a game presents them with—the term "player" is predicated on this supposition. A fundamental feature of games is their arrays of feedback systems through which game and player respond to one another—a player acts in response to a situation and the game responds, often in ways that lead a player to understand their action as either helpful or unhelpful toward achieving a winning condition (or at least not failing in some way). In this sense, players expect games to be predictable, rule-based entities; players suppose feedback and we can consider feedback as an "event" in the computing and design processes of game, which grates against Lovecraft's coordinates of the weird. In addition, what the player is able to do in a game, the possibilities open to them are yoked to other prescripted narrative events that are causally linked. Games are therefore "event" heavy, even in the most ambient of games. In games, the entire construction of place, time, and mise-en-scène is dovetailed with affordances for action both in terms of what the player is able to do and how the game feeds back. Games then are largely event based, and, more than that, events are very often predictable and regulatory. In this sense, the logical and purposive construction of games, with their stable currencies and balances, and our pleasure in their regularity and predictability, is very far removed from the anti-human irrational dissonance of the weird. *TSW* inevitably draws on this normative vocabulary and indeed formal characteristic of games. As an MMORPG, players build their character's powers through the accumulation of skill points gained from killing enemies and running quests of various types. In skilling up, new areas of the map open up to players and more difficult quests and dungeons become available. The quest and dungeon structure that constitutes the principle mode of gameplay are event based, even if there are many atmospheric devices throughout the game. Regularity and predictability are built in to gameplay so that players are able to plan the trajectory of their character and manage risk; the game provides much information to help the player in these regards (maps, location of quests, health bars, "xp" tracking, numeric hit statistics, etc.). Like many games, there is an ethos of building knowledge and skill toward an increase in purchase power in this game's world. There is however a considerable attempt in *TSW* to shift the game away from the traditional dungeon-crawler, where gathering loot is emphasized in a very clearly coded fantasy world, toward a play experience that has depth and atmosphere. The game is thickly encrusted in a web of atmospheric intertextual details, drawn from a huge range of sources, thereby acting as a Lovecraftian counterweight to the event-based form of games. In weighting the game against events toward intertextually laden atmospheric detail, it begins to coincide with Harman's definition of "weird realism," where the medium of games is used against itself to flout normative expectations of guaranteed winning conditions and player mastery (of which more later in the chapter).

Unlike other MMORPGs games such as *Star Wars: The Old Republic* (BioWare, 2011–present) or *World of Warcraft* (Blizzard Entertainment, 2004–present), *TSW* is set in a version of the "real" world in which the supernatural and the occult have become manifest, making the familiar strange as is instrumental to the weird and current in popular texts such as *Buffy the Vampire Slayer* (1997–2003), *True Blood* (2008–14), or *Penny Dreadful* (2014–16). The real-world context helps a move closer toward Lovecraft's requirement for "psychological verisimilitude." There is no doubt that the supernatural exists and that lack of ambiguity in the game frames it squarely as "occult fantasy," thereby shoring up a basic distinction between real and imaginary, although some features of the game do chip away at these markers. In terms of existing game grammar, the game overturns the expected RPG alignments of "lawful good" and "lawful bad" or neutral and chaotic and aims for far greater moral ambiguity. It is hard to judge if the three institutionalized factions (Templar, Dragon, and Illuminati) are good or evil, neutral, lawful, or something quite different. All three have at least dubious moral standing, the details of which are well beyond the sphere of knowledge of the player-character. This works against the usual "knowable" and quantified world of system-based games. The factions' shaded history provides a further layer of enigma that plays into the conspiracy hermeneutic. Psychological verisimilitude arises out of this in congealing a sense that the player-character is simply a mere speck on vast opaque canvas. Here, different rhetorics of monstrosity crowd into the scene, and there are many and various intimations that call into question the "humanity" of the individual factions and what we might as player-characters do under their aegis. Although operating in secret, the various factions are in conflict, struggling to gain or retain power even as other forces are seeking to destroy humanity. This precarious situation is the premise on which the atmospherics of "malign tensity" are created as well as providing motivation for the standard MMORPG practice of Player versus Player (PvP) gameplay.

The format of PvP in the game has three flavors (termed Battlefields, Warzones, and Fightclubs) and there is no world-based PvP or specialist server. Warzones differ little from standard "Capture the Flag" and "King of the Hill" formats, while the persistent Battlezone offers something different in that faction buffs can be won that reach into Player versus the game Environment (PvE), arguably representing an invisible/occulted force that underlines the game's conspiracy milieu. The player-character awakens at the start of the game to find that they have acquired a strange power that emanates from their body and are called to join one of the factions: Templar, Dragon, or Illuminati. Players have already chosen a faction (based in the first instance on little knowledge of the nature of that faction) in a previous starting screen. Character name, look, race, and gender are also chosen from set options, choice-making that helps bind player to character. In terms of the player-character narrative arc, joining a faction is justified as their only option if they are to develop their nascent powers and help in the fight against the forces seeking to destroy humanity. There are no playable fantasy races dividing the game off from other science fiction or fantasy-based games: all available characters are coded as human, are gendered with wide range of racial characteristics available. In addition, the game is very fashion-conscious, with clothes and accessories stores in a vast range of styles available—and paid for with in-game or out-of-game currency—to help players express themselves in the game world. The world might be in peril yet players are strongly encouraged to look stylish in the face of adversity. The palpable sense of humanity that is created through these (inevitably normative) elements is aimed at bridging the gap between player and character but differ from the polarization of human and monstrosity of much fantasy fiction (in games as elsewhere). Creating a bond between player and character and at least intimating something of the vulnerability of the human is, however, important if the full effect of the weird is to come into play.

In the game's realization of the Lovecraftian weird, particularly his principles of "creation of atmosphere," "malign tensity" (which we might read as the creation of a palpable sense of dread) and "appeal to impressionist imagination," audio has a strong contribution to make. Central to all these elements is the generation of the mood of pensiveness and foreboding, which helps players experience malign tensity as a property of the game's visual context. The branding motif of the game is a clutch of notes played on the high end of the piano in which lies a dissonant note resonant of disturbance and grating against the laws of the human harmonic scale. Music also deepens the game's sense of scale: it opens up impressionistically unknown dimensions and in a hallucinogenic way mythologizes events and actions (largely this is actioned through the use of "epic" and "cosmic" orchestral and electronic music found in relevant film genres). The high piano key motif becomes accompanied by a high, soft, soaring yet distant human voice (connoting both the human and the angelic) or the scything sounds of dulcimer, evoking John Barry's haunting theme to the TV Show *The Persuaders* (1971), to which is added a low-end horn section that threatens "something below" and a soft and insistent drumbeat that inexorably counts down to doom and suggests a brewing storm. Ambient sound in the game's gothicized version of London builds a sense of place, yet the cawing of crows forewarns malice, calling on Poe's raven harbinger (ravens/crows are everywhere in the early part of the game, doubling also as a reference to Norse and Celtic mythology). Audio, story, and graphics each pull their weight in building a palpable sense of tension.

Weird Mediation: Working Against Itself?

While ostensibly the game world is signified as the world we live in, distortions in the space-time continuum are evident from early on, giving the otherwise gothic signification a science fiction feel, yet nonetheless creating the vertigo that is emblematic of the weird. Very early on in *TSW*, the player is treated to a cut scene where they stand on a tube train platform but look out into the infinite void of cosmic space. This spectacle scale treated the spectacle of is intended to give generate a sense of vertigo, physically, psychologically, and metaphysically. As established in Lovecraft's story "The Dreams in the Witch House," the "mathematical significance" of "odd angles" (Lovecraft 2005: 303) in non-Euclidean geometry alongside juxtapositions in scale become a sure fire means of raising the weird. It is in this mode that atmosphere and psychological verisimilitude take center stage in the game—even if both are generated through the evocation of (oddly) familiar signs of the weird. If the game did not use such devices so reflexively in the context of the grammar of an MMORPG and as a means of undermining the position of the conventional hero, then the experience offered by the game would be simply quotidian. However, there is a problem that arises between the expectations of player agency and mastery in the context of an MMORPG and the intention of the weird. Let Lovecraft be our guide, once again.

Walter Gilman, the central character of Lovecraft's "The Dreams in the Witch House," is beleaguered by dreams and haunted by increasingly alienating sounds and visions. Rather than the active hero, he is largely passive and terrified throughout the story, occupying the role of "false hero"—unable to act, to save the day, as is common to gothic fiction. Gilman becomes a somnambulant participant in a satanic pact, and when he finally finds the wherewithal to react to prevent the sacrifice of a child, he is bested; and at the end of the story, he lies dead with his heart eaten out. Alongside this passivity, and indeed by virtue of it, Gilman is involuntarily flung beyond normative space and time, boundaries between waking and dreaming collapse in an affective context of paralysis and bewilderment. These are signified by disarranged perspectives, impossible geometries, and unplumbed voids causing certainties to fall in a welter of unresolved enigmas. Compounded by drumming cacophonies of sounds and dim memories of agreements without agency, Gilman is left dumfounded and confused. He is subject to an occult conspiracy that he has no grasp of and thereby becomes an emblem of paralysis and involuntarism. This affective palette is counter to the normative, positivist trajectory inherent in most games. Given that human activity, technology, and computing are often integral to a belief in progress, it is not too far off the pace to argue that the weird in games works against its own medium (or least the discourse that surrounds that medium).

The experiences of gaining mastery, problem-solving, and improving skill are principal pleasures for players that drive the design of many digital games. This is a problem for games that follow gothic or weird pathways and particularly so given that the "false hero" is so fundamental to them. As Manuel Aguirre (2013) has written: "A key to Gothic thus resides in its centering the flawed character as protagonist . . . [while] the standard hero of traditional tales is often demoted to a helpless or passive stance" (Aguirre 2013: 11). Even in *TSW*'s opening cut scene, the player-character's newly found power comes at the price of visions and dreams that disturb the borders of knowability, reality, and fixed identity. When considered in the round, the representation of humanity conjured by the game is far from "good" or heroic; humans are either in a state of banal denial or foolishly questing for the acquisition of knowledge and power over others. This is evident in the design of the game's PvP supports. While PvP differs little from the usual structures that support for players a sense of mastery and skill, in their act of "killing" other player-characters from other factions while the world burns, morally ambiguity is already raised—more so because of the general context of moral ambiguity that the games constructs. Nonetheless, at some level the "human" is still valued in all its fallen and confused state; it is even defined by such. This conception provides the door for the game's entry into the types of affect and atmosphere associated with romanticism, pathos, and tragedy. To this is added a distinctly Schopenhauerian pessimism, much as would be expected of any text that makes a claim on weirdness. In this even though perhaps obliquely, the game is at least somewhat consonant with Lovecraft's weird counsel for a lack of sympathy for the human. This is apparent and contextually drawn out through the presence of the other Lovecraftian components in the absence of anything more than short-term resolutions, the absence of redemption, and the blatant presence of entropy. There is of course as an MMORPG just the endless return of only temporarily slain monsters and striving for more skill points. The tensions and oscillations between game form/grammar and the weird are now explored through a closer look at gameplay and the way that it constructs its conspiracy hermeneutic.

The Secret World: Gamifying the Weird

We will start with a general sense of the design and experience of the game space, seen through the lens of the Lovecraftian weird (players of the table-top RPG *Call of Cthulhu* may well be very afraid to look through said glass!). Players find their first mission on Solomon Island, located off the coast of New England, where, in a geographically appropriate manner, there is an outbreak of Lovecraftian mythos. In this area, the game draws on a very specific and highly influential regional accent of the American gothic to create its ludic version of the weird tale. The ingénue player-character arrives in the area's main town, Kingsmouth, to discover a running battle between living and dead townsfolk—seemingly a classic zombie-apocalypse situation. Players are requisitioned by the local Sheriff to run errands as well as to fulfill the factional requirement to investigate the nature of this manifestation. It soon becomes plain that zombies are the least of the town's troubles and symptomatic of a far more dangerous threat to humanity. While later the player will be sent to investigate other locations, Egypt for example, the player spends a lengthy period in the New England area, pursuing a range of goals and engaging with a range of appropriate myths and texts. The game is much more open than, for example, *Alan Wake* and players are free to quest, indulge in exploration, shop, gather, or fight other factions. Players can also easily visit other areas of the game world by virtue of a kind of fast travel device known as Agartha, a kind of mystic, faster-than-light underground railway system wherein a distortion of the space-time continuum is harnessed generously to enable players to travel quickly and easily. Accumulative, slow-burn character development and world-building is where emphasis lies in this game and the sense of progress that this implies does sit incongruously with the intention of the weird, although unlike most MMORPGs there is no expression of level that consolidates the progression system. Nonetheless a polyphony of gothic accents are collated as a means of creating a strong sense of "worldness" for players; and indeed that world is never what it appears to be; nor are players ever afforded full revelation of what governs the world. Polyphony abides there in the range of signification mobilized by the game, creating a fabric of competing narratives and intertexts that add complexity and mitigate across narrative closure: in addition to the American gothic, we encounter throughout the game a plethora of references to Steampunk/Victorian gothic, Eastern mysticism and martial arts, witchcraft and various versions of folk magic and Folk Horror, occultism and occult systems, ranging from John Dee through to post-Quantum theory Chaos Magic. The presence of all these intertexts, often used as a source of enigma and to help support the creation of a sense of "world," also helps to make individual game events seems less important than imaginative engagement with the game's fictional premise.

The New England area locates the game firmly within the literature of the weird as an offspring of American gothic, and this location is ripe with stories and histories well suited to a strongly accented weird theme. As in Magic Realism, myth and reality are interlaced. What the player encounters in Kingsmouth is a catastrophe that has objective reality in diegetic terms. It is not a subjective projection of a delirious author, as with *Alan Wake*, which revisits a similar scenario in the film *In the Mouth of Madness* (John Carpenter, 1994). As suits the formal specificity of a multiplayer online game, players of *TSW* fight collectively and ostensibly for the survival of the human race, within which the player plays their small part by trying to make meaning from their place and limited agency in this world of enigma and obscurities. *TSW* is a game woven from many fragments and in that sense it is consciously multiply authored. The game's environment is testimony to this. The closeness of the name Kingsmouth to the Innsmouth of Lovecraft's short stories "The Call of Cthulhu" and "The Shadow over Innsmouth," respectively, is enough to alert the literate player to an important legacy requisite to the American gothic and to Lovecraft's "fictionalized New England landscape" (Joshi 1990: xvii). Entry into the town also reveals street names, visible collectively on the in-game map, such as Dunwich Road,

Arkham Avenue (probably more widely known in the contemporary imaginary from the Asylum of the Batman franchise, yet a key fictional place in Lovecraft's geographic mythos), and Lovecraft Lane. Other popular American gothic texts are evoked in the names of landmarks such as Poe Cove and Elm Street. A short trip down the Dunwich Road confirms that we are knee-deep in Lovecraft's mythos: boxes of rotting squid lie abandoned yet half eaten on a zombie-infested street, and if we follow the trail of empty boxes, we arrive at the sea, to be greeted by a large tentacular sea monster, who seems to regard the player as a large and tasty squid. The boxes state in bright lettering: "Fresh from the deep to your door" and "Product of the USA"—subtlety suggesting, rather against the ethos of Lovecraft's cosmic horror, that human activity may well be implicated in the plight of the town. The first group task (the Polaris dungeon) that the player encounters is, of course, to defeat an enormous tentacle sea monster: Cthulhu in all but name (although Lovecraft aficionados might suggest that given the location it should really be the much less well-publicized Dagon). The game is thickly populated with many and diverse intertexts. The effect of which is to create a "rich" text that helps to interpellate the player into the game space by making use of their prior knowledge of horror and gothic texts. In this the game is tailored to a genre-literate audience (genre is applicable in terms of gothic, weird, and horror as well as MMORPGs/RPGs) who already have an investment in the subject matter.

In making use of the weird's psychological verisimilitude, *TSW* achieves a distinctive blend of fact and fiction. This is underlined through the structures and properties of conspiracy theory and the type of reading that is intrinsic to conspiracy theory. The game, and indeed the player, forges connections that traverse usual boundaries, paying little attention to their signifying frameworks. All signs regardless of their status—iconic, symbolic, or indexical; real or imaginary—are texts to be read and decoded as components of a great hidden (occulted) system. The game environment is itself a "text" to be read in this way, as is clear from an early quest "The Kingsmouth Code" in which the player must seek out signs inscribed into the fabric of the town's infrastructure left by the founding fathers of the town, who were Illuminati members and which indicate their secret activities and quest for power. Games rely heavily on properties of the game space to convey story, thereby placing the player in the role of investigator. Playing any game requires of the player, at some stage, acts of close reading. In the context of a game drawing on the gothic, close reading not only is constitutive of a ludic mode of engagement but also fuses that engagement to thematic syntax. The requirement of close reading has in particular a special resonance with Poe's detective, Dupin. The investigative act of gathering and attending to fragments in order to construct story is a central mechanism of the game and one that is infused with aspects of a conspiracy-style approach to reading. "Lore" fragments are scattered around the gamespace, often hidden in hard to locate places or encountered randomly while undertaking other tasks. These provide an extensive back story, often contextualizing places, people, and situations. If collected, players can then read, for example, about the plight of the trawler The Lady Margaret at dock in Kingsmouth's harbor, what its crew encountered at sea and brought back to the town, all delivered in the same peculiarly encrusted enunciative style of Lovecraft's writing. This story arc dovetails into another strand of lore entitled, "The Fog," a clear homage to Stephen King's novel, detailing the arrival of the fog in Kingsmouth. Players can also learn about the how the town was founded by members of the Illuminati and the presence of the character Beaumont, who sought to steal from them, providing is a large cog in the main story quest chain. There are still many enigmatically charged gaps however; the lore fragments never quite give the whole story—just limited perspectives and are never authorial, omniscient statements.

In addition to the use of lore as a coded means of storytelling, the area is also peopled by some staple figures of American mythology, each of whom have their individual story and add color. Sandy "Moose" Jansen is free-wheeling, philosopher-biker, repurposing himself as explosives expert. Daniel Boon is an old-fashioned, modern-day Cowboy positioned to advise the ingénue player in their fight against evil. Norma Creed is an old lady with a smoking rifle and a gritty attitude, resembling Lillian Gish's character seeing evil off her land in *The Night of the Hunter* (1955). The horror writer, fast becoming a staple figure of American gothic, is also represented, in homage to King yet also to *Alan Wake*. Here, however, he appears as Sam Kreig, a hard-drinking, world-sour writer notably, with regard to Wake, living in the Kingsmouth lighthouse. Not only does *TSW* refer to a plethora of literary and cinematic weirdly texts, but also to other games with a bearing a similar cast. Story here is a multidimensional assemblage of fragments and remnants, and is more powerful, far-reaching, and enigmatically rich for this. It is more than simply a means of giving meaning to progress bars; instead, it is a complex and carefully constructed tapestry aimed to locate the player in terms of place and time, geared toward encouraging a close engagement with the game *as* text. Like the conspiracy theorist, the player of *The Secret World* is invited to put together an assemblage of signs in order to ascertain and elaborate on underlying patterns— as such, the game constructs the weird world of conspiracy where "Everything is True," thereby following the tagline of Shea and Wilson's conspiracy-based *The Illuminatus! Trilogy* (1975). Nowhere is this principle made more apparent than in the game's investigation quests.

There is a limited range of different types of quest activities available for players, clearly designed to appeal to different play styles. Some involve stealth-style missions, others collection-type activities, while others send the players down a central story arc, but the most innovative and weirdly laden are the investigation quests. These conjure with materials similar to those that are at work in Poe's tales of ratiocination. Of all the quest types, these are most well suited to the "gamification" of the weird. There are several in each geographical zone of the game. One example of many is recounted here but I have to warn you, dear reader, that I am spoiling the game here in the name of analytical investigation. The quest is undertaken in the Egypt zones and is entitled "Angels and Demons." The player seeks to find out if a company operating in the zone is a front for something more "murky." On entering their offices, the player encounters a dead employee, an ID card can be retrieved from the corpse. This provides a clue to gaining access to the man's email system and it is delivered as a type of riddle, reading: "My surname is common in classic literature. And my clearance level is the key." The ID card shows that the man's name is H. Glass and his clearance level is: Gold-Bug. "The Gold-Bug" is a short story by Poe (1989) written to be published in episodes in 1843; players are more likely to find this out by googling, using the game's inbuilt web browser. Poe's story has within it a cryptographic code, made up by Captain Kidd, to disguise the location of his treasure in written form. The player must codify "Glass" to gain entry to the computer. This quest is neatly emblematic of the way that *TSW* translates weird fiction into digital game form, without losing sight of either its investigative and overdetermined hermeneutic dimension nor its wider textual heritage, and, at the same time, goes some way toward using the medium of games against itself to create at least for some players a weird sense of paradox and ambiguity. The choice of "The Gold-Bug" as the basis for the quest here is interesting. Not only is the Gold-Bug part of the family of scarab beetles, relevant to therefore to the Egyptian location, but the story has a puzzle at its heart, a cryptographic puzzle that Poe challenged readers to solve. In many such missions, the player must gain a good knowledge of the geography and have a decent graphics processor in order to get a good view of all the signs and notices that litter the gamespace, as with the mission "The Kingsmouth Code" mentioned earlier. In addition to the game's wiki, the in-game internet browser is designed to help players make sense of the more abstruse clues, looking up verse and chapter in the Bible, for example in the case of "The Kingsmouth Code," or hunting down the source of the Gold-Bug. In bringing the internet into the game, the borders of fiction and fact are softened, in accord with a central plank of gothic fiction and strengthening the sense of conspiracy. This is exemplified when undertaking a mission to find out Sam Kreig's backstory where the player is channeled into looking for a clue on a cover of one of his books that can only be found online. One of advantages of the blurring of fact and fiction is that it adds depth and diversity to a given fiction, and it is often the case that horror has often tried to convince the reader in various ways not just to suspend disbelief, but instead to read psychotically and believe, providing a further association with conspiracy-style reading. The presence of puzzles, enigmas, and fragments invites the player to go deeper into the text, the ludic hermeneutics of which can be regarded as an innovation in the way that players are engaged and marking a significant and powerful addition through the use of game media to weird fiction.

Conspiracy Hermeneutics across Media

To conclude, the type of paranoiac reading that successful weird fiction generates is produced by the conspiracy hermeneutic but is also the outcome of an individual's subjective inclinations and serendipitous correspondences. The investigation quests and intertextual flurries of *TSW* are geared to appeal to those sensitive to such pleasures; for those players less inclined to such, the game provides other more immediate means of creating atmosphere. However, the game has not done well commercially, suggesting a limited market. But I would claim for the game a welcome innovation in MMORPG design, which is had through the lens provided by weird fiction, elements of which are used to push the boundaries of what game media by disrupting normative game conventions and player expectations. *TSW* occupies a space that has been hollowed out by books such as *Foucault's Pendulum* (Eco 1988)—a book that features in another *TSW* investigation quest, by nineteenth-century magical systems including Crowley's database of correspondences *Liber 777* (1987), by post-Crowleyean fiction such as *The Illuminatus! Trilogy*, Kenneth Grant's conspiratorial reading of Lovecraft's fiction as reality (1997), and by more recent New Weird fiction such as the novels of China Miéville. Within such contexts, conspiracy and magic are closely bound, hidden connections are sought out and imagined, fictions are regarded as true, perspectives become deliberately distorted, and, thereby, normative distinctions, and assumptions become challenged. *TSW* goes some way toward that by sewing such chaos into its design, going well beyond simply style and aesthetics. Following Lovecraft's coordinates of the weird, the game creates its media-specific version of the weird through the deployment of a vertigo of overdetermined correspondences in which imagination and reality become fused. Intensifying all this is the way that the "real" internet is seamlessly woven into the fabric of the game, breaking the fourth wall of the game and allowing a sea of tangential connections, interconnections, paranoia, and conspiracy to rush in.

Notes

1 As noted in the Acknowledgments, this contribution has previously been published, in the journal *Well Played: a Journal on Video Games, Value and Meaning*. Reprint by permission.
2 "Let's designate as hermeneutic code . . . all those units whose function it is to articulate in various ways a question, its response, and the variety of chance events which can either formulate the question or delay its answer; or even, constitute an enigma and lead to its solution" (Barthes 2004: 17).

References

Aguirre, M. (2013), "Gothic Fiction and Folk-Narrative Structure: The Case of Mary Shelley's *Frankenstein*," *Gothic Studies*, 15 (2): (November)..

Barthes, R. (2004), *S/Z*, Oxford: Wiley-Blackwell.

Crowley, A. (1987), *777 and Other Qabalistic Writings of Aleister Crowley*, London: Red Wheel/Weiser, 1987.

Eco, U. (2007), *Foucault's Pendulum*, Boston: Mariner Books.

Grant, K. (1997), *Nightside of Eden*, London: Skoob Books.

Harman, G. (2012), *Weird Realism: Lovecraft and Philosophy*, Winchester/Washington: Zero Books.

Hoffmann, E. T. A. (1982), *Tales of Hoffmann*, trans. R. J. Hollingdale, Harmondsworth: Penguin.

Holdstock, M. and Edwards, R. (1983), *Realms of Fantasy*, Limpsfield: Paper Tiger.

Joshi, S. T. (1990), *The Weird Tale: Arthur Machen, Lord Dunsany, Algernon Blackwood, M.R. James, Ambrose Bierce, H.P. Lovecraft*, Austin, TX: University of Texas Press.

Lovecraft, H. P. (1973), *Supernatural Horror in Literature*, New York: Dover.

Lovecraft, H. P. (2005), *The Dreams in the Witch House and Other Stories*, Harmondsworth: Penguin.

Peterson, J. (2012), *Playing at the World: A History of Simulating Wars, People and Fantastic Adventures From Chess to Role-Playing Games*, San Diego: Unreason Press.

Poe, E. A. (1989), "The Gold-Bug," in *The Complete Tales of Mystery and Imagination*, 104–27, London: Octopus Books.

Shea, R., and Wilson, R. A. (1998), *The Illuminatus! Trilogy*, New York: Raven Books/Robinson Publishing.

Stevenson, R. L. (2008), *Treasure Island*, Harmondsworth: Penguin.

17

Afterword

Weird in the Walls

Roger Luckhurst

Julius Greve and Florian Zappe, the editors of this collection of essays, asked for an afterword, a genre that has always been something of a puzzle to me. Is it part of the book, continuous with it, on the same level as the chapters, or is it separate, with a distinct temporal and spatial distance from the chapters it follows? Isn't it implicitly, given a higher authority from all that precedes it, always able to have the last word? Gérard Genette's exploration of paratexts, those elements that surround, frame, and locate a text, starts by calling them "an undecided zone" (Genette 1992: 261) but ends up giving them a greater "illocutionary force" than the text itself. The paratext, he says, is "the fringe of a text which, in reality, controls the whole reading" (262). Given the diverse strengths of the contributors to this collection, and averse to claiming any greater authority than the contributors, I was reluctant to take on the quasi-authority of that position.

Yet something about the weird itself consistently dethrones conventional assertions of textual authority. China Miéville contaminates the operation of the afterword by penning an "Afterweird" instead, a short postscript to *The Weird: A Compendium* that subtly undoes all that volume's earnest work of po-faced canon formation by denying any final closure. Greve and Zappe begin this collection by quoting Michael Moorcock's "Foreweird" from the same compendium. These simple puns hint at an insistent lexical and conceptual contagion that marks the operation of the weird on the genres it touches and, by touching, transforms. I started to be interested again in the possibilities of an afterword if it could acknowledge the strange topology that is key to the weird: its overflow of rigid boundaries, its slow but sure undermining of textual authority. "The law of genre cannot hold," Greve and Zappe's Introduction warns quite early on—and that insight survives into these last, brief comments.

Johnny Murray's chapter in this volume, "The Oozy Set," heroically stages a struggle between the need for capsule definitions of contiguous genres—SF, fantasy, gothic, and horror—and the *viscosity* of the weird, its distinctive rheological flow that defies taxonomical fixity. The weird has what Ben Woodard has termed a "slime dynamics" all of its own (Woodard 2012). "Ooze," after all, was the title of the story by Anthony Rud that opened the first issue of *Weird Tales* in 1923, about "a slimy, amorphous something which glistened in the sunlight" that comes back from the swamps to slime to death its mad-scientist creator (Haining 1990: 257). It's as if the weird was already from the very beginning remarking on the quintessential horror of the formless and disgust at overflowing ooziness that would help define the genre.

Anne-Maree Wicks in a later chapter appeals to Derrida's essay "The Law of Genre" (1980), which reminded me of the philosopher's exhaustive (and often exhausting) reflections on weird textual topologies throughout his career. Perhaps because weird fiction has been subsumed by object-oriented ontology over the last decade (debated again here by Daniel Fineman and Graham Harman) and Lovecraft has been elevated to a case of what François Laruelle would call "non-philosophy," the weird's Revenge of the Object is meant to move beyond the fatal complicities of deconstruction with the philosophical tradition. The weird and the eerie were forms of "hauntology" in Mark Fisher's brilliant theorizations (see Fisher 2016), but this term was borrowed from Derrida's *Spectres of Marx* without any of the apparatus of deconstruction, and the term as used by Stephen Prince (2018) and others has only drifted ever further from its source. Yet Derrida's topological investigations of textual margins, borders, frames, and genre remain, I think, incredibly useful for theorizing the location of the weird.

"The Law of Genre" takes on the neat structuralist taxonomies of figures like Genette to propose that all those marks that might define a genre are precisely *re-marks* that travel and overflow individual textual boundaries and thus always smuggle in impurity. If the law of genre is that "genres must not be mixed" to stay pure, then the secret law of the law of genre is intrinsic impurity. Many of Derrida's works harped on this aporia. Texts were doubled, presented in two columns to be read simultaneously (*Glas*) or with a continuous band of a footnote running underneath the main body ("Living on: Border Lines"). These tactics undid hierarchies, putting the inside of "pure" discourses (philosophy, literature) into contaminating contact with each other. The margins of philosophy (the title of one of Derrida's earliest collections), where footnotes, parenthetical addenda, or parergonal additions resided were to be moved to the center of focus. The very frame of the text or artwork is put into play in *The Truth in Painting*, where

Derrida notes that the frame is "a form which has as its traditional determination not that it stands out but that it disappears . . . melts away at the moment it deploys its greatest energy" (Derrida 1987: 62). Instead, he affirmed, "No 'theory,' no 'practice,' no 'theoretical practice' can intervene effectively in this field that does not weigh up and bear on the frame" (61). Where does it start and end? Is it inside or outside the work itself, peripheral or central? The paratextual topping and tailing of texts by titles, author names, copyright statements, prefaces, signatures or postfaces, afterwords, or afterthoughts are all subject to sustained interrogation in Derrida, who points to "the essential parasitizing which opens up every system and divides the unity of the line which purports to mark its edges" (7). This is what he later calls a *limitrophy*, a study of "what abuts onto limits but also what feeds, is fed, is cared for, raised, and trained, what is cultivated, on the edges of a limit" (Derrida 2008: 29). In his other coinage, *invagination*, Derrida talks about the structure of a topological fold in which "the inverted reapplication of the outer edge to the inside of a form" means that "the outside then opens as a pocket" that may be larger than the inside ever was (Derrida 1979: 97). The border is no longer a line of demarcation, but a strange *volume*, full of hybrid, transitional things, neither objects nor subjects.

Although Derrida had absolutely no interest in popular genre, assuming only that the modernist avant-garde could reveal the secret transgressions at the heart of the law, I find it amusing that these topologies almost exactly describe the interstitialism of weird texts. He might have known this if, like Gilles Deleuze and Felix Guattari, he had actually read some Lovecraft. Much of Derrida's work could be wondering around the vast topological fold, the labyrinth that opens up inside the tiny Navidson House in Mark Danielewski's *House of Leaves*—a compendious book that swallows Derrida's work whole and spits it out again. Weird texts are marked by their intermixing of contiguous genres, such as science fiction and the Gothic, where the boundary was policed by scholarly border wars for decades even as the texts themselves always slyly undid those overtidy definitions of cognitive *versus* noncognitive estrangement, or scientific *versus* theological worldviews or framings. Weird texts also consistently remarked on their condition by explicitly thematizing impossible topologies and strange, invaginated zones. A line runs directly from the zone in *Roadside Picnic* by Boris and Arkady Strugatsky (filmed by Tarkovsky as *Stalker*, twice, of course, the lost double haunting the second attempt) through M. John Harrison's *Empty Space* trilogy, with its nonsensical fragment of alterity, the Kefahuchi Tract, slicing through Newtonian space and narrative causality, and up to China Miéville's cross-hatched cities overlaid on each other in *The City & The City* (2009) or

Jeff VanderMeer's Area X in his Southern Reach trilogy of 2014. I have written about this line and these zones in other places (see Luckhurst 2011 and 2017), but now I can add to this list the weird spaces of David Lynch's *Twin Peaks: The Return* and all the other unnerving spaces explored in the latter half of this collection, from Lily Amirpour's weird western landscapes to the spatial logic of the computer game *The Secret World* to Jordan Peele's mainstreaming of the weirdness of The Sunken Place in *Get Out*. Absurd zones or impossible pockets that leave inside and outside folded together in knots are central to both the weird and even more so to its recent incarnation as the New Weird.

If this is too abstract, too mathematical in its spatial obsession, the challenge set down by Tim Lanzendörfer and Dan O'Hara in this collection is first to historicize the weird and then try to think of it as a distinctly *American* formation. Lanzendörfer attempts to think through the Old Weird and the New with Fredric Jameson's injunction "Always historicize!" The weird then becomes the cultural form of distinct yet comparable conjunctures of capitalist crisis. The unknowable horrors of Lovecraft, his tortured, self-cancelling pileups of adjectives that describe the indescribable, articulate the aftermath of the First World War or the Crash of 1929, while the New Weird was championed in Miéville's 2003 manifesto as a "post-Seattle fiction" (Miéville 2003: 3), referring to the first major protests against the forces of neoliberal globalization at the World Trade Organization in 1999. This argument intensifies after the 2008 global debt crisis, where gothic figurations of "zombie capitalism," a system dead yet somehow living on, suggests that the weird sensibility, a feeling of an occluded totality that acts with hooded agency, more than chimes with the times. If capitalism shudders in crisis—symptoms mistaken by some as death throes—then the closed system of capitalist realism is thrown off its axis. Suddenly, there *is* an alternative struggling to be born, although whatever it is, to cite John Carpenter's *The Thing* (1982), it's weird and pissed off.

This can be a compelling argument, although for my taste the further it moves away from Jameson's tactic of often reductive homologies the better. We have also seen the weird persuasively tied less to short-term market crashes and more to the longer cycles of climate crisis that mark the emergence of the Anthropocene, as in the reflections of Timothy Morton on the meaning of weird in the opening pages of his *Dark Ecology* (2016). This also features in the companion volume to this one that Greve and Zappe have edited, *Spaces and Fictions of the Weird and the Fantastic: Ecologies, Geographies, Oddities* (2019). Even if the climate crisis is of course tied to the Capitalocene, as in Jason Moore's work, the longer, chaotic cycles of climate change mean that the weird cannot be programmatically read off as a cultural symptom of the American century in any straightforward way (see Moore 2016). The weird twists and veers: it is *busted allegory*, often obtusely resistant to depth hermeneutics.

Dan O'Hara's take on the *Americanness* of the weird turns away from economy and heads toward the apocalyptic theology that the white settler Puritans brought to the New World. In this, O'Hara follows Lovecraft's characterization of the weird emerging "from the keen spiritual and theological interests of the first colonists," who were haunted by "hordes of coppery Indians whose strange, saturnine visages and violent customs hinted strongly at traces of infernal origin" (Lovecraft 1973: 60). In this key passage from *Supernatural Horror in Literature*, Lovecraft equates the distinct cosmic horror of the American Weird to an imagination "given the free rein under the influence of Puritan theocracy to all manner of notions respecting man's relation to the stern and vengeful God of the Calvinists" (Lovecraft 1973: 60). The American historian Paul Boyer (1992) has followed the revival of apocalyptic and eschatological thought in the United States after the publication of Hal Lindsay's premillennialist *The Late Great Planet Earth* in 1970 (a book which has sold in America in its tens of millions), and O'Hara is right to follow the traces of this apocalypticism, however displaced, into the mainstream literary fiction of Joseph Heller, Thomas Pynchon, and Don DeLillo as well as the popular horror of Thomas Harris's *Red Dragon* or more weirdly tinged genre writing.

These scattered reflections on topology, history, and eschatology can be pulled together, I think, if we insist on the intrinsic link of the American Weird to the question of race. Race returns to the American instantiation of the weird with a kind of mute insistence throughout its history. Of course, we know that Lovecraft's racism is absolutely integral to his conception of the weird: "Wherever the mystic northern blood was strongest, the atmosphere of the popular tales became most intense," he wrote in *Supernatural Horror in Literature* (Lovecraft 1973: 19). Eugenie Brinkema's strong chapter in this collection on Jordan Peele's *Get Out* suggests that the film slyly rewrites Lovecraft's definition of weird fiction as a "breathless and unexplainable dread of outer, unknown forces" to become, for the black protagonist navigating structural racism, a breathless yet *entirely explainable* dread of outer, *known* forces. This "common weirdness," Brinkema suggests "is precisely and paradoxically its obviousness, what exists on the surface" (Brinkema, 127). This subversive rewriting of the nativism of Lovecraft's weird is what has allowed Victor Lavalle to rewrite the Old Weird from the African American perspective in his 2016 novella, *The Ballad of Black Tom*, or Matt Ruff to interweave the Old Weird with Jim Crow laws in *Lovecraft Country* (2016).

These are not one-offs. I would propose that there exists a line that is traceable through the lineage of the American Weird that uses a distinct topology to figure the disavowal of racial violence that underpins what Dana Nelson calls the formation of an "American national manhood" (see Nelson 1998). This is the trope of something weird and horrifying pushing through the walls of the home. With a relentless insistence, the American Weird is full of things that live (or live on, undead) in the walls, interstitial horrors that at the edges of the secure borders of the home turn that defensive line into a weird and wonderful volume. This is the signal generic remark of the American Weird.

It is there in Edgar Allan Poe's tale "The Black Cat" about the fatal mistake of inhuming the vengeful creature along with the body of a murdered wife in the walls of the house. This is a story commonly understood to carry ambivalent racial resonances (see, for example, Ginsberg 1998 or Kennedy and Weissberg 2001). Poe's weirder tales keep returning to this topology: corpses under the floorboards in "The Tell-Tale Heart," inhumations in cellars in "The Cask of Amontillado" or below the ancestral home in the crypt in "The Fall of the House of Usher." It recurs with a similar kind of compulsion in Lovecraft's stories: the structure of subbasements and sub-subbasements that underlies the house of the evil genius Robert Suydam in the crucial transitional story "The Horror at Red Hook," his delirious portrait of racial miscegenation and devil worship in Brooklyn's degenerate docks. In "The Rats in the Walls," this structure peals away successive layers of infested walls, hidden basements and, even further below, hidden caves that hide a disgusting family secret under the ancestral mansion. In "The Dreams in the Witch House," the angles of the attic rooms reveal a non-Euclidean geometry which is continuous with the obsessions of the unfortunate lodger, Walter Gilman, who specializes in the Higher Mathematics, the fourth dimension, and "freakish curvatures in space" (Lovecraft 2013: 291). This trope drives right through the postwar Gothic, in Shirley Jackson's *The Haunting of Hill House*, whose walls, "holding darkness within" (Jackson 2010: 243), subverts space and exerts such malignant otherworldly pressure that the bedroom doors and walls bow under the weight of its undying fury. This lineage, with its undertow of foundational yet disavowed racial violence, continues right through Stephen King's *The Shining* and *Pet Sematary*, and into the 1990s with the bizarre racial phantasmagoria of the horror films, Wes Craven's *The People Under the Stairs* (1991), and Bernard Rose's *Candyman* (1992). In Craven's film, a grand family mansion of the miserly white overseers of the black ghetto outside is a house riddled with passageways hidden in the walls, the twisting path through which, eventually, the black ghetto will overthrow their landlords. Just as an extra weird twist, the white couple (incestuous siblings) are played by the same two actors who played Ed and Nadine Hurley in *Twin Peaks*. In Rose's *Candyman*, the suppressed history of a lynching is avenged in the haunting of the Cabrini-Green housing project in Chicago, a notorious black ghetto used in its last days before it was pulled down by the city. The Candyman is always reaching through walls, or framed in holes busted through brick, toying dangerously with the myth of potent sexualized black man menacing white feminine virtue.

If anything, this trope seems to have intensified in the 2010s, bubbling up alongside and often intertwined with the rise of the New Weird. Aside from the home invasion fantasies that drive so many contemporary horror films (*The Purge* franchise and *Don't Breathe* foreground specific racial resonances of the trope through their settings: overrun affluent suburbs or the catastrophic ruination of Detroit), there has been a spike of films that seem to play on the memory of Lovecraft's "The Rats in the Walls." These include *The Man in the Wall* (2015), *Behind the Walls* (2018), or even the children's fantasies, *The Wolves in the Walls* (2003) or *The House with a Clock in the Walls* (2018). A creepypasta Halloween micronarrative on Twitter went viral in 2019, presented as a childhood memory of discovering a man living in the walls of the family home, a secret sharer often seen by the narrator but that no one else believed in. One of the freakiest passages in Jeff VanderMeer's Southern Reach trilogy, so far the quintessential American New Weird text, is not the Thing found writing the interminable sentence on the wall, but the man who folds himself into the attic space of the government offices that sit on the border of Area X. It is a moment that tells us that the border is on the move and the instrumental rationality of government bureaucracy has become wild at heart and weird on top, contaminated by the expanding zone.

In their invaluable study, *Horror in Architecture*, Joshua Comaroff and OngKer-Shing speak of the gleaming white rational spaces of modernist architecture as doubled by "unspeakable cavities" and "obscene and recessive spaces" that "contradict the resolved bourgeois exterior" (Comaroff and Ker-Shing 2013: 7). For every white cube or minimalist atrium, the walls are stuffed with ducts carrying shameful wastes, tangled wiring, hidden service elevators and backrooms, functional emergency exits, and basement entryways. These "machines for living in," as the modernist slogan had it, carry doubled or weirded volumes where the spectres of history implacably return to haunt.

In the opening scenes of Denis Villeneuve's film *Sicario* (2015), an FBI raid on a known Mexican cartel safe house just inside the American border appears to be fruitless until the team starts to pull down the plaster walls. Inside, the team finds dozens of inhumed bodies, trafficked Latinos that have been murdered by their smugglers. This is emblematic of how the house can figure for the state, in this case offering a racial phantasmagoria distinct to the politics of global migration in America in the twenty-first century. In Trump's populist rhetoric, which owes much to the nativist discourses of the 1920s, the rats in the walls, the global south's "vermin" and "scum," are the hordes of rapists, murderers, and drug dealers slipping insidiously across the border and folding themselves invisibly into the homeland. The border wall is the nationalist fantasy of a clear line drawn in the sand, a demarcation that defends purity. But the wall is also, and inevitably for the political theorist Wendy Brown, "only the imago of sovereign state power in the face of its own undoing" (Brown 2014: 25).

What is weird—truly *topologically* weird—is that this American/Mexican border wall has demonstrably become a *borderscape*, a dynamic volume that is not a fixed line but "an elusive and mobile geography" marked by an unpredictable "elasticity of territory" (Mezzarda and Neilson 2013: 8). These volumes multiply into strange "exclaves," pocket territories of internment or holding that operate extralegally (see Easterling 2016 or Rajaram and Grundy-Warr 2007). They are "states of exception" that suspend national and international laws on human rights. The border is no longer a line to be transgressed but a distributed zone situated at once, as Étienne Balibar states, "everywhere and nowhere" (Balibar 2002: 78). Like the weird zone of Area X, the border has expanded to swallow the homeland entire. There is, now, only this borderscape, this interstitial edgeland, where citizenship and even bare life itself is only precarious and provisional.

This weirded logic of expanding, engulfing borders is a global phenomenon of course. Walls and their extraterritorial ecosystems multiply across the planet. But I would propose that the American Weird has flowered because it offers a kind of "weird realism" that best articulates this contemporary imaginary in popular cultural form. And where better to argue this than in an "Afterword," this curious pocket, this paratextual exclave smuggled into the outer wall of the main body of the text? This collection insists on the importance of thinking through the Americanness of the weird even as it always overflows or oozes out of that deluded frame of nationalist thought.

References

Balibar, E. (2002), "What is a Border?," in *Politics and the Other Scene*, trans. C. Jones et al., 76–85, London: Verso.
Boyer, P. (1992), *When Time Shall Be No More: Prophecy Belief in Modern American Culture*, Cambridge: Harvard University Press.

Brown, W. (2014), *Walled States, Waning Sovereignty*, New York: Zone Books.
Comaroff, J., and O. Ker-Shing, (2013), *Horror in Architecture*, Novato: ORO Editions.
Derrida, J. (1979), "Living On: Border Lines," in H. Bloom (ed.), *Deconstruction and Criticism*, 75–176, New Haven: Yale University Press.
Derrida, J. (1980), "The Law of Genre", trans. A. Ronell, *Gylph*, 7, 202–32.
Derrida, J. (1987), *The Truth in Painting*, trans. G. Bennington, Chicago: Chicago University Press.
Derrida, J. (2008), *The Animal That Therefore I Am (More to Follow)*, trans. D. Wills, New York: Fordham University Press.
Easterling, K. (2016), *Extrastatecraft: The Power of Infrastructure Space*, London: Verso.
Fisher, M. (2016), *The Weird and the Eerie*, London: Repeater.
Genette, G. (1992), "Introduction to the Paratext," trans. M. Maclean, *New Literary History*, 22 (2): 262–71.
Ginsberg, L. (1998), "Slavery and the Gothic Horror of Poe's 'The Black Cat,'" in Robert K. Martin and Eric Savoy (eds.), *American Gothic: New Interventions in a National Narrative*, 99–128, Iowa: University of Iowa Press.
Greve, J., and F. Zappe, eds. (2019), *Spaces and Fictions of the Weird and the Fantastic: Ecologies, Geographies, Oddities*, London: Palgrave.
Jackson, S. (2010), *Novels and Stories*, J. C. Oates ed., New York: Library Classics of America.
Kennedy, J. G, and L. Weissberg, eds. (2001), *Romancing the Shadow: Poe and Race*, Oxford: Oxford University Press.
LaValle, V. (2016), *The Ballad of Black Tom*, New York: Tor.
Lovecraft, H. P. (1973), *Supernatural Horror in Literature*, New York: Dover.
Lovecraft, H. P. (2013), "The Dreams in the Witch House," in R. Luckhurst (ed.), *Classic Horror Stories*, 285–319, Oxford: Oxford University Press.
Luckhurst, R. (2011), "In the Zone: Topologies of Genre Weirdness," in S. Wasson and E. Alder (eds.), *Gothic Science Fiction 1980-2010*, 21–35, Liverpool: Liverpool University Press.
Luckhurst, R. (2017), "The Weird: A Dis/Orientation," *Textual Practice* 31 (6), 1021–41.
Mezzarda, S., and B. Neilson (2013), *Border as Method, or, The Multiplication of Labor*, Durham: Duke University Press.
Miéville, C. (2003), "Long Live the New Weird," *The Third Alternative*, 35 (3).
Moore, J. W. (2016), *Anthropocene or Capitalocene? Nature, History and the Crisis of Capitalism*, Oakland: PM Press.
Morton, T. (2016), *Dark Ecology: For a Logic of Future Coexistence*, New York: Columbia University Press.
Nelson, D, (1998), *National Manhood: Capitalist Citizenship and the Imagined Fraternity of White Men*, Durham: Duke University Press.
Prince, S. (2018), *A Year in the Country Wandering Through Spectral Fields: Journeys into Otherly Pastoralism, the Further Reaches of Folk and the Parallel Worlds of Hauntology*, n.p.: A Year in the Country/Amazon Publishing.

Rajaram, P. Kumar, and C. Grundy-Warr, eds. (2007), *Borderscapes: Hidden Geographies and Politics at Territory's Edge*, Minneapolis: University of Minnesota Press.

Rud, Anthony M. (1990) "Ooze," in Peter Haining (ed.), *Weird Tales*, 248–63, London: Xanadu.

Ruff, M. (2016), *Lovecraft Country*, New York: HarperCollins.

Woodard, B. (2012), *Slime Dynamics: Generation, Mutation, and the Creep of Life*, Winchester: Zero Books.

Contributors

Maryam Aras is a doctoral researcher in Iranian Studies at the University of Bonn. She received her M.A. in Islamic Studies, Political Science, and North American Studies from University of Cologne and has published academic articles and essays on literature and film, modern Iranian history, diaspora and identity, postcolonial culture, and Gender Studies. In her doctoral research, Maryam focuses on the politics of cultural memory in Shiite eulogy rituals of contemporary Iran. Her latest publication is entitled "Vampires, Veils and the Western Gaze—Gender Images and the Notion of Beauty from Qajar to Postrevolutionary Iran."

Eugenie Brinkema is Associate Professor of Contemporary Literature and Media at the Massachusetts Institute of Technology. Her research in film and media studies focuses on violence, affect, sexuality, aesthetics, and ethics in texts ranging from the horror film to gonzo pornography to works of art cinema. Her articles have appeared in the journals *Angelaki, Camera Obscura, Criticism, differences, Discourse, film-philosophy, The Journal of Speculative Philosophy, qui parle*, and *World Picture*. Her first book *The Forms of the Affects* was published in 2014.

Daniel D. Fineman is Professor of American Literature and Theory at Occidental College in Los Angeles. His primary fields of interest are American literature and literary theory. The authors who have garnered most of his time are Melville and Dickinson. His secondary fields are gender studies, film, photography, science fiction, and British literature.

Fred Francis works as a narrative designer for an interactive fiction publisher. He was previously Assistant Lecturer in English at the University of Kent, where he also earned his PhD. He has published articles and book chapters on the American Romance in comic books, and has organized the comics exhibition *There Is an Alternative! Critical Comics and Cartoons*, and is co-editor of *Comedy and Critical Thought: Laughter as Resistance?* (2018).

Alexander Greiffenstern is an independent instructor and scholar who studied comparative literature, history, and computer science at Bielefeld University.

In 2008–9, he was a member of the international research group "E Pluribus Unum" at the ZiF (Center for Interdisciplinary Research), Bielefeld. He is the coeditor of the essay collection *Interculturalism in North America: Canada, the United States, Mexico and Beyond* (2013), and he is a member of the editorial board of the *European Beat Studies Network*.

Julius Greve is a lecturer and research associate at the Institute for English and American Studies, University of Oldenburg, Germany. He is the author of *Shreds of Matter: Cormac McCarthy and the Concept of Nature* (2018), and of numerous articles on McCarthy, Mark Z. Danielewski, François Laruelle, and speculative realism. Greve has coedited *America and the Musical Unconscious* (2015), *Superpositions: Laruelle and the Humanities* (2017), "Cormac McCarthy between Worlds" (a special issue of *EJAS: European Journal of American Studies*, 2017), and *Spaces and Fictions of the Weird and the Fantastic: Ecologies, Geographies, Oddities* (2019). He is currently working on a manuscript on the relation between modern poetics and ventriloquism.

Graham Harman is Distinguished Professor of Philosophy at the Southern California Institute of Architecture. He is the author of twenty-two books, of which nineteen have already been published and three are in press. He has also published over three hundred articles in twenty-four languages, and has given over three hundred and fifty lectures on six continents. In 2015, he was listed by *ArtReview* as the #75 most powerful influence in the international art world.

Tanya Krzywinska is Professor of Digital Games at Falmouth University, Cornwall, UK. She is the author of books and many papers on digital games as well as horror, weird, and the Gothic, and is the editor of Games and Culture. Her recent research area is augmented and mixed reality design for museums, working with a number of museums in Cornwall, and she has been writing about the implications of mixed reality for conceptions of time and space. In her spare time, she paints.

Tim Lanzendörfer is Heisenberg research fellow at the University of Frankfurt, where his research is on contemporary literary theory and literature as well as on the mediation of literary studies to the public. He is the author of *The Professionalization of the American Magazine: Periodicals, Biography, and Nationalism in the Early Republic* (2013) as well as *Books of the Dead: Reading the Zombie in Contemporary Literature* (2018). His forthcoming third book is entitled *Speculative Historism: Utopian Pasts and Futures in the Contemporary Novel*. He is also editor and coeditor of several collections of essays and special journal issues. His most recent work includes special issues in contemporary literary theory and genre theory.

Roger Luckhurst is a professor in Modern and Contemporary Literature at Birkbeck College, University of London. His books include *The Invention of Telepathy* (2002), *Science Fiction* (2005), *The Trauma Question* (2008), *The Mummy's Curse* (2012) and *Corridors: Passages of Modernity* (2019). For Oxford World's Classics, he has edited *Late Victorian Gothic Tales*, Stevenson's *Strange Case of Dr Jekyll and Mr Hyde*, Stoker's *Dracula*, and H. P. Lovecraft's *Classic Horror Tales*.

Oliver Moisich studied English and American Literature and German Literature at the Friedrich-Schiller-University Jena and the University of Aberdeen. Since 2015, he has been a research assistant in the Early-Career Research Group "Hybrid Narrativity" at the University of Paderborn. He is currently writing his PhD on empirical and experimental narratology with a focus on comics and visual literature.

Johnny Murray is pursuing a PhD in English at Boston College. In 2017, he received his master's degree in English Studies from Manchester Metropolitan University, graduating with distinction and earning the Head of Department's Prize for Outstanding Achievement.

Dan O'Hara, B.A., M.A. (Warwick), M.St., D.Phil. (Oxon), is a literary historian and philosopher of technology. He has taught at the Universities of Oxford, Cologne, and NCH London, and is one of the founders and director of Virtual Futures. His DPhil was a history of the idea of the machine in literature, art, and philosophy since the Enlightenment. He has written on British and American novelists, on Critical Theory, and on the evolution of technology. His most recent books are *Extreme Metaphors: Interviews with J. G. Ballard* (2012–14) and *Virtual Futures: Near-Future Fictions* (2019).

Stephen Shapiro is Professor of American Studies in the Department of English and Comparative Literary Studies at the University of Warwick (UK). His books include *Pentecostal Modernism: Lovecraft, Los Angeles, and World-Systems Culture* (with Philip Barnard, Bloomsbury 2017), four critical editions of Charles Brockden Brown's romances, *Wieland*, *Edgar Huntly*, *Arthur Mervyn*, and

Ormond (with Philip Barnard, Hackett, 2004–8), *The Culture and Commerce of the Early American Novel: Reading the Atlantic World-System* (2008). He belongs to the Warwick Research Collective and its authorship of *Combined and Uneven Development: Towards a New Theory of World-Literature* (2016). Currently, he is coediting with Mark Storey the forthcoming *Cambridge Companion to American Horror.*

Paul Sheehan is an associate professor in the English Department at Macquarie University, Sydney, Australia. He is the author of *Modernism and the Aesthetics of Violence* (2013) and the editor of "Post-Archival Beckett: Genre, Process, Value" (2017), a special issue of the *Journal of Beckett Studies*. Most recently he has published articles on writing technology, cryptographic modernism, and post-human bodies.

Anne-Maree Wicks is a doctor of Philosophy candidate at the University of Southern Queensland in Australia with a research project that focuses on Weird Fiction's concerns of genre and form, and the feminist frictions within weird fiction's phallogocentric concepts.

Markus Wierschem studied Philosophy, German, Media Studies, and English and American Literary and Cultural Studies at the University of Paderborn and St. Olaf College (Northfield, MN). In 2017, he received his doctorate degree for his dissertation "An American Apocalypse? Myth, Violence, and Entropy in the Novels of Cormac McCarthy." He is the author of numerous articles as well as the anthology *Patterns of Dis|Order: Beiträge zur Kulturgeschichte der Unordnung* (2017), and has been teaching courses on American literature and culture—including courses on American Film Noir and David Lynch—since 2011.

Florian Zappe is an assistant professor of American Studies at the Georg-August-University Göttingen, Germany. He is the author of books on William S. Burroughs (*"Control Machines" und "Dispositive"—Eine foucaultsche Analyse der Machtstrukturen im Romanwerk von William S. Burroughs zwischen 1959 und 1968*, 2008) and Kathy Acker (*Das Zwischen schreiben—Transgression und avantgardistisches Erbe bei Kathy Acker*, 2013), as well as the coeditor of the essay collections *Spaces and Fictions of the Weird and the Fantastic: Ecologies, Geographies, Oddities* (2019) and *Surveillance|Society|Culture* (2020). In addition to that, he has published widely on literary and visual culture. Currently, he is working on a book on the cultural history of atheism in America.

Index

Amirpour, Ana Lily   5, 8, 139–53, 251
apocalypse   15–27, 66, 240

Bakhtin, Michail
   chronotope   8, 154–72
Barney, Matthew   5
   Cremaster Cycle   9, 187–200
Blackwood, Algernon   7, 29, 31–7, 72, 78
Burroughs, William S.   202, 208–14

Camp   66–9, 232
capitalism   7, 143, 222, 225, 251
   combined and uneven
      development   62–4, 68, 70
   subsumption   56–60, 69
Captain Beefheart   5, 8, 9, 173–86
   Trout Mask Replica   174, 176–7, 181, 183

DeLanda, Manuel   94–5, 97, 109, 114
Deleuze, Gilles   7, 8, 89–104, 105–18, 197, 201, 250
   Difference and Repetition   91, 96
Derrida, Jacques   40–54, 98, 105, 113–14, 130, 134, 249, 250
   "The Law of Genre"   40, 249
Dickinson, Emily   8, 89–90, 92–3, 99–102, 105–8, 116

eschatology   21–4, 141, 252

feminist criticism   7, 41, 53, 69
Fisher, Mark   9, 64–5, 67, 72, 74–80, 82, 86–7, 129, 140, 143, 146, 166–7, 169, 188, 190, 195, 210, 213, 218–27, 249
   The Weird and the Eerie   4, 49, 55, 76, 163, 175, 194, 219
Foucault, Michel   58, 155–7, 159, 163, 201
   heterotopia   8, 155–63, 167, 169

Freud, Sigmund   30, 121, 125, 127, 167

gender   9, 65, 68, 193, 219–21, 237
genre theory
   fantasy   6, 28–34, 36, 232, 237, 249
   gothic   6, 8, 28–31, 34, 36, 40, 42, 44–5, 50, 63–6, 93, 99, 139–41, 217–18, 230–4, 238–45, 249–51, 253
   horror   3, 6, 28–30, 34, 40, 42–5, 50, 128, 154, 160, 230, 232, 234, 242, 249
   mythopoeia   189–91
   science fiction   3, 6, 28–32, 34, 36, 40, 45, 55, 156, 232, 237–8

Harman, Graham   7–9, 72, 74–80, 89–104, 105–18, 194, 196, 225–6, 232–6, 249
   Weird Realism: Lovecraft and Philosophy   4, 89, 94–5, 136, 232
Heidegger, Martin   76, 92, 94–5, 99, 107

Joshi, S. T.   3, 33, 42–3, 47, 51, 87, 211, 233

Lovecraft, H. P.   3–9, 29–32, 34, 36, 43, 49, 50, 55, 67–8, 73–87, 90, 98–101, 105–6, 136, 190, 196, 201–13, 217–18, 226, 232–46, 249–54
   Supernatural Horror in Literature   3, 77, 127, 230, 234, 252
Lynch, David   4, 5, 8, 154–72, 180–1, 184, 189, 251
   fan reception 162–3, 167, 169
   nostalgia   162–70

Machen, Arthur   7, 28, 29, 33–6
Marx, Karl   7, 56–62, 65
   crisis   72–87

media studies   1–10, 122
    mediation and remediation   1, 5, 63, 158, 238
Miéville, China   28, 31, 47–53, 55, 72–9, 245, 248, 250–1
millennialism   18–21, 151
modernism   42, 179–83
Moore, Alan   5, 9, 201–15

Ngai, Sianne   1–3, 10
    Our Aesthetic Categories   1, 10

object oriented ontology   4, 55, 73, 76, 105–8, 111–16, 249

Peele, Jordan   5, 8, 121–37, 251–2
Poe, Edgar Allan   5, 99–100, 105–6, 203, 234, 238, 242–4, 253
Puritanism   6, 16–18, 20, 23, 25, 141, 148, 150, 252

race   10, 56, 68, 237, 252
    violence   125–35

Sontag, Susan   66, 67, 201, 212
speculative realism   4, 93, 94, 101, 107, 136, 226

technology   18–21, 25, 33
Thacker, Eugene   1, 5, 72, 141, 145, 146

Thrift, Nigel   224–7
transgression   6, 28–30, 34, 40, 47, 49, 51, 146, 190, 250, 255

uncanny   16, 30, 35, 81, 85, 106, 121, 127, 146, 159–60, 167, 188, 217
utopia   6, 18–20, 23, 25, 31, 66, 67, 81, 84, 85, 156, 157, 163, 174, 225, 227

VanderMeer, Jeff   5, 28, 43–4, 47–9, 55, 72, 78, 85–7
    the Southern Reach Trilogy   7, 74, 82–4, 216, 251, 254

weird
    common weirdness   8, 121–38, 252
    digital games   230–47
    fashion   9, 216–29
    fiction   7, 33, 35, 40–54, 72–82, 85–6, 127, 160, 218, 232–4, 244–5, 252
    film   21–5, 55, 121–38, 139–53, 154–72
    Marxism (*see* Marx, Karl)
    New   7, 41–2, 45–9, 51, 82–5, 197, 246, 251, 254
    Old   7, 41–2, 47, 50, 51, 251, 252
    postcolonial   139–53
    space   8, 85, 154–72, 251
    woke   7, 55–71

www.ingramcontent.com/pod-product-compliance
Lightning Source LLC
Chambersburg PA
CBHW072133290426
44111CB00012B/1869